11/01/2020

# MY EXILE
## *to the*
# WORLD

*A Citizen of the World*

Everything is possible

Faustin Rusanganwa

# MY EXILE
## to the
# WORLD
## A Citizen of the World

FAUSTIN RUSANGANWA

Palmetto Publishing Group
Charleston, SC

*My Exile to the World*

First Edition

Printed in the United States

ISBN-13: 978-1-64111-897-2
ISBN-10: 1-64111-897-0
ebook ISBN: 978-1-64111-219-2

In memory
of my father, Camille Buyenge,
of my mother, Marie Mukarukore,
of my people carried away by men with evil in their hearts.

To my beloved Claudette Umutoni,
to my dear children, Arnell, Ariane, Arvin, and Arcel,
to all the great souls I met on my journey,
to all those around this earth that, against all odds, still believe
in love and fraternity among mankind.
To all, I dedicate this book.

# Contents

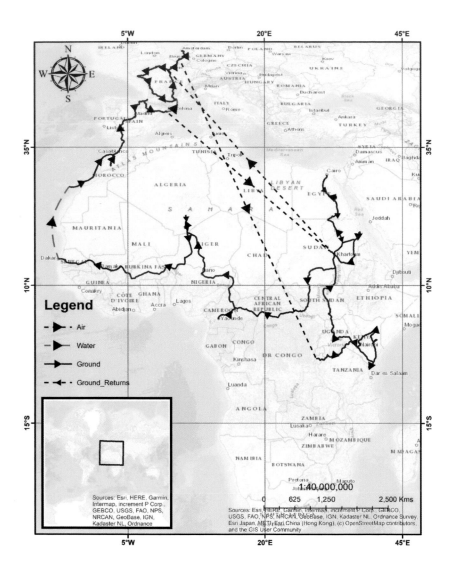

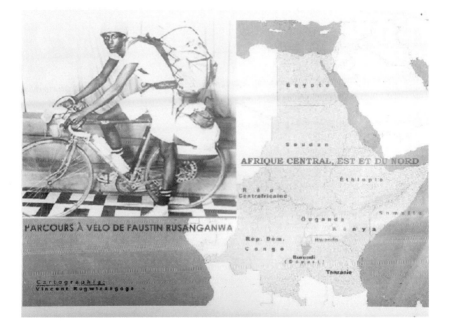

PARCOURS À VÉLO DE FAUSTIN RUSANGANWA

AFRIQUE CENTRAL, EST ET DU NORD

Égypte

Soudan

Éthiopie

Rép Centrafricaine

Ouganda

Somalie

Kenya

Rép. Dém. Congo

Rwanda

Burundi (Dépait)

Tanzanie

Cartographie:
Vincent Rugwirangoga

# Prologue

The year 1973 was the one that changed my life. I was nineteen years old when I left Rwanda for the safety of Burundi to escape the terrible tribal conflict between the Hutus and the Tutsis. After five years there, sick of the hatred of the world and ready to search myself out, I decided to leave Burundi on a bicycle bought with borrowed money. Not quite destitute but already in debt, I set off toward adventure. What was meant to be a two-month trip through four African countries gradually took on globe-trotting proportions: a five-year adventure across two continents over savannas, rain forests, steppes, and deserts.

At the time, the only threat I prepared myself for was the threat of being without. I was a traveler with restricted papers, which only granted permission for me to go to Tanzania for three months. I was without money, family, a sponsor, or a benefactor. I was even without a proper education, being only schooled up to the third year of primary education. I barely knew how to read and could not write, though I did know how to speak Kinyarwanda and Kirundi (twin languages from twin countries), a bit of Swahili, and enough French to help me get around.

There were countless threats I was not prepared for, which would end up making the trip more than just a little precarious. I look back now and wonder how I did not think once about the threats of the natural world. At one point, I found myself buried by desert sands, semiconscious, mumbling a prayer, and preparing for death. Another time, it was elephants that nearly crushed me beneath their giant feet in an equatorial forest. Though I don't think I could have ever expected or prepared for the threat of being eaten by an African serpent or being swarmed by vultures (it was only until much later that I learned of their attraction to the red color of my backpack),these natural threats were nothing compared to the threat posed by governing men, which turned me into a refugee and made me more handicapped with each border crossing. The men in the employ of these held me at gunpoint more than once. I must admit that my innocence and ignorance about what I was undertaking with this journey still astounds me.

However, the journey was also filled with wonderful things that still whisper through my days in the random moments of life. What scenery and creatures! During moments of stress in my life now, I think of the magnificence of the animals and landscapes. I am humbled, remembering how grand life is, that stress is not anything I want to carry. And what beautiful people and cultures! Humanity showered me with kindness, as many benevolent souls housed me, fed me, clothed me, and even employed me. This kindness saved me and stood in stark relief to the atrocities I witnessed. Without their generosity, I do not know where I would be today likely decomposing in the Sahara Desert or in a mass grave in Rwanda.

Begrudgingly, after ten years of being on the road, I was forced to bring my tour to a close in 1982. The harshness of a Dutch winter cut into my momentum. By then I had crisscrossed the better part of Africa, crossed over to Europe, and wanted to go farther to China, India, and even Australia if it were up to me. A proverb from my land says, "The path does not speak to the traveler. On his journey the traveler always encounters unforeseen challenges. Sometimes he overcomes; sometimes he succumbs." This time I had to succumb. So, I buckled my backpack and returned to Burundi, just the same as I had left five years earlier: without luggage and without a dime. However, in some ways, I was returning with much more than just the same bike I had left with. I was returning with refugee papers from Sudan, and I had found the inner strength and awareness that only comes from surviving for so long on the road. Little did I know that my journey had only just begun, and I would spend another three years making my way to my current home in Davis, California. If someone had read my fortune and told me I would find myself at home in a small college town in the United States, I would have laughed at them! Yet here I am, in my lovely Davis house.

The inception of this story began when I returned to Burundi in 1982. I had told my story many times on the road but wanted to finally put it down, to have a definitive record of my journey. Sure, there were newspapers and TV stations that interviewed me, but I wanted a version all my own out in the world. Being illiterate, I couldn't read or write; this presented a significant obstacle. Because I was a Tutsi, the government stole my childhood from me, including the single most important thing a child could get: an education. I often reflect on just how much that theft handicapped me and the other Tutsis of Rwanda. But I still had all of the memories fresh in my mind. I asked around and eventually found a man named Aimable Ruzindana, who was able to read and write both in Kinyarwanda and French. For a few months, we sat down together in the afternoons, and I dictated to him my story, to which he listened very carefully. He reacted with joy at the surprises, wept with me at the tragedies, and wrote every little detail in his thick notebook. He was enthralled by my adventure and gained perspective through my experiences.

He told me I was giving him an education. His receptiveness and love for my life story made the process very enjoyable for me as well. We continued working together on and off.

When our jobs separated us, I found others who would transcribe my story, but they were only looking to profit off me. When Aimable and I were reunited in Bujumbura about half a year later, we got back to work for another few months, but then I had to go to Kenya to work on Lake Turkana. I left the manuscript with him. It was about eighty pages long and captured roughly half of my story. Then a tragedy struck. I am often astonished at the sheer amount of tragedy and fortune that has been scattered throughout my life. In this case, Aimable had moved to Canada while I was away in Kenya, and he took my manuscript with him. I got back to Bujumbura in the summer of 1983 and went straight to Aimable's house. He was gone, I was told, and I had no way of reaching him. I thought I had lost all of our work. I felt empty inside and had no idea how I'd connect with him ever again. I was deflated. Later, in 1985, when I was living in North Carolina, I got a phone call out of the blue. It was Aimable. He had gotten my information from connections in Burundi. The joy we both felt was overwhelming. I was so happy to hear his voice after so long. There are some feelings that are beyond description, so I will not even try. I thought I had lost the manuscript, and I had given up. Then this call came up out of nowhere. It was a miracle day.

Within a few months, I caught a plane to Ottawa, and our project was back in business. I stayed with Aimable for two weeks, and we made incredible progress. I would venture back to Canada one more time to make further progress, but we would eventually continue working over the phone when I settled in Davis. Aimable would also visit me twice in California. Then the project lost steam. The time required and the distance, not to mention my two jobs and my family responsibilities, became hurdles that constantly pulled my attention away. I picked up the manuscript intermittently over the years, but it always got put back down when I thought about the difficulties I would face when writing alone. Then Aimable passed away. I was devastated. Not only did I lose a good friend, but I also felt the project had died with him.

Over the years, I had a handful of people work on my manuscript—UC Davis students, other Africans in the community, and even a French professional in Belgium. I dictated in French, and they typed out what I said on a computer. Finally, in 2015, I finished the first draft. I was happy for a whole minute before I realized that I had my extraordinary life story written in the wrong language. I was in the United States now, and I had kids who didn't speak a word of French. I needed to get the draft translated. That same year, in 2015, my old friend Jean François Duriex connected me with someone who could take the draft and hire the right people to translate it and turn it into a publishable manuscript. This kind and generous woman has done a lot of incredible work for refugees and the world. Her help sparked a lot of progress.

After four years of working with a writer, I had a complete manuscript in my hands, but it didn't reflect my story. Somehow, it had evolved into a political statement, with a lot of references from a lot of books. It was no longer about me. I really believed I had a good story to tell the world. I wanted it to be in my voice. I got it back from the writer; then I went back to the original French, found a translator on my own in Sacramento, and started all over again. After the new translation was completed, I worked with a few writers and editors who have helped me to bring this story to you.

I don't regret a day of my adventures. While I would warn young people not to go on long journeys without financial means as I did, I can't discourage them completely. One needs to leave in spirit before their feet can take them anywhere, as movement starts in the spirit and then follows in the body. The desire to leave has to be more pressing than everything else. You have to really want to go, or else you'll never leave.

But even when we don't know where we are headed, we must not forget where we came from. The bird may flitter and fly, but eventually he will have to perch, always on the branches of a tree. I know I am an American with Rwandan roots. I live in Davis, California. I have my own landscaping business and worked as a senior custodian at the UC Davis campus. I have become, even without a predetermined course, a man comfortably settled in a beautiful life, although it doesn't look anything like the future of my childhood dreams. But can my peaceful home heal the scars of racism, the scars of the genocide of my people? Can material comfort make up for a stolen childhood? I now have a family of my own, and I think perhaps, yes. As long as my children may be spared, so they can bring help and comfort to others.

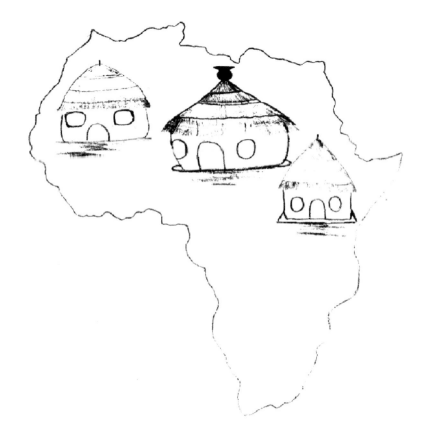

# Part One:
# A Childhood with
# Broken Wings

# CHAPTER 1

# Jabana: My Lost Paradise

I was born on July 17, 1954, in Jabana, Rwanda, the third in a family of seven children. I had two sisters and four brothers. My oldest sister, Mukabuzizi Specioza, was four when I was born. She was the fastest in our family, and she loved dancing. The second oldest was my brother, François Rusinzigwa. He was usually nice and friendly, but sometimes had a temper. I was next; then after me came my brother Celestin Kabisa. What I most remember about him is how much he loved the girls! In 1958, the fifth child in our family was born. Her name was Martha Mukabazayire. She was my soul sister. She was a tomboy, and everything about her was fun or funny. She was the queen in the family. My brother, who was next, ended up as a gentle giant. His name was Damacent Rukumba. He was very strong and a hard worker, ready to help anyone. Lastly, in 1960, my youngest brother, Emmanuel Hitayezu, who was always infatuated with animals, was born.

Growing up in the village created some of my fondest memories. We played together and always helped the younger ones so everyone could have fun. My parents, Maria Mukarukore and Kamili Buyenge, were very happy, building a life for us all. Mama was the foundation of the family, and she made everything feel like home. My dad was the roof. To make a home, you have to have a foundation and a roof. We were lucky to have both.

At six years old, I started school, but had it been up to me, I would have started earlier. I don't know what caused my precociousness. It might have been my exposure to the violence that had erupted in 1959 between the Hutus and the Tutsis in my village. It could've been the bedtime stories my papa told us as we all huddled in our one bed, four of his sons, dozing off to the sound of his voice. His stories were about growing up and how to stay out of trouble. They were stories his parents told him when he was a child.

Rwanda is known as "the land of a thousand hills" and is among the smallest countries in Africa. It sits below the equator between another of Africa's smallest countries, Burundi, and the Democratic Republic of Congo. Bordering Rwanda is Uganda and Tanzania. The country has two basic seasons: the rainy and the dry. We are known for our bananas, some of which are grown for cooking and others for beer. Rwanda also produces sorghum, beans, cassava, sweet potatoes, corn, peas, coffee, and tea.

Jabana, my native village, is on one of those thousand hills, which sits about twelve kilometers outside of Kigali, the country's capital. It had a good community for us as children to grow in. There was a lot of giving, sharing, and celebrating. One thing we always celebrated was the naming of a newborn. About a month after the birth, all the children in the village were invited into the home so the parents could introduce this newest member to their community. Each child was expected to give the newborn a name. The names were silly, funny, and sometimes didn't even make any sense. This big traditional ceremony tended to last at least half a day, and it was something everyone looked forward to. After all the kids had given the newborn a name, the parents would raise the child above the crowd and introduce him or her to the whole village. They would use the name they had already chosen before the ceremony, usually the name of a relative, like a cousin from a distant village.

The way of life in my father's house was the same as life was in most homes in the surrounding villages. We grew enough food to cover our needs, thanks to benevolent seasons. Rwandans live on what falls from the sky and what grows from the earth; the rain falls upon it seven to nine months a year, and we depend on this to live. The door of my father's house was always open, open to everyone. As children, we played without paying attention to whether we were part of the Hutus or Tutsis. As a matter of fact, no one worried about it at the time. It was a blessed time, but it ended without warning. The first signs of trouble came when my father was fired from his job as a policeman in 1959. He wasn't alone. Office workers, teachers, postal workers, and all Tutsi professionals were fired for being Tutsi. This was only the start of change in Rwanda.

Historically, in the late 1800s, Rwanda had three main African tribes: the Hutus, the Tutsis, and the Twa. We shared everything: our culture, religion, morals, and customs, and even our common language of Kinyarwanda. Our oneness was emphasized by the fact that we united under the same flag and national song as well. The Hutus and Tutsis were like the biblical brothers Cain and Abel. We intermarried, and our kids enjoyed the same lives. We were all Rwandan, even though the Hutus made up the majority of the population at about 85 percent. The Tutsis made up 14 percent and the Twa just 1 percent. Even with much shared, there were differences; the most basic difference between the tribes was based on how they made their livelihoods. Hutus were traditionally farmers, Tutsis were herdsmen, and the Twa were hunter-gatherers and potters. No one is quite sure where the inequality sprouted from, but many hypothesize that it was due to cattle being the most valuable asset in the lands. Since the Tutsis were herdsmen, they were richer than their counterparts, making them the de facto elite. Their power grew further when the Tutsi king, Kigeli IV Rwabugiri, expanded his territory and consolidated his power across Rwanda by appointing Tutsi chieftains in his newly acquired lands. In 1897, two years after his death, a window opened for Germans to directly colonize a weakened and unstable Rwanda. The Germans harnessed the divisions between the Tutsi chiefs and Hutus, their feudal subjects, before passing the reins to the Belgians after the First World War. By 1933, the Belgians had issued ID cards for each tribe, which emphasized minor ethnic differences such as heights and nose sizes, sowed deep tribal divisions, and solidified the apartheid system that continued to bring privilege to the Tutsis, but not to the Hutus. The separation of the population through different Identification Cards was the main root of all evils the peaceful and beautiful Rwanda went through.

Since I was a boy, I knew that the Belgian colonizers divided the tribes for their own purposes. Looking to profit from the colony, they forced farmers, regardless of their tribes, to grow coffee crops and forced both Hutus and Tutsis to leave their livelihoods to work on development projects like building roads. The Tutsi ruler at the time, King Mutara, eventually refused to cooperate with the Belgians in forcing labor on his people. He demanded independence from Belgium in 1956, two years after I was born, while tensions were rising with the Hutus. The Belgians provoked Hutus to violence, and the Hutus eventually rose up and revolted, took the Tutsi king out, and put their own Hutu in power.

In 1959, things reached a boiling point. Caught up in their rage and rebellion against the Belgians, Hutus raided Tutsi homes and forced them out of the country. We were forced to forget our lives' work and our lives altogether, leaving without fully being able to run from the danger, with so many of us left behind. This was the start of not only the anti-Tutsi discrimination, but the whole dehumanization of a people.

Our crime? We were Tutsi.

I always saw or heard talk of it. From whom? The Hutu government, which wanted our death, all our deaths. Most of the populace would just reluctantly bow and obey. Note that the Hutu majority wasn't extremist. Some would offer clothing, others tools, and still others something to eat.

The 1962 ethnic regime of the Hutu Grégoire Kayibanda, the first Rwandan president after independence from Belgium, would not be kind to Tutsis. Tutsis were banned from schools and jobs. We were stripped of our rights and were not even allowed to leave the country legally. We couldn't do anything, so we were forced to start growing food for ourselves in order to survive. Most of these people were not farmers; they were professors, bureaucrats, and doctors, so farming did not come easy. In my world, there was no ethnic hatred, not among my friends. Not in my paradise. I didn't even know by the age of nine that there were labels to describe those of us who lived in Rwanda as different people. In Jabana, we considered ourselves all Rwandans, children of the universe. Before I left school, we proudly sang "Our Rwanda," our national anthem.

Home-born Rwandans all, beat the victory drums!
Democracy has triumphed in our land.
All of us together we have striven for it arduously.
Together we have decreed it—Tutsi, Twa, Hutu,
with other racial elements,
This hard-won independence of ours,
Let us all join to build it up!
Let us cherish it in peace and in truth,
In freedom and in harmony!

When my father lost his police job in 1959, I was only five. We suffered worse living conditions, and my father fell back on agriculture to help feed his large family. But on what field, oh Lord! It was too small to sustain an African family, and my father had to start from scratch. He had never grown a vegetable in his life. There were a few good souls around who lent us a hand, but besides that, we were on our own.

The discrimination against the Tutsis only worsened as time went on. Hutus started seizing our land, arbitrarily carving out the lion's share for themselves, but it was unclear why they were acting so brutally toward us. As a child, I couldn't understand. Who or what were they avenging? We spoke the same language, shared the same culture, and ate the same food. We were one and the same. But the Tutsi king was a good king who wanted to protect all the people in his country, and the Belgians wanted to enact unfair labor practices. By printing identification documents that emphasized our tribal background, the colonizers caused us to turn against each other.

Having been brainwashed by Hutu extremists, even our own neighbors betrayed us. My father gave one of our neighbors a half acre of land as a wedding gift, helped build his house on the land, and treated him like family. However, the Hutu revolution changed everything. This same neighbor, whom my Dad had been so generous with, saw his chance to grow richer at our expense by stealing our land. My father was a well-respected man in the village and tried to rally the community to our protection. He brought them to our home and showed the land markers that demarcated our land, but even this failed because the movement against Tutsis was too strong. The ungrateful neighbor ripped out our land markers three different times, and we were forced to leave our fields and possessions behind to find shelter far from our ancestral lands. Though the plundering of our land forever remains etched in my memory, even this did not prepare me for the genocide that would occur thirty-five years later. It was without a name and without precedent in my homeland.

After we lost our home and our land, we had to move four miles away. My dad also had land here. We had to build a new house, but at least we still had land. In 1962, things got worse. My parents decided to send some of my siblings to live with different families in nearby villages in case of an attack on our home. That way, our family would have a better chance of survival. They sent me to a village around two miles away to live with an older couple, Pierre Tukokora and his wife, Euphraise, who were distant relatives of ours. I was nine when I was with them and in my third year of primary school. When not in school, I occupied myself with helpful chores like bringing water from the river and collecting wood for the stove.

One summer day started out like so many others. I went to the river to get water, came back, and did my chores; I cleaned and hung the laundry to dry and collected and stacked wood. Then I went on to enjoy a meal and pleasant conversation with Pierre and Euphrasie. I remember the exact moment things changed. We were laughing at something Pierre had said; he was such a jovial soul, always laughing and making jokes. We were all sitting in the house when suddenly, we heard piercing whistles and shouts outside. We ran to see what was going on and saw in the distance a raging mob of around forty Hutus storming toward us from the hills with clubs and machetes. We knew right away we were in trouble, but we didn't have anywhere to go. I had no time to think, so I just took off toward the banana plantation down from Pierre's hut. I hid behind a banana tree and watched as the mob dragged Pierre out of his home and beat him with clubs. I'll never forget the groans and shouts of the old man. My heart was beating faster than ever before, and I was sweaty and shaking. Then they dragged Pierre to the creek, where they hacked him to death in a rain of machetes. For the first time in my life, at eight years old, I saw a man die. It was not a natural death, and not just any man; it was the violent death of my beloved guardian, Pierre, at the hands of evil Hutus. In my terrified mind, I remember wondering, *Why? Why so much hate?* It didn't make sense. I didn't understand why he had to die just because he was a Tutsi. Just as the natural world is diverse, with mountains, trees, flowers, and rivers, humans come in all shapes, sizes, and colors. That's what made the world beautiful to me. That's what still makes the world beautiful to me.

I didn't know what to think. I didn't know whether to pray or not. I knew that the executioners must have been baptized, so it occurred to me that maybe I should pray to a demon instead of a saint.

I was worried about Euphrasie. Did she get away? Was she also dead? I didn't stay to find out. In Rwanda, we say that the gods of misfortune are also the gods of good fortune. I hoped that she was on their good side.

I ran for about forty minutes until I got back to my family in the hills. My nine-year-old mind kept repeating the same horrible vision of what I had just seen. I would be unable to wash that horrible image from my dreams for the next six months. Everything I was seeing before me—the trees, the bananas—all looked dangerous, as if they were evil Hutus trying to kill me. I just kept running. The tears in my eyes made it impossible to see clearly. In that moment, I was not myself; I was a being of pure panic and pain.

When I got to my family's hut, my father was nowhere to be seen, but everyone else was there. My mother and my siblings were panicked, ready to flee. They were grabbing clothes and putting them on, one on top of the other. I was in tears, having cried the whole way back. I told my family what had happened to Pierre, and we feared that the Hutus had killed our father in the same way, as the Hutus were at the moment targeting males fifteen or older.

We didn't have time to wait around; as my brother was seventeen, he would surely be the next target. We were all aware that they could have come any minute. My mother took the reins of the family without my father there and deemed it was time to go. That moment was the strongest I had ever seen my mother. It had been all of five minutes, and throughout it all, I just stood there, violent flashbacks playing out in my mind. We broke up into smaller groups and fled toward the next village. I traveled with my eleven-year-old brother. We carefully spaced our groups and parted onto different trails. We would all meet up at our local church, which was roughly a forty-five-minute speed walk from our home.

François and I were together on a trail that gently and quietly climbed up, then down, then up again, and so on for what felt like hours. My memory of it has us surrounded by darkness, though in truth, it was a bright, sunny day. We didn't dare talk—maybe a few whispers here and there, but we were terrified of what awaited us over each hill. The school associated with the church came into view first, then the church itself. Its cement-walled exterior, painted white, greeted my fearful heart in a way that I think only other religious folk can understand. A flash of comfort for just a second, then I urgently scanned the surroundings. My thoughts were on the rest of the group. François and I were the first to arrive, but then we had to wait for my mother and the rest of our siblings. My mind raced. Would they be OK? Would the Hutus find them and do what they did to Pierre?

After about an hour, we could stop. When we finally got there, we rallied at the Catholic mission of Kabuye. We had all made it, thank God. We arrived in the churchyard, where there was already a crowd gathered, and more people were coming over the hills, from every direction. You could see everyone, some carrying things, some crying, some holding and comforting their loved ones...some were injured and some frozen still in a state of shock, but everyone had darkness in their hearts; everyone was grieving. Suddenly, I saw Pierre's wife in the crowd, mourning and crying softly to herself. When I lived with them, she was always so happy, but seeing her now, without her husband of more than fifty years, the love of her life, she looked like a completely different person. The sorrow was unimaginable. I burst into tears again. Euphrasie was like a mother to me and her devastation on top of the loss of Pierre was too much for me to handle.

Other Tutsis from surrounding regions started to stream into the Kabuye Mission. I felt utterly devastated, thinking about everything my family had lost—our home, our cows, goats, clothes, everything we had owned. Then I heard other people's stories and saw blood streaming down people's faces from the beatings they endured at the hands of the Hutus. The blood was not their own, but their children's, their husbands' or wives', sometimes even their entire families'. Mothers had been forced to leave their children behind, as Hutus would take and kill Tutsi babies. My loss felt small in comparison to others', as aside from our father, we were all alive and together. Yet, as the cries filled the air and more and more victims joined the mass, I felt hopeless for us all.

What standard of living could we even expect at the Kabuye Mission? Without basic supplies, we slept on the floor, without mattresses or sufficient blankets. Because we didn't change out of our clothes—we had left everything behind, and many of us had only enough time to flee in what we had been wearing—we recognized each other by our single dirty outfits. We wore the same things everyday, as we had no options for obtaining new clothes in the refugee camp. Some people walked around in rags, their clothes having been torn to shreds by bands of Hutus. At night there was so much commotion that I slept at most three or four hours. I kept imagining how much worse it was for the children, who had to make their way through this chaotic crowd of hundreds. Still today, I wonder, where are they now? What became of their lives after all this? How sad and terrifying it must have been for them. Still today, I am haunted by this all. I cannot even imagine what the children, who went through worse, must have felt if they ever made it to adulthood. In terms of food, we had little to eat. Sorghum was scarce, but the grain was our only source of food at that point. People would try and go home to bring food back for the group. Sometimes they were caught, but when they came back, we all shared what we had. Conditions were not sanitary; there were no toilets, and there were hundreds of us. Within a week, dysentery set in, and infections and contagious diseases of all kinds and severity threatened to take more lives from one moment to the next.

But my family still had our health—as did my father, it turned out. We were playing soccer with other kids on the field. We had quickly bonded with many other children, just as you'd expect from such a situation. We were having fun together in the game, despite our dire circumstances. My brother was playing next to me when he suddenly screamed and took off. I followed him to see what it was, and there was my dad. He was walking toward us. I was so happy that I forgot the pain of my scraped shin, which had been scratched when I was fleeing from Pierre's hut. He was just as happy to see us because he'd had no news of us at all. It was the greatest relief in the world to see him. We surrounded him immediately with a joyful group hug, then we all took off to see my mom. My mama could not stop crying tears of joy. We were all very emotional. Later on, we asked where he hid, and he told us only that he'd been in the banana fields, but he would never speak of what he had been through. Very few indeed would have had my father's luck. It was three days after we had arrived at the mission. I still have the scar; it will always remind me of that terrible period in my life.

After three weeks, some government officials came to the mission and told us that peace had been made between the Hutus and Tutsis. We wanted to believe them, since we had no sense of peace or security. We had nothing to hold on to. When we returned to Jabana, it was just me and my family walking the five-mile trail together. We passed several Tutsi houses that were reduced to ash, the houses of people we knew. As we neared the end of the five or six hills between the church and our home, we saw black smoke rising into the sky, our neighbors' homes. I was aware of a strong sense of foreboding mixed with fear. We had a mud and brick home with an aluminum roof, so I figured they would not have been able to burn it. I was surprised to find our home in ruins anyway. They had chopped it up. When we returned to our home, we found it empty. The Hutus had taken our livestock, furniture, windows, and doors. Everything that could have been stolen was gone. We were the poorest in the world in that moment. What were we to do? Where were we to go? We still slept in our house, even though the tin roof was broken through with machetes, letting the shining stars stream through in the nighttime. When my siblings and I lay down at night in our bedroom, we gazed in amazement because we could see the stars through the roof! Even though my father tried to stop us, we kept having fun pointing at them, laughing and playing. His face was expressionless. He never smiled once, for all was lost for him.

After 1959, for the rest of his life, I never saw him return to his joyful self that I once knew. I wonder now if every morning when he opened his eyes, if the first thing he thought about was how his family would survive the day. How *he* would survive the day. What we would eat, how would we get the supplies necessary for protection, not only against more Hutus, but against the basic elements of the world? Storms would be coming soon, and we were not prepared to stop the rain from pouring through the holes in the roof. Every day I watched him slowly walk around the house, again and again, inspecting it, analyzing it, angrier each time. Angry at the evil people who took everything from him, from us. This ate at me.

Just as not all Germans were murderous to Jewish people, not all Hutus were bad. Some of them saved Tutsi lives by hiding them, protecting them, or giving them information—at times, even risking their own lives. In the night or early in the morning, before sunrise, some Hutus in the village brought us food, pots, plates, and household supplies. In Rwanda, we have a saying that if you have two friends, and you have just one cow, and if only one friend likes you, but you like the other, to which friend would you give the cow? You would give it to the one who likes you. These Hutus gave us just what we needed in our time of need. It helped me to see the true goodness in these people. In this critical moment after the trauma we had suffered, the most comforting realization was discovering that some of these Hutus were still close friends, like family, or even just simply good people, who did not support the trauma being done to us by other human beings. We could not have survived without their generosity. I imagine my parents were more than grateful. Little by little, our lives became more peaceful, but they would never be the same as they were before the waves of violence in 1959. After that, things were forever changed for the Tutsis in Rwanda.

Before the violence, the stereotype for Tutsis was that they were herders and intellectuals, while Hutus were stereotyped as ignorant farmers. This changed after the massacres, as Tutsi employees were fired from their jobs and their children expelled from school. One day, when I was in third grade, the principal came into my classroom and asked all the Tutsi children to raise their hands. He counted us and then left the classroom. I wondered why he didn't count the Hutu kids. For a second, I thought we were getting candy or some treat, but I told my mother what happened, and she wasn't nearly as excited. She knew what would come next, and sure enough, after the semester ended, when I went to sign up for the next semester, I found out that I couldn't. Along with most of the other Tutsi children, I was told to go home. They said they would let me know about registration, but they never did. This was the strategy of the government to deprive the Tutsi population of schooling. Not only did this impact our intellectual potential, but it set the stage for us to become seen as "others" to be despised by our own society. Even though my father had helped build the school, as well as the Kabuye church, and was key to the growth of the community, it did not matter in the end. He was Tutsi, and that was all the government needed to know to deprive him and his family of basic human decency.

Even as a policeman, my father was never feared, but rather respected for his work in the community, as he was committed to his people and his country. My father was a beacon of the community; whenever people had a problem, they would come to him. He would offer advice, offer to be a middleman, or even offer to help personally. His honesty and wisdom helped us through these dark times. What the Hutu government did to him, to us, to all our relatives, was something my father never forgot. Because of his reputation, my father's life was saved many times by neighbors who were willing to hide him during the escalation of violence against Tutsis. None of us were wounded or killed, which was rare, given the fact that most Tutsis suffered losses of limbs or lives altogether.

After being kicked out of school, my siblings and I had nothing to do. We tried to be useful by helping out with daily chores like planting beans, weeding, housecleaning, or fetching water and firewood. For the moment, we were useful, but that didn't make up for not being in school and having our paths to an education blocked. What a loss for the country's future! Instead of helping us fulfill our potential, the state abandoned us to the streets. I believe there are four stages in a human's life. The first is birth to twenty-five years old, which we don't appreciate, even though it's the most important. You don't know much. The second is twenty-five to fifty. These are important years because you build your whole life, including marriage, a job, a house, kids, and the rest. From fifty to seventy-five, you kick back, relax, and enjoy what you've built, peacefully. However, if you haven't learned what you needed to learn by then, there's little chance of you experiencing the peace of this stage. The last stage, however long it lasts, is a bonus. The Tutsis of my generation are in the third stage, humbled or crippled because of shallow political division that ended up destroying the peace between three good tribes.

Being kicked out of school meant my life consisted mostly of play, outside of the chores. It was a period of relative peace, though we didn't know for how long. I readjusted and regained a sense of ease. We lived day by day, month by month, and year by year. Tutsi children explored the countryside, bushes, and hills and killed time while most others were at school. I was always drawn to the rivers and forests, where I went fishing, climbed trees, hunted for food, or used a slingshot to shoot down birds, which we would grill later for dinner because there was not much else to eat. But there was never any pressure on me to bring home food; anything I gave to the family was a bonus. The fields on the edges of the village were their own paradise, their tall sorghum shoots hiding us from the rest of the world. A place where we could build small fires to grill sweet potatoes, corn, and other vegetables. These wild and beautiful places fed my young dreams, but more so, they subconsciously gave birth to an as-yet-unspoken desire to adventure, which would manifest itself just a few short years later.

The master wanderer was my youngest brother, Emmanuel. We called him Njumberi, which has no direct translation, but roughly meant "explorer." At three or four years old, he couldn't reach the plank of wood we used to bar our door in the night, but as soon as the door opened, he sprinted right out of the house to be gone until the evening. Nothing could keep him at home, not even my mother's scolding or even my father's spankings. Sometimes Njumberi would come back after the evening meal and go to bed without eating. My mother, worried that he wasn't eating enough, came up with a plan. She tied a string around his waist after he had eaten a full meal, only then letting him loose to the village. When he came back, she would check on how tight the string was. If it was tight, she would let him go to bed, but if it was loose, she would force him to eat. All of us stood around him, laughing and making fun of him. Every time I think of Njumberi's escapades, I think of my mother's soul and how she always showered us with love.

So what was my mother like? She was one the most selfless people I knew, and a role model to everyone in the village. Both my mother and father were devoted to improving our community. People visited her constantly for advice, mostly young girls, and my mother was always ready with wisdom to share. She also shared whatever meager amounts of food we had and helped other families weed fields, grind sorghum, and prepare banana beer and sorghum beer. Someone once told me a line from a

French poem (I can't remember which). The poem said, "The humble life of the mundane daily tasks is a labor of choice that requires much love." The poet surely must have been describing my mother. Reserved, generous, hardworking, my mother was loved and respected in the village. But it was for her children that she reserved the most love. This is how she was and will always be in my memories. Just recalling these memories makes me feel like a child again.

Though I had many fond memories from my youth, by the age of twelve, I was already tired of life, a life without a future in a country that rejected me. I was starting to think about my future, a common thing to do in Africa. I know it is different for American preteens. I wanted to fly with my own wings, hold my destiny within the palms of my own hands. So when I managed to get a seasonal job guarding rice fields from birds who pilfered the crops, in a project directed by the Chinese in Kabuye, I got a hint of what it felt like to be a man. They hired anyone who came, and they did not care whether I was Hutu or Tutsi. And best of all, I did not need an education. For a second, I almost believed I could land a career. I got a hint of what it felt like to be a man. Then, not only did I learn the job was only to last three months, but I was also only to be paid pennies, maybe ten cents for a whole day, from sunrise to sundown. The money I took home would have barely fed a bird, ironically. But even at that age, with all I had witnessed, I was glad to be alive.

But again, misfortune brings fortune. At around the same time, my father found a job on an irrigation project led by a Belgian developer who did not care about ethnic distinctions, but only about ability and job performance. This man promoted my father to supervise workers digging trenches. The job was another blessing for us.

When my job in the rice fields was over, I started selling roasted peanuts on the side of the road near where my dad worked. At this point, I was expected to contribute to the family income. We needed every cent. It was the only other thing I could do to survive. Every morning, as the sun rose, I'd walk about five kilometers to the market to buy one to three kilograms of fresh peanuts. I'd walk back to my house with the sack of peanuts, grill them in a pot over the fire, and then I'd either walk back to the market, around the village, or near my father's worksite to sell them. I gave half the profit to my family. That's how we did things in my family—you sank or swam as a group. I spent every second working, while kids my age played soccer. But the money I brought in was essential to my family. I felt like a hero; I was proud to be a significant help to my family. Where other kids were relaxing, I didn't have time for leisure or entertainment and never spent a penny on sweets. My siblings did the same as I did. They did chores, fetched water, gathered firewood, or helped out in the farm. Everyone had some role to play in the family; there was no time for mere play. Just being alive was more than we had hoped for as Tutsis.

For two years, I was able to scrape by and help my family in a small way. I was making pennies but still felt the bliss of being alive. Since there were some who didn't even have the opportunity to sell peanuts, I felt privileged. I also felt grateful for my family; we were brought closer together because of the struggles we faced and thus shared everything, small or big. It strengthened our bonds and our spirit, and it opened our hearts to each other and the world. We were full of smiles despite everything.

But, as we say in Rwanda, the sky became jealous of our happiness. The worksite moved away from the village. I had to start over, once again. There was no future in that village; we would never be able to thrive. At age fifteen, I was a young Sisyphus, carrying my boulder up the mountain to watch it fall and roll down to the bottom. Sisyphus was a king in Greek mythology who tried to outwit the gods and cheat death, and so was forced by Zeus, the king of the gods, to roll a boulder up a hill, but just before he could reach the top, it would always slip from his grasp. Then he would have to start all over again. I'd gotten a taste of his struggle. Maybe I was also paying for escaping the clutches of death, as I barely escaped the Hutu machete just seven years prior. My oldest brother, François, seventeen years old, knew just as well as I that the horizon would never be open to us in the village. So, at the young ages of fifteen and seventeen, my brother and I left our home village and went to Kigali, the capital of Rwanda, where we tried to start a new life.

## CHAPTER 2

# Kigali: Leaf in the wind

Kigali was a new world for me. It was very diverse, not only full of Hutus, Tutsis, and Twas, but also mixed race people and those who came from all over. Europe, India, China, Burundi, Uganda—it seemed like whole world was in Kigali. Kigali is a hilly city, much like any other place in Rwanda, small but bustling with restaurants, markets, and shops, though I didn't have much of a chance to shop here, even though I wanted to. Walking the streets, I remember gazing in wonder at the rainbow of fruits: mangoes, bananas, oranges, all laid out on the ground and in baskets. My brother and I slept on the streets as we tried to find our way. During the first few days, we picked flowers from the side of the road and sold them to the Muzungus (the white people) and rich Rwandans, but we hardly made any money. François decided it was best we sell fruit. We would buy fruit from the marketplace, then we would sell them to people at a slight premium. We did not make much money, but any money helped. François would stay at the market, selling bananas, avocados, and mangoes, and I would go door to door, selling in the richer neighborhoods where government employees, diplomats, and businessmen lived. Usually François would bring in more money; the marketplace was the place to sell. But it really depended on the day. Some days, a blessing would visit me, and one person would buy my whole basket.

One rainy April day in 1970, after a month and half of being a fruit salesman, I was going about my business and knocked on a white door of a large red-brick house. The personal chef of the house answered the door. My price was cheap enough to get him to buy a pineapple and a mango. Then the housekeeper walked up to the door and asked whether I knew anyone who could do gardening for the master of the house. I jumped at the chance to get myself hired. I told them I could do it, and they told me to come back in the morning to talk to the boss at 7:30 a.m. I was beyond excited. I was sixteen and ready for a career! I was also anxious about speaking to the boss. I knew he'd speak to me in French, and I only knew my native language, Kinyarwanda, and I wasn't going to learn French overnight. When I returned to my brother and told him of the wonderful news, he was ecstatic for the possibility of a better life for me. I don't think money even factored into his happiness; he was just happy for my gain.

François and I often changed the locations we slept in, whether it was because of the weather or the people that came to clear us out. Two weeks after we had moved our lives into Kigali, we had already found a group of boys of all ages who were in our situation. We stuck together, we slept together, and when people came to beat us, we ran together. The next morning, I got up early and arrived with a big smile on my face, despite being nervous. I got to the house half an hour early and went to the back door outside the kitchen to meet the chef. His name was Mousa. Judging from his looks, he was in his fifties; even now, I cannot picture him without his apron on. He was quiet, too, but always kind. He told me the boss was at breakfast, finishing up his coffee. Within a few minutes, a large white Belgian man came out to meet me. He greeted me with his chubby but clean-shaven face. He was wearing big glasses, his brown hair was specked with gray, and he was wearing a long-sleeved shirt with light-blue stripes, clean trousers, and dress shoes. He said, "Bonjour" to me, and I replied with the same, knowing well that I had already exhausted a third of my French vocabulary in the conversation. Thankfully, he turned to the chef right away, pointing to different sites in the backyard. I didn't know what he was saying, but I soon realized that I had been hired already. It didn't make sense to me. I didn't have to convince anyone. What luck! As soon as the boss stopped talking, the chef turned to me and translated the boss's instructions.

I was to wash the boss's car at seven o'clock every morning before he left for work. I would take care of the garden once he left. This meant weeding and planting flowers, vegetables, papaya, pineapples, and *marcoutcha*, a type of passion fruit popular in Rwanda. I gladly accepted the job and started working right away, getting a tour of the outside. It was the perfect size for a lone gardener like myself. My boss was called Jean Trudel. He was an official with the European Economic Community. That was all I needed to know. I felt blessed to be employed. Overnight, I went from a street urchin struggling for survival to a houseboy in the wealthy Kiyovu neighborhood. Things were still difficult; life as a Tutsi in these times could never be easy, but I felt at least a little safer. To be a houseboy for a European—what a point of pride! It didn't matter that I was essentially a servant. Isn't the king's dog the king of dogs? In Rwanda, we say that God spends the day in all parts of the world, but when the sun sets, he comes to sleep in Rwanda. That day, I was sure he had come to sleep in our land, and I was thankful for the blessing he brought me.

My monthly salary working for Jean Trudel was almost double that of my last job. I was guaranteed $12 per month, and I felt lucky. For the first time, I knew what it was like to have modern plumbing, electricity, and refrigeration. Halfway through my first workday, after Jean had lunch, the chef called me over to the kitchen and offered me lunch with the rest of the house staff. I joined the staff to a delicious meal of meatballs, fries, and salad. I was shocked that they were feeding me. Then, after lunch, I had my first glass of water chilled by a refrigerator. This was not something I ever expected to happen; these kinds of luxuries were beyond what I could have even dreamed of just weeks before. Best of all, not even a penny was taken out of my salary. Even though I now realize that was just a typical act of kindness, something anyone should be extended, at the time, I felt like a king. My family always said that the more you give, the more you gain. I truly believed it too.

There were, however, downsides to the job. Once I had my employment secured, my brother and I moved back home. It seemed like the violence had died down a little bit. I had to walk from my village, Jabana, to Kigali daily, which was a round trip of about twenty-four kilometers. I left before sunrise and did not return until after sundown. It was exhausting, but it was worth it. The salary allowed me to save a little money, and eventually I decided to buy a bicycle, which made the back-and-forth easier on me.

I had learned to ride a bicycle when I was nine or ten. At that time, people would bike from other villages and, with my father's permission, leave their bikes near my home along a fence since it was too hilly in my area to ride easily. Eventually, I started climbing onto the bikes when people left them there to learn how to ride. Thankfully, I was never caught in the act; it would have been like taking someone's car out for a joyride. They were big bicycles that we called "Chinese bikes." The first time I grabbed one, I couldn't reach the handlebars from the seat, so I just stood on the pedals with one foot going through the frame. It took me a while to learn to ride, but once I did, the kids thought I was a hero. I would cruise through the village on the bike for everyone to see. By the time the villagers got back to retrieve their bikes and head home for the night, I had placed them where they had left them, like no one had touched them. I couldn't wait for the next day, when they'd leave their bikes for me again.

Now, at sixteen, I was able to buy a bike with the money I had saved up working for Jean Trudel, and I was already an expert at riding. Soon after I got the bike, I found out about a race sponsored by a wealthy Rwandan businessman. Because I was commuting every day on the bike, I was in good shape to compete, so I signed up. The race was populated entirely by Rwandans, too, but none of us were professionals. When I looked at my competition, which was maybe one hundred other bikers, I knew I didn't have much of a chance at winning, but I decided to have fun with it anyway.

The race spanned downtown Kigali, but the hills would prove the most difficult part. Even though I was an expert commuter, the hills of Rwanda could slow down any man. But as I zoomed past the crowds cheering me on, yelling, "Look at the kid go!" I got a little energy back each time. I was happy to compete and afterward even received an honorary mention, since I was the youngest, and probably the skinniest, competitor in the race. Although I was certainly among the last to finish, I still look back on the race fondly.

Two years later, in the summer of 1972, Jean Trudel left Rwanda to return to Belgium. His contract had ended. I was thankful for what he did, since he treated me like a man and gave me two major skills that would serve me in the future: biking and gardening. I was also thankful because he had written me a letter of recommendation before leaving. A black man with a recommendation from a white man was a powerful force in that time. I went door to door offering my gardening services, and before long, and because of that letter, I was eventually offered a job. A German criminologist named M. Fredman hired me, though for Fredman, I was just a gardener; I did not plant any fruits. That made me a little sad because even today, my favorite part of gardening is seeing things grow. The patience it takes is something I have always valued. Under Fredman, I ended up making just a little more than I had under Jean Trudel, but all the money I made went straight to helping my family.

This period of relative ease was not to last. Once again, ethnic troubles quickly came to disrupt our lives. The year was 1973, and I was nineteen years old. The regime of President Kayibanda, the first president of Rwanda upon our newfound independence, decided to continue the harsh treatment of the Tutsis instead of promoting universal prosperity. I will not hide my disdain for Kayibanda and his regime. Under him, my life and the lives of all Tutsi people were torn apart in the worst kind of way. Before violence against all Tutsi people erupted again, the period in between was far from peaceful. Kayibanda and his men took Tutsis randomly, jailed them, killed them openly, or made them disappear, especially the few organized activists who remained—the intellectuals, students, small businessmen, and officials. But 1973 marked the year that violence broke out in full force again. As had become the custom, there were deaths. There was another wave of exiles. The main difference this time was that it was more difficult to escape than it had been to escape in 1959, as there were new checkpoints on all the major roads of the country. Vehicles were stopped and carefully searched, and passengers identified as Tutsi were sent back, imprisoned, beaten, or killed.

Considering the situation, I thanked my boss and gave him my resignation. The long road from Jabana to work in Kigali had become dangerous. It was impossible to get to work safely with all the ID checkpoints, as I was Tutsi and would get caught, and who knows what they would have done to me. The Hutu government had gotten out of control. Tutsi homes were already being burned. Each day brought new stories of killings of Tutsi in one place or another, increasing the angst and fear already so great within us. I was no longer a child but a grown man; I was beginning to critically assess the insanity of it all. Must one kill another because they come from another tribe? We were still of the same country, the same race. We spoke the same language and shared the same culture. Our lives were being controlled by pure evil again, and I knew I had to take them seriously. I had no other choice but to leave the country. My family also pushed me and my brother to leave. It had been a while since my family all slept under one roof. We had been sleeping apart for safety, either in banana plantations or in the forest. Each day or night that passed without incident was a divine blessing. We lost count of the dead in our extended family. Other relatives were forced into exile, including my grandparents, who were separated by the violence. My grandfather was still with us, but we assumed my grandmother was dead at this time.

The relationship between Hutu and Tutsi had gone from bad to worse. In Jabana one morning, we heard noises of whistles everywhere. Since 1959, we had known that whistles meant that it was time to flee. This was the final signal, the final warning. The day of total extermination of Tutsis had rung. My family split apart and ran into the woods, and fortunately, we found each other among the banana trees where we knew to meet. As lightning flashes and is immediately gone, we had a rapid family meeting to make important decisions and then flee. The conclusion of that meeting was one of the most difficult moments of my life. It was an intense situation full of panic for all of us. Split decisions were made. In fact, François and I were to go from the village, to leave the family immediately, to escape. Our family was falling apart but we had to quickly choose life or death.

I asked my mother, "Mom, am I a Tutsi?"

She paused to think about it before she answered, as all Rwandans were technically the same people; and as a child, it was hard for me to understand what could cause all this hostility. My mom looked at me with her eyes full of tears and said, "Yes, hundred percent Tutsi."

"But what have we done to deserve this? And where should I go? I want to stay with you, Mom," I said. My mind raced. *Why should a Tutsi die because of his race? And what is the difference from being colonized and having independence if these atrocities would continue?*

"You must go. Go far from here. I don't want you to die. I don't want my children's blood to flow in front of my eyes."

"I cannot go anywhere without you, Mom."

"Go, my child. Don't ask too many questions today. Don't talk too much." She screamed at me in her rushed, terrified voice.

I looked at my father one last time. By this time, he looked different, no longer the man I knew. No smile, no jokes. Even though he was trying to hide it, I could see his seriousness, his fear, his rage. The situation was finally too much for him. I realized, suddenly, that he had broken. This made me all the more anxious; I was trapped in a dilemma. I could run away, but what would I be leaving behind? It wasn't only my parents, brothers, and sisters, but the knowledge of their existence. The ability to find them again. Once I left, I knew it would be nearly impossible to be with them again if they were never able to return to Jabana, to our home.

My father and my mother held us as they tried to convince us to accept the decision.

"You know, you are so young, and you have life in front of you. You don't deserve to be killed. But don't worry; nothing will happen to us. We will meet when things go well," my mom said through tears. This remains one of the greatest heartbreaks of my lifetime.

We left with little Innocent Bayijahe, a cousin who had just arrived, fleeing his own village previously set ablaze. He came to us in tears and told us that he had watched as his village had been slaughtered. These were the darkest days of my life so far, having to say my goodbyes to my mother and father, having to leave them behind. The decision felt too swift. None of us—my parents, my brother, or I—were at all prepared for the separation, but no choice remained. We had to leave, and we had to leave right away. As it was excruciating for everyone, we were still dragging our feet when a Hutu woman came running up to us in the field, sweating and screaming that the Hutus were coming to our farm next. "Run away! Killers are coming to you with machetes! You are the next victims!"

It was a headlong flight; everybody ran in different directions like nesting birds surprised by a hunter's gunshot. Dogs were barking. We didn't breathe anything other than smoke, and fire shot up from everywhere on the hills and valleys. If you had a bird's-eye view of our village, you would be able to tell who a Tutsi was just by the location of smoke going into the sky.

# CHAPTER 3

# Rwanda: Escape

François had just turned twenty-one that day. Innocent was sixteen, and I was nineteen when we fled our former oasis. We headed north toward Gisenyi, Zaire, known then as Goma and now called the Democratic Republic of Congo (DRC). The strategy was for Innocent and me to meet François in Goma, but we were to take different routes to get there. We always found it easier for a group of two to sneak through the grass unnoticed. The elders would say the trail doesn't speak to the traveler. In other words, we were embarking on a journey without any certainty ahead of us. On this adventure, our fates would separate us so that in the end, nothing would work out as we expected, except that François would make it to Goma and wait for us there.

Up until this moment, we had never left Rwanda before, never needing to and, truly, never wanting to. I'd had everything I needed in my native Jabana home. So when I stepped on DRC soil for the first time, I was officially a foreigner, a refugee separated from my parents, my culture, and my own identity. Innocent and I knew nothing of Goma, the small town with its trails made of crystallized volcanic lava flows. We had imagined it bigger, like the Congolese country. All we knew was that we needed to find the Roman Catholic church, which, since 1959, had been the catchall for Tutsi refugees from Rwanda.

A young Zairian (Congolese) was kind enough to guide us. Hundreds of refugees from all over Rwanda had preceded us, and more were still pouring in. The young man took us to an office where we had to register our refugee status. While we waited in the line, Innocent and I asked everyone we could get ahold of if they knew or saw François. After we got registered, the two of us launched into the search for François. Not a trace. But people who knew him assured us he passed through and had gone on with his journey, to an unknown destination. We guessed Burundi, the country just south of Rwanda, where we believed we had family who had fled in decades past. For many of us refugees, Goma was only a waypoint on a much longer journey. Some hoped to go to Uganda, while others planned their exile to Burundi, each picking their destinations based on places they were most likely to find family links from the first wave of refugees that left in 1959.

We opted to search for François in Burundi, staying in Goma less than a week. It seemed the most likely place for François to go, as we had always thought some of our family lived in Burundi, forced there after the events of 1959. We were among a large number of refugees going to Bujumbura, Burundi's capital. It was a place of refuge and served as a hub for those headed to safer destinations like Uganda, Kenya, or Tanzania. Innocent and I then had no choice but to leave again. So, after five depressing days of searching with no answer, we decided to follow that same route to look for François.

We found a truck headed toward Burundi by way of Bukavu and Uvira in Eastern Congo and were able to take the journey in the truck bed. The journey was long, tiring, and emotionally trying, taking all night over some of the worst roads I have ever been on. It had so many potholes, which made the truck tip back and forth all night, and kept us jostling among the truck's goods, fearing that we would be crushed by the truck's load of empty bottles. But after two terrible days, we reached Uvira safe and sound, if not a little bruised. After our truck trip, we had to walk the rest of the way to Burundi. Uvira is a small town in Eastern Congo on the edge of Lake Tanganyika across from Bujumbura. Unlike Rwanda, it was as flat as could be. Innocent and I walked from Uvira to the border of Burundi, all the while withstanding the booing by Zaire locals who shouted, "Refugees! Refugees!" At the Zaire border, the guards refused to let us pass because we had no papers. It took us a long time to convince them we were only refugees bound for Burundi, but finally they let us pass. I think that they just tired of us and finally let us through, not wishing to deal with us anymore. The final walk into the country that would become my home for several years took us another three hours. But after that, we had finally made it to Burundi and hoped we could now find François. At the time, having just been through the terrors in Rwanda, I was scarred but not deterred by the cruel taunts of the Zairean natives, nor by the difficulties we faced along the journey. Crossing borders was something I would become well accustomed to later in my life. Had I known the extent of my journey before beginning it, I don't think I would have ever left!

# CHAPTER 4
# Burundi: My Home Away from Home

FAUSTIN AND ISABEL OUTSIDE IN THE GARDEN

Like the longed-for land of Canaan to the Jewish tribe, so was Burundi to Innocent and me! The whole journey was quiet between us; our only discussions were about dangers, worries, and fears. It was June 9, 1973, the day we arrived as refugees. Entry into this country had been easy, and the request for asylum was well received. The issues for Tutsis were well known to

Burundians who had wrestled with similar demons the previous year. But we knew we would be safe in this new country; the fights between the Hutus and Tutsis within Burundi were not our own.

Burundi is a small country similar in both size and ethnic composition to Rwanda, (with Twas, Hutus, and Tutsis). It was also a former Belgian colony like Rwanda. The two countries were like siblings: the same size, people, and geography. And like Rwanda, Burundi was no stranger to ethnic conflict. The country had just gone through a bloody war between Hutus and Tutsis, which they called "The Events of '72."

When we arrived in Burundi, we heard on the radio that the Rwandan president, Grégoire Kayibanda, had been removed by a coup led by Major-General Juvenal Habyarimana. He was now in power, which marked the beginning of the Second Republic, the fifth of July 1973. The new president called for peace and social harmony between the various ethnic groups. All this time, François had been waiting and looking for us in Goma for about a month. I still don't know how we missed him. Sadly, destiny would keep us apart for another ten years.

We took care of the red tape at the High Commission for Refugees office. Innocent and I went through the exhausting process of registering again. There were such long waiting lines for nothing more than a safe place to sleep at night! We were so many Rwandan refugees meeting in those lines!

The camp was already overcrowded when we got there, and refugees continued to stream in every day. Babies, youths, young women, men... all kinds of people living in a depressing, tiny space. Conditions here made malaria and other ailments certain. Every person we met had a story that would make your hair stand on end. All could recount the vicissitudes of their experiences, the acts of miscreants and bandits, the theft of possessions, the rape of young girls and women, deaths along the way, and aban-doned corpses without the simple courtesy of a marker. It was a butcher's bill of indescribable horrors.

After a week at the camp, we still felt alone in the immense crowd, having no luck finding other family members or acquain-tances. It was under these difficult circumstances that I ended up meeting a young girl. She was a resplendent beauty of nineteen, average height, slender, elegant, and light skinned. She had big eyes and long lashes, a broad forehead, and velvety soft skin. Her beautiful smile was a sort of relief against the desperate condi-tions we endured.

The first time I saw her, she approached me asking for infor-mation. She told me her name was Marie-Cécile, and she asked me where she could find water and get food. It was clear that she was dehydrated and starving, like many of us were. In our very first conversation, I was blessed that she shared her story with me. She had only been there two days so far, after a long journey with the same struggles that I had faced with Innocent: roadblocks, border guards, and too much death. She told me of her long and perilous journey. There had been many obstacles, and she'd had a number of near misses that could have ended in her death. She'd lost everything, including her parents, broth-ers, and sisters. When she exploded into tears at the end of her story, I hugged her, trying to console her, but I knew nothing I could do would repair the pain she felt. I looked into the distance and thought of my own parents. My own eyes flooded with tears. This girl and I were living similar lives. Listening to her story brought my own memories into clear focus. I took her by the hand—it felt both cold and wilted, like a dying flower—and we walked away from the crowd's prying eyes. On the streets outside the refugee camp, we walked and talked and shared stories alike. She showed me her legs and joints, swollen and bruised from the journey. She showed me her back, badly beaten after trying to escape. Back at the refugee camp, I massaged her scarred skin with hot water and oil, hoping to heal her damaged tissue. After the massage, she turned to me, looked into my eyes and said, "I am sorry, Faustin, that I cried in front of everyone. I couldn't hold it in; it was all too much."

I assured her, "Oh! Nothing to apologize for. The hurt is great. You are right to cry; it's even best in this type of situation, as it helps express the pain. Know you are not alone. Know that all in these camps are crying as we are in similar situations."

She took a deep breath, cleared her knotted throat, and asked, "Tell me, Faustin, what of your parents?"

I told her our story and then said, "I don't know if any of them are still alive."

She buried into my chest, crying. My throat knotted up. I offered more. "Let's hope all will go well for our families and our country."

"You are right," she said. "Better, let's think of those people that are suffering more than us in this moment."

I could see clearly, while holding her, the suffering and grief deep in her heart. I knew this deep suffering was echoed in the hearts of all my people. The thought overwhelmed me.

The more time I spent with Marie-Cécile, the more I learned about her. She was vibrant, smart, and full of ideas. She filled my heart with joy and love in those dark times. We spent a lot of our time together on the beach of Lake Tanganyika and walked around the town.

Bujumbura city is a gorgeous, flat town that sits on the edge of Lake Tanganyika and is decorated with palm trees and coconut trees that lend to its beauty. It is surrounded by tall mountains of West Congo and those of East Burundi, easily the prettiest mountains of the African Great Lakes. Its climate during the summer was warm and sunny twelve hours a day, but it was never miserable. We enjoyed these moments together.

But the wonderful time we spent together on the beach did not distract us entirely from the reality of our situation. If we wanted to survive, we would have to find work. Thankfully, it only took us all a few weeks to get jobs. Innocent had found his half sister in Bujumbura, who helped him find a job working in a boutique, while Marie-Cécile got a job as a babysitter. The fact that we were all able to find jobs so quickly was truly a miracle.

One morning passing through Kabondo, one of the higher-end neighborhoods on the east end of town, I noticed a dozen people pacing around a house. They seemed clearly of a different class than the neighborhood's residents. They were standing in front of the house, respectfully, as though they were awaiting orders. My sixth sense started tingling; it smelled like a prospective place of employment. I could smell a job.

I had been praying continuously to the Almighty, that he may grant me his blessing. I approached the group. A white man, they told me, needed a chef. I thought, "Really! I wonder if this could be my lucky day. This white man probably just landed in the country. If what he needs is a gardener, I am as good as in, thanks to my experiences in Kigali, and if he needs a cook, well… why not try my luck?" I waited with the others.

The European came out of his house. He began asking the others about their work experience. When it came to my turn, I didn't beat around the bush. I had taken the letters of recommendation from my former employers, the Trudels and Fredmans, and kept them close as I traveled to Burundi. I always took care to keep everything of importance on me since my exile, but the letters were by far the most important. To me, they might as well have been diplomas. The gentleman adjusted his glasses. He read them, popped into the house for a minute, and returned with his wife to let me know I had been selected. They told me they were looking for a boy, but it was my credentials they ended up valuing. What luck! My joy was immeasurable; I wanted to hug the man and his family for taking me on. The other candidates walked away empty-handed, largely from their lack of French and references. Lesson learned. More proof for me that everything works out according to God's plan.

## CHAPTER 5
# Bujumbura: Wanderlust

M y new employers wanted me to start working right away, in that very moment. Finally, after years of atrocities, I began to feel as though my luck was changing. God had heard me and handed down this job to me, answering my prayers. I remember humming old and joyous tunes learned in Jabana. I spent a few minutes meeting the people of the house, introducing myself and explaining I had only been in Burundi around two months, but really, I could tell I was supposed to begin working. My boss's name was Jean-Pierre Amande, and his wife was Danielle. Their daughter, Isabelle, was six years old at the time. By their names and their perfect French, I assumed they were from France, but I would later discover that they were originally from Belgium. Since Jean-Pierre taught chemistry at the Collège du Saint Esprit school and was gone most of the day, Danielle was the one to tell me the tasks that I would be undertaking. That involved anything like sweeping, mopping, doing the dishes, peeling potatoes, washing salad ingredients, and other jobs of that nature. I was elated to have work and felt grateful to go from having nothing to something.

To show my gratitude, I often worked harder and with more joy than was necessary in order to please the family that pulled me out of abject poverty. There was no limit to the hours that I was willing to work. The Amandes family was thus satisfied with my efforts and started to have faith in me, allowing me more and more time with their little Isabelle, who ended up becoming one of my greatest friends during the three years I worked for the family. She was very amusing, and we enjoyed each other. She drove away the dark thoughts that cropped up when I was alone, far away from home. In these moments, my thoughts drifted to the search for relatives. I missed my family that I left behind in the homeland so much. Little Isabelle allowed me to focus my thoughts to lighter things. But she also taught me French, all the while laughing at my accent and correcting me often. She did not even know that she gave me some of the greatest gifts I ever received: the French that would let me navigate the world, and a renewed joy that I had lost somewhere along the way to Bujumbura.

What did Isabelle appreciate about this humble servant? She was six years old, still learning about the world herself. I was comfortable with Isabelle and didn't hesitate to ask her to repeat words I did not understand. And she would always oblige me, but best of all, she never got tired of me. The best educators are undoubtedly those that have kept childlike ways. Could my time with Isabelle have been anything but a gift from God?

One joy rarely comes alone. It was at the Amande home that I would purchase one of the most important things in my life. Its acquisition was by itself an accomplishment, as I never could have had the spare money for such a jewel. The price of the bicycle was 15,000 Burundian francs, my entire monthly salary. I decided to share my dream with my employers in hopes of getting a loan from them. The generous Mr. and Mrs. Amande accepted. I rejoiced at the thought that I would return home on a bicycle, a bicycle all my own.

My new bicycle was very different from the ones I rode in my youth. Those were of Chinese make, large, heavy, and black. They had gigantic frames, with flat handlebars and fat tires. But this new one was so pretty! A race bicycle made by Peugeot with a thin frame, like that of a young teenage beauty in full bloom, and curved handlebars, like the offer of a kiss. This little marvel gave me more freedom of movement than I had ever had. Now in possession of a race bike, I found the doors of cycling clubs were open to me, and I could participate in races whenever I wanted.

About five years had passed. I still hadn't heard anything about my family, which weighed on me every day. Being in Burundi, so close to Rwanda, in a country so similar to my own, made me want to get away. I wanted to try something different. I planned a three-month absence from Burundi for myself to go on an adventure. It was something that only could have popped into my young and stupid head. I shared my decision with the Amande family, then planned to leave a few months later.

During my time in Burundi, I had built a life for myself and a new group of people who cared about me. But it never could completely take my mind off my family. All my friends tried to discourage me from leaving, but seeing my determination, they finally gave up. They had mentioned everything from wild animals to cannibalistic tribes, dangers of the forest, and Lord knows what else to try and discourage me. Nothing worked. Innocent worked the hardest of all to try and keep me from going. We had survived so much together, and he thought I was throwing it all away by leaving. They all thought I was crazy, and I likely was, but the insanity of youth made me feel invincible. However, they were unaware of two things: my youth in Jabana and early exile. Those two elements forged in me a heart of stone that even Isabelle and the Amande family could not see. At the same time, I developed an audacity and an open spirit of discovery! What ties did I have around me that would stop me from exploring elsewhere? I had fled my country at a dreamer's age. A new dream I did not yet have a name for was calling me. At least this time, I was hunted by no man. I wasn't drifting aimlessly. It was a choice. My own choice. When I thought of the possible dangers ahead of me, I knew I had seen worse. How could I imagine anything worse than what I had already gone through? I would go toward other people to discover our differences. I was, in my own way, on a search for man, as I hoped and wanted to believe in his humanity.

But one problem loomed heavier than all the rest: How would I announce this crazy idea to Marie-Cécile? My greatest friend in those darkest times had always been there for me, and I had always been there for her. I felt guilty about what I had to do, but I knew I had to go. There was no choice for me; the call of adventure was too great. When I told her, she threw herself into my arms and broke my heart, her goodbye undoing me. I cried, too, asking myself why I even wanted to undertake this mad adventure. There she was, standing there in front of me, ready to give me her heart and receive mine, whereas the adventure hadn't even started. Still, I could not deny adventure's magnetism! It was a real dilemma. I curse myself for breaking the heart of this frail jewel of a woman, but unshakable, I remained faithful to the demon that hungered for something else. She could sense it; my mind was made up. She accepted it in the end. Despite her sadness, she could see the reason for my decision. My deepest wish was that even from afar, the flame of our love would not go out. Before I left, she said to me, "Do not forget, you are the ambassador of all refugees; you will open doors for them. You have our blessing. Go forth and tell the people of the world of our situation."

Marie-Cécile had secretly held out hope that I would eventually renounce this adventure in the days before my departure. I knew it. After the last kisses, I saw her eyes redden. I looked away. She could not restrain herself. She melted away into tears.

She undid a bracelet from her wrist to put it on mine in memory of our love. Somewhere along the way, this love bracelet was lost. In the equatorial forests? In the deserts? I will likely never know.

# Part Two: Whirlwind of Adventure

# CHAPTER 6

# Tanzania: In the Forest

On the rather torrid afternoon of September 1, 1977, I set off toward Tanzania with the naivete of being only twenty-three, but with the wisdom that all of those years afforded me. My intention was to pass through Tanzania from west to east, up to the Kenyan border, passing through the town of Mwanza along the way. My khaki Bermuda shorts, white T-shirt, and baseball cap were new and felt just fine to me. In my backpack, I was carrying three spare tires, two inner tubes, a water bottle, a spear, a knife, and other useful items. The spear was tied to my bike, always facing forward. The backpack felt rigid, but I had filled it only with the essentials. Carrying more than you needed was the quickest way to make your journey more difficult. The oppressive sun of Bujumbura toward the edge of town made me sweat endlessly. My mind was sure, but my heart was uncertain. As I rode, I sometimes touched the Saint Christopher necklace hanging around my neck, a parting gift from Marie-Cécile. Saint Christopher is the patron saint of travelers, so I was told, so just touching it calmed my nerves and reminded me of Marie-Cecile. According to folklore he was extremely tall and spent his life searching to be in service of the most powerful. Meeting a hermit who told him of Christ, he was told that by helping travelers cross a dangerous river he would please the Almighty. He carried a child across who became so heavy that he almost did not make it. The child revealed himself to be Jesus. I didn't know his story at the time, but when I did learn it, I truly felt that Saint Christopher's guidance must have helped me. I believed that if Saint Christopher could carry Jesus across a river safely, he could carry me across Africa.

On September 3, I set course for Tanzania, the first country that would host me; its familiarity would be a good starting point. The wind and animals still sang familiar songs, and the men had familiar names. I even knew the language and clothing. I had picked up a bit of Swahili while living in Burundi, but just enough to get by. At this point I had no worries; the familiarity of the country gave me comfort and confidence. But I knew that soon enough I would be in foreign territory, where I recognized nothing and knew nobody.

I entered the border of Tanzania through Kobero. Everything that surrounded me felt foreign, the exact opposite of what I was expecting. The way the leaves rustled, the thousands of unidentifiable sounds. I had never experienced anything like that. I felt like a newcomer to nature. On one side, there were elephant droppings and immense termite mounds; on the other, new faces and foreign languages. The differences were captivating. Between my Rwandan roots and this new country that I would inhabit for less than a month, I felt a great contrast. Tanzania's population size was significantly larger at nearly 17 million people while Rwanda contained just over four million. Swahili and English were its two main languages though there were over 100 languages spoken and numerous tribes that called the country home. This was surprising to me because I was used to places where only one or two languages are spoken and at most three tribes present. Tanzania was also home to Mt. Kilimanjaro, the tallest mountain in Africa, and known for its vast wilderness and abundant wildlife both inland and offshore.

After understanding that Tanzania was not to be as I expected it, I moved on to the next stage of my journey. Towns flew by quickly. Crushing sun, oppressive heat, and a disastrous road made me start to regret going on this journey at all. I expected a flat tire soon enough, but knew I had enough spare parts to make it where I needed to go. The potholes in the road resembled the craters made by shells, though this country had known no war. The worst was yet to come. By this time, I was deep in a dense forest. I did not know how far it reached, or when I would escape it.

My thoughts touched on African mythology: the first animal formed by the Creator is the lion. Beautiful for man, but ferocious against man and not to be approached. God also created the cat, less fierce, a sort of miniature lion that man can hold in his arms and rock. As for the snake, it is dangerous, but does not harm infant humans, as they are defenseless. Animals of all species in this forest may or may not leave me be. I was defenseless. My fear grew as recollections of African myths multiplied in my mind. I would have liked to cycle fast, fly through, fly out and away, come out sooner. I quickly realized that the forest would not end soon, and it was getting dark. I rolled slowly, hoping to leave any trap unsprung. The tunnel was long; I racked my brain for any protective action I could take in the dense forest. The locals taught me that the animals were nocturnal and to be careful at night. During the daytime was safer as the animals were asleep. Around three or four o'clock in the afternoon, the sun began its daily retreat. I searched for shelter and attached my bike to a tree, as massive as it was gnarly. I climbed this tree to spend the night without having to worry overly about climbing leopards.

The Tanzanian forest was for me a baptism by fire. The night felt longer than a whole twenty-four hours! My night started at 4:00 p.m. The sun would not rise until 9:00 a.m. the next day.

But what a sun! In this night without end, I fidgeted with the Saint Christopher's necklace constantly. There were nocturnal murmurs, frightening in these parts: roars, howls, squeals, hooting, cries of agony, scampering, scattering. There was a plethora of unique sounds blending into a soft cacophony all over the scale; even the mosquitoes with their incessant buzzing joined into the orchestra. By some miracle, I was left untouched by any large animals. I appeared to suffer more fear than harm in my insane whim of a trip, risking my life without the need for it.

After such a terrible night, I still had to endure another day and a half before I made it out of the forest. The terrors finally let me be once I left the forest, but it was still another day before I would reach Mwanza.

Just as I left Mwanza, I was already exhausted and incapable of carrying on. I felt like I would collapse. In the village of Magu, I saw at the road's edge a robust man in his forties, of average height and sporting a pointy little beard. His name was Youssouf, and he carried in his hand a small bag. He had an air of friendliness and forthrightness. Exhausted as I was, I decided to ask him for shelter. When I told him I was traveling from Burundi to Kenya, he offered me his home and family. They were a poor family but rich in heart. The wife was of average stature, friendly, rather pretty, in her thirties, kind, and always smiling. Each time I looked at her during my stay, she smiled. The family also had a pretty girl who was around fourteen, and she had three little brothers between the ages of eight and ten.

I was invited to take part in a very joyful communal meal. The rice and smoked fish was shared by young and old alike, and it was delicious. The next day, however, I woke up with a fever, body aches, and a splitting headache. I quickly realized. My body, weakened by fatigue and the numerous mosquitoes of the dense forests I had just crossed, had given me malaria, a plague in the region. I rested all day to see if I could sleep it off, but the following morning, I was still unable to get up! I took niva-quine, malaria medicine that I had brought from Burundi, which seemed to help. I hoped the culprit was the anopheles mosquito and not another venomous insect. I was very lucky to have been sick with Youssouf and his family rather than alone in the forest. Here, in this welcoming home, I was taken care of. Mrs. Youssouf prepared corn porridge for me and even went to get sugar. This treat likely rarely entered the Youssouf household, except maybe in cases of ill health or holidays. It was quite an honor that was bestowed upon me! They also bought me whole wheat bread, another sign of their fidelity. Despite their heartfelt concern for my health, I was unable to swallow anything.

Youssouf returned in the evening from his smoked fish mar-ket to find his guest ill. Everything was interrupted so that the whole family could pray for me. Youssouf and his family slaugh-tered a chicken for me and attached it to my heart. It was in-credible generosity. They turned east and began worshipping in a monologue led by the head of the household. They did a litany of prayers. Some of these practices were new to me as they were Muslim, and I Catholic; but though our style of prayer differed, it felt as though we were one in the same in our belief in a higher power. I had no idea how beautifully poetic the Swahili language could be. It was unbelievable, even for the healthy. Would Allah grant me a prompt recovery? Based on the way the children looked me over, it seemed more likely that they were reciting prayers for the dying. The mother no longer left the house, pam-pering me endlessly. When I tried to give them a bit of money, they would all cry out with reproach, despite their clear need for it. I started walking with some difficulty and got around their attempts to stop me. Three days later, I made it to the market. There I bought sugar, bread, and meat. For the six days I spent in Magu, I tried every time to bring something pleasant home to share with them, at the end of each healing walk. On the morning of the sixth day, their prayers for my health were answered. I could pedal anew and finally get back on the road. For an intense minute, we were all overcome with emotion when I embarked on my journey again. I shared my gratitude for their hospitality and bid them adieu.

Having traveled narrow and tortuous roads, I arrived in Musoma, a small town built of giant stones that gave it unparalleled tourist appeal. I ran into the market, where I was greeted like an alien. Old and young alike yelled, *"Mutali wa Afrika!"* which meant "An African tourist!" I was such a rare breed! They pushed each other for a chance to touch me, pull on my clothes, arms, ears, and touched anything else they could. They turned my handlebars, felt my backpack, commenting all the while. I was so surprised and so happy to receive such a big welcome. I felt humbled by the excitement, especially after having come from living in the forest and sleeping under the trees. It was the first time in my life that anything like this had ever happened. I was given water and soda to quench my thirst. I was stunned; could I, a refugee, be so important? I didn't believe my eyes. This welcome strengthened my morale and took me from feeling like a wandering exile to a hero in mere moments—what a gift!

The going was difficult, trying to make my way through the crowds swirling about shouting, "A black tourist! Unheard of!" English, French, Americans, and Canadians, of course, were typical to them. But a black man! They were also surprised to hear me speak their language, Swahili, even if I spoke it with an accent. It was this common language that helped endear them to me even more.

I rushed into the entrance of a motel on the edge of the marketplace, the crowd following me. The attendant struggled to push back the crowd, but finally I was able to find protection and peace. At this very small motel, I showered and enjoyed a good chapati, a Tanzanian specialty, like crêpes. The sauce uses a goat meat base prepared with tomato, onion, and a bit of pepper. This delicious dish is highly prized in Tanzania. Traditional Tanzanian cuisine includes staples like samaki (fish), wali (rice), mshikaki (grilled meats) and abundant spices and is renowned for being flavorful and delicious. After my meal, I went on a walk for fresh air, during which I discovered the great Lake Victoria. This blue jewel, so beautiful, was the greatest of lakes I had ever seen, the largest in Africa and fourth largest in the world. Around the lake were very skilled artists, and I was filled with admiration in the face of the creativity surrounding the lake. I wondered if the natural beauty of the lake inspired the birth of human beauty in the form of ideas. Being so taken with Lake Victoria and all its surrounding stories, I lost myself into the evening, and thank God, for I was able to witness the stars reflecting on the glinting waves under a beaming moon. It was what I always imagined Eden to be.

Habari, ndugu. Meaning "How are you, my brother?" in Swahili.

I turned around to find myself in front of a man fixating on me with malicious eyes. The first thing I noticed was that he walked with a cane. My first feeling was a pity that was quickly erased by the man's cunning expression. He looked at me sideways, one crooked eye. He seemed to be in his early 20s, had short hair and a stocky build. He was wearing shorts and a short-sleeved shirt. His eyes were red and he seemed like a smoker. A sideways smile flashed on his big lips, turned white by dehydration. He told me his name was Mustapha and asked me for money, but I had no money to give him. I told him I was going to Kenya. Seeing an opportunity to instill superstition in me, he tried selling me a little tree twig that I was supposed to chew and spit out upon arriving at borders. If I used it, he told me, all barriers would be lifted before me. "Make your decision, quickly," he said. "And consult with Mustapha. Everyone"—he made a circular gesture—"knows he is never wrong. My brother! Make your decision!"

*The poor guy!* I thought to myself. I took a long look at him. He misunderstood the direction of my decision and told me the twig would only cost 250 Tanzanian shillings. In my heart of hearts, I didn't believe it. I was shocked. Who did he think I was? I can get visas and know where the embassy is, and as far as I know, these had nothing to do with wood twigs. There are people like him in every part of the world. They live off those who listen and trust in them. Down with this miserable man and his twigs. Only Saint Christopher needed watch over me. I tell him that my decision was that I needed no consultation, to which he yelped, "Then forget about Kenya! You shall not pass. You will die like a dog on the road. Mustapha can help you; you know?"

Discouraging the huckster, I told him what the so-called seers of my native Rwanda would do to extract money from the more naive among us. I knew one who, to impress clients, would surreptitiously place one or two frogs in a canteen. He would then bring it out in public, turn it over to show his marks that it was empty. In reality, the frogs were too large to pass through the narrow opening. He would then put it back right side up. Having riled up the frogs, he would start making predictions and got the money he desired quickly. His predictions would vary based on the movement of the canteen left or right, depending on the movements of the excited frogs inside. Seeing that I was unshakable, the huckster finally left me alone, and I continued to pass through the town on my way to Kenya.

## CHAPTER 7

# Kenya: The Green Country in the Sun

W hen I arrived at the Kenyan border, they asked the usual questions. Where I was going? What I was doing? How long would I be in Kenya? And finally, they asked for my papers. However, having no legal entry permit for Kenya, I presented my old pass received in Burundi that only gave me a right of entry into Tanzania. I was merely trying my luck, hoping upon hope that I did not get found out and stuck at the border. I watched with bated breath as the officer put my entry visa on my paper, allowing me entry into the country without asking any further questions. The document itself was written in French, and this officer was clearly a native English speaker. I counted myself truly lucky that day, because I do not think the man could read my documents and he just let me in.

On my route, I passed farms, intensive agriculture, tea plantations, mountains, valleys, and grass-grazing big sheep with thick wool like I had never before seen. I was in awe of the land's obvious fertility with crops ranging from flowers to coffee, mangos, chiles, and sweet potatoes. The weather was beautiful, and the people greeted me with open arms, warming my heart. I pedaled, pedaled, and pedaled some more. I took fruits and vegetables here and there to keep myself going. I took anything from pineapples, to maize, and even oranges from the fields along my route. I cherished them all. The splendor of fruits is that I did not have to grill them. This harvesting is permitted in the authentic African tradition, a sharing spirit that remains in the hearts of Africans. Near a cornfield, I stopped and cut down a few stalks and lit a fire with a few dry leaves and wood. Then, starving, I grilled myself some maize. The field's proprietor and his daughter, who I quickly discovered were named Benjamin and Bahati, respectively, found me there and proceeded to sit down near me to see who was in their field and what they were doing. Even though I was only doing what I needed to do, fear grew in me. The feeling seemed to be mutual. When they saw my bicycle and baggage, however, they realized that I was just a traveler in search of sustenance. "Have no fear. Make yourself at home, and eat as much as you can," the man told me while sitting on the trunk of a tree.

Having introduced myself and shared some pleasantries, I surprised Benjamin with my story.

"Are you sure you're going to Nairobi, on a bicycle? It is not possible," he said.

Considering the journey I had already made by my bicycle, and the state of the bicycle itself, the man came to understand that I was an uncommon traveler. He continued. "You are still very far from Nairobi. You could spend the night with us and continue on your way tomorrow."

Without hesitating, I accepted their generosity. I waited as I watched him. Then, he climbed back up the hill, cut some maize, and made a bundle for his daughter to carry, while saying, "Let's head home." On his return with the maize, he simply told his daughter and me to follow him. We walked in a line along a narrow trail, till it split in two. Then, we climbed up a small path and arrived in front of a great gray house, his home, surrounded on all sides by a garden, the likes of which I had only seen in monasteries. It was very clean, with neat and well-kept surround-ings, which I would not have expected of a farmer. I was even more surprised upon entering and finding that the interior was more impressive still. He expressed his regrets that his wife was not there, as she had gone to Molo with her elder sister, who was in labor. But the generosity of the two was more than enough for me, as they could have received a trespasser with much more ap-prehension and hostility.

The young girl first brought me a thermos containing tea, then bread, cheese, and papaya jam. Between sips, Benjamin told me that he was an agronomist and had won several prizes for his agricultural business. I quickly learned that this entire family was studious, as Bahati was also attending school on her own. Benjamin also told me that the jam and cheese were homemade, though I was able to tell just from the intensity and boldness of the flavor. Benjamin even had honey that he exported to neigh-boring Tanzania. I then shared parts of my own story, during which our conversation continued. His daughter hung on my ev-ery word. I mostly told my story for this young and pretty woman. I was truly struck by her beauty, but more than that, I simply loved spending the night in their home. I enjoyed the sense of community and camaraderie; but as always, very early in the morning, I set off on the next stage of my journey, basking in the generosity and hospitality of such a warm family. What comfort to have had the chance to meet such a kind souls!

# CHAPTER 8
# Nairobi: The Impossible City

O n November 10, 1977, I finally made it to Nairobi, the capital of Kenya. It was late when I came into town, probably around 10:00 p.m. Everything dazzled me here, with the lights and skyscrapers, and the cars passing like speeding comets while I huddled, both amazed and afraid, on the side of the road. I had never seen anything like it; Bujumbura and Mwaba could never compare to this metropolis. The worst part about coming into the city so unaware was that the cars drove on the opposite side of the road compared to what I was used to. And the roundabouts! At nighttime, I was risking my life biking with all of the cars. After a long and tiring journey, I had to bike through an unfamiliar city whose drivers drove on the opposite of the road. As amazed as I was, I was still toil-worn with fatigue after a long day of pedaling. My entire body was one great wound, and I looked awful and terrifying, covered in sweat and dust, with my Bermuda shorts and T-shirt falling apart at the seams. They hadn't been washed since leaving Bujumbura, more than a month ago. The soles of my shoes were only hanging on thanks to pieces of rope picked up here and there, the rest of my shoes having failed after about twelve hundred kilometers of my journey. The bicycle was also no longer in the best condition after all this time on rocky roads. The tires were worn, and the inner tubes no longer held air. My backpack was of no comfort either; on the bike's basket were two water jugs, and on my person a bag crusted with dust. On my bike were attached spare tires, flopping and overflowing on all sides. I was worried that, being in this town, I might be mistaken for a scarecrow with my dirty and dusty hat!

Fed up with being dirty, I dragged myself into the Esamin Hotel. It was one of countless Indian hotels in Nairobi, but it was truly a miracle that I was able to find it. As I wandered through the streets, I asked people where a hotel was so I could get some rest and some food. Many of them said the Esamin Hotel, but I had no idea where it was or how to get there. But then all of a sudden, through the twisting streets of Nairobi and what I think was a great deal of luck, I found myself there. The hotel was small and cheap in a very crowded area. The lodging was upstairs, accompanied by a restaurant downstairs. It was great to find both in one place. A good shower gave me the strength to slink down to the restaurant, where I pounced on the available food. In front of me was chapati, goat curry stew, and all the rice I could eat. Immediately after, I returned to my room and reflected on the surreal conditions of my long course from Bujumbura, on my journey through Tanzania, and finally to where I was now in Kenya. The beauty of everything around me, the incredible luck I experienced, and all the people who showered me with kindness, generosity, and charity. Just in these few dozen days, I had experienced so much of the good in the world. But my mind did not just dwell on the good. I thought of the forest, where I felt fear and thought I might die, but then my mind moved back to just how lucky I was to meet the people who helped me survive all of this so far. Soon enough, I passed out on my bed, with not a care in the world.

The next day, I decided to go exploring, thinking a little bit of walking would be good for my body. Most importantly, I needed new shoes to replace the ones I had been overworking since my journey began. Biking was out of the question after my harrowing experience the night before. I knew that my sore body needed to warm up, and I wanted to explore this beautiful city I found myself in. Instinctively, I decided to keep to the main avenue; I knew it was where my hotel was. And just looking around at the city, I knew I would quickly get lost if I ended up on some other street. I followed the avenue with slow and cautious steps. Everything was new, and I was continually solicited by a variety of shops, street barbers, shoe shiners, music shops, and people of all stripes reflecting the world. I discovered River Road, a lively neighborhood that raised my morale with its musical and festive cacophony. Every store played a different kind of music than the next. Indian, Kenyan, Congolese—each store had its own radio and its own style. It was the first time that I had seen such a lively street, and my heart rejoiced though at times it was a sensory overload.

What an astounding world at times! My Rwandan country boy background had been turned on its head. Along the way, I had forgotten the warning principle to stay on the main avenue. Step by step, I traversed one avenue, then another, without realizing, lost in the music. I was sucked in as if by a giant bellow. Looking behind me, a few minutes later, I quickly lost sight of my avenue. Panic! I attempted to retrace my steps but found myself utterly lost. *Where has the hotel's avenue gone?* I asked myself. *My avenue! The only avenue I could not lose track of!* I searched, made a large circle, and worried to no end. I eventually recognized that only a miracle would get me out of this trouble. When I asked people if they could tell me where the Esamin Hotel was, they asked which one I was talking about. Apparently, there were multiple Esamin Hotels, and I did not know what street mine was on. What to do? I launched blindly up streets, wandering in circles, and by luck ended up smack dab in front of the building.

I recognized it by my bike; it was unmistakable. My hotel indeed. God is good!

My time in Nairobi passed quickly. I rested up for about a week, healing my tired body, but then I knew it was time to continue. My adventurer's heart could not be stopped, even when my legs begged it to. One place in Nairobi stood out from all the rest, and that place took me to the next leg of my journey. I had never seen a train before Nairobi, but while in the city, they were impossible to miss. If you could not see them, then you could certainly hear them, whistling from afar. That magical machine called to me like nothing else. My plan was originally to travel from Burundi, to Tanzania, to Kenya, to Uganda, to the DRC, and then back home. But when I saw the train, it threw all my plans into flux. I had to go where it went; there was no choice. My planned three months were coming nearer to an end, but I could not return just yet. Not when there was so much more to see. And besides, going home was not an option. This truth was both empowering and heart-rending. As the master of my destiny, I was free to go with the winds of change. When I saw the locomotives, I knew it had to be.

On the last day of my stay in Nairobi I checked out of the hotel and ran to the station with all my belongings, bought a ticket, and was on board in minutes, embarked for Mombasa, riding an overnight train for the first time ever. I was nervous to ride in the mechanical beast that made such unfamiliar sounds, but after I had survived forests, malaria, and border crossings, a train was not going to stop me. The train ran through the night, and somehow, I was able to sleep through it all. Early in the morning we arrived, with my belongings intact. Long live the train!

# CHAPTER 9

# Mombasa: At the Ocean's Edge

Mombasa and Nairobi are two different cities, not only in size but also in culture. Nairobi is a huge city; and Mombasa, a humid, smaller city, has old buildings abutting the sea but is well kept and bordered with palm trees along the oceanfront. Beyond the tourist interests such as vibrant cultures, safaris and beaches, the town has one of the largest ports of east Africa, and is drowned in a forest of coconut trees and flowers, each prettier than the next. Two memories of Mombasa that stand out among the others: the coconuts, those wonderful fruits that give you drink as well as food and many other uses—it was almost the perfect food, filling all my needs. And the Twiga Lodge, which I chose from the many possibilities to stay in at the ocean's edge.

Twiga Lodge is a camping spot approximately seventeen kilometers from Mombasa. Kind souls told me it was the cheapest lodging in the area, mainly because you have to take the ferry at the city's edge to get there. I was able to board with my loyal, silent, and reliable partner, who always carried me without complaint through this interminable quest. After the ferry, we traveled a road that meandered toward the ocean's shore, and I finally saw it for the first time. From afar, at first. The coconut trees bordering the road through the hills still sometimes obscured the sea. The ocean still hid from me as I reached for it.

Along the road, people were smiling, relaxed, less reserved than those who had met me elsewhere, with more of an air of ease.

I arrived at the Twiga Lodge campground. The ocean spread out below, immense, free, to infinity! I ran down to it, contemplating the deep blue for the first time in my life. What came first was the impression, and then the certainty of infinity, in my mind. I think I could see the end of the world through the light mist and its acrobatics, practically immobile over the mass of water. Enclaved by land as I was in Rwanda, the Country of a Thousand Hills, it was a privilege to stand next to the deep blue immensity that joined worlds, the sky and the earth. My joy was great. What paradise! What majesty! I got such a shock from the ocean that I didn't dare to even wash my hands in it. Years later, I still have strong memories of that moment.

I spend a few hours roaming at the water's edge. In the end, I settled next to a coconut tree below the main campground nearest to the ocean. The rustling of coconut tree leaves at sunset, bordering the ocean and sandy shore, were enchanting, as were the murmuring of a thousand birds and a thousand more insects. The glistening of rocks, the lights dancing everywhere, stretching out beyond wide waters, glittered my eyes.

When I woke in the morning, I looked upon another planet. Where had the ocean gone? How had so much water disappeared all of a sudden? Was there something wrong with my eyes? The coconut trees were all solidly at their posts. The campground hadn't moved. But the water's lapping sounds had gone. Only the sand and rocks remained to testify to the water's existence before it pulled up stakes. Using my hand as a shield against the sun's rising rays, I caught a glimpse of the fugitive but, oh, so far! So I was not crazy, or on another planet. I asked around, and people told me about the tides. I was born in the Thousand Hills region and had attended very little school. My geography lessons were, consequently, very limited. I know only of the hills, not the ocean.

Soon enough it was Christmas. So by my count, I had been five months on the road already. And sometimes, off the road. I had already blown by the three months I had set for myself. Christmas reminded me of the midnight Mass sung in the church at Kabuye, but also of my family left back there so long ago. The house of God sat squarely in the foothills of Mount Jari, near Jabana.

In Rwanda, where the Catholic religion is dominant, I recalled the single-file line heading for the church. All, or nearly all, were dressed in white, in traditional loincloths. The costumes came out of deep suitcases with their strong odor of naphthalene (mothballs). Their lightness against hills embalmed in a thousand wildflower scents accorded it with the divine majesty.

The Kabuye site was splendid, as only priests know how to pick. It left a mark on my childhood. The immaculate procession of the numerous faithful converged toward the church. A worm was already munching at the apple, however, as priests divided the Hutus and the Tutsis.

Here, too, in Mombasa, Christmas happened outside. Twiga Lodge organized the festivities with games and incredible carousing. Dances to the rhythm of tom-toms and horn blowers, ropes on fire that twirled on the naked bellies of men, dancers spinning around till exhausted. It was so beautiful. And delicious! Christmas with fried fish, lamb and whole broached goats, and fountains of drinks. In Europe and North America, Christmas might be snow and holly trees and extravagant shopping, but the holiday is about joy and celebration there, too, just like in Africa.

I left the next day for Malindi, my next stop, about 120 kilometers from Twiga Lodge to the north-east. The road was flat the entire way, which I was grateful for, and was lined with palm and other tropical trees. While pedaling, I encountered an enormous, immense snake, bigger than me. Surely it was a boa barring my route. As soon as he saw me, he stopped, and I did the same. I did not know at the time, but we had scared each other. But I was not the one who made him backtrack. I think he was already full; otherwise, my time might have come. Heavily and slowly, he moved up toward the tall grass of the savanna, moving and shaking everything in his path. Ouf! It was not to be my last close call.

AFTER SWIMMING IN THE INDIAN OCEAN, 1977.

# CHAPTER 10
# Malindi: The Garden of Eden

A rosary of modern hotels and campsites ticked by along the ocean shore up to Malindi, a tourist town in the Arab style. There was a mosque at the center of town, and coconut trees were everywhere. This life cost me virtually nothing, as I ate and slept for free at the ocean's edge. It was first-class hotel level living near the ocean! I asked a fisherman to lend me a net, and he gave it to me happily. But not just their net—I even used their boat when they were not using it. I fished for my own supper: fish marinated in salt and lemon juice. Nature fed me, and the culture too. On the beach, in the water, under the stars, I lived like a king.

The weather was sunny, and several people joined me on the beach; these beaches of the Indian Ocean are among the prettiest in the world. The water was clean and blue, and a fresh wind blew upon them. Sitting on the fine white sand under the coconut trees, I contemplated the blue sky. I then noticed a majestic young girl walking in my direction. She walked right up to me, shocked as I was, and introduced herself as Jane. I told her my name and that I was from Rwanda but lived in Burundi. She thought she was dealing with someone who spoke English, as Kenya was a former British colony. She then launched into a long sentence I did not catch a word of. My English was just enough to say hello and introduce myself, but beyond that, I was hopelessly lost. I had no choice but to reply in a plodding French, thinking she would not understand either, but once again, the woman surprised me. She spoke French, and even better than mine. I invited her to sit with me, and she happily obliged, and I saw that her eyes were as blue as the ocean facing us, her hair blond like the sun, this pretty, white English girl. She was breathtaking. I had never been so close with a white woman before. It was clear that we had excellent chemistry, so I just decided to go with it. We spoke French to each other, and the fear I was feeling disappeared quickly. Our conversation took on a serious tone. Very quickly, we were close to each other. While we spoke, I was making a ball out of coconut tree leaves, and Jane was happy to see my creation. Then we decided to improvise a soccer game on the sand. This young girl played well; it wasn't much of a surprise—she was from England, after all.

Later, we walked on the beach, taking breaks beneath the trees, conversing all the while. We entered a bar, where we ordered two Tuskers, a very popular Kenyan beer, and spent a long time drinking and dancing to African music. It was more than pleasant. In between dances, she would ask me questions, each of which I answered happily. One of which was why I lived in Burundi if I was Rwandan. I once again shared my story, never tiring of telling it. "A tragic war has broken out in my country. It has spared neither the young, nor the old. Many have lost their lives. The luckiest ones, like me, have found refuge in neighboring countries, where they live as refugees." I saw Jane's blue eyes turn red and tear up. We talked about the war, this horrific, dramatic thing, but we did not stop at just Rwanda; our conversation spanned the entire planet. "My people are responsible for what is happening to you," admitted Jane. "Africa is a peaceful place, but since the arrival of whites, to supposedly bring civilization, it is now war all around. It is so sad. I apologize."

We continued our night by going to the stadium to see a local soccer match. The crowd was excited, and we took on the energy of the crowd. Once again, she surprised me.

"Thank you, Faustin, for these moments spent together. Now, would you accept my invitation to a restaurant?"

"No, it is you who must accept mine, but not to a restaurant. I cannot afford it."

"Where, then?"

"At my place, on the beach, under the coconut trees, where I live."

We both burst into laughter at these words. *At my place, on the beach.* I had never said anything so silly. "I caught some fish this morning in the ocean, and it is already marinated. There is enough for the both of us. All we need is the condiments."

We went to the market to pick up our needs for our meal: fruit for dessert and *fufu*, a doughy Kenyan main dish made of maize flour. It was incredibly delicious and healthy too. Back at my "place," we made a fire using branches and dry coconut tree leaves and proceeded to cook our fish on the hot coals. It was delicious. Afterward, we lay down on the sand, and she moved to kiss me. She was incredibly affectionate, open, and loving. Jane stayed with me on the beach for about ten days, which was much longer than I was expecting to stay. But each of those days were wonderful. Our daily activities were spontaneous walks and swimming, heading into the village for beer, and fishing for our food. My life was a paradise. Unfortunately, before long she had to return to work, and I had to continue my adventures.

Upon our goodbye, she stood near the bus that was supposed to take her away to Nairobi, but she didn't want to leave. We looked at each other without saying a word, and I admit, it was a difficult goodbye. It was with a broken heart and a choked throat that I picked up my bicycle and, with determination, started off for Somalia. Somalia—a country I knew to be dangerous due to continual wars and wild animals that roamed the roads. I opted for a detour to the west, toward the village of Garissa, north of Malindi.

# CHAPTER 11

# Garissa: In White Hell

I arrived at Garissa, 111 kilometers to the north of Malindi, on January 2, 1978. One hundred and eleven painful challenges on a road without mercy. At least I had just spent a month in an earthly paradise at the edge of the Indian Ocean, the best part of that with Jane. Just before I arrived in Garsissa, I was surprised to run into several giraffes. Their long necks peeked above the trees before I could even see the rest of them. Even today, I am astonished every time I see the raw beauty of a giraffe. I noted their incredibly long necks, and their tan skin with brownish spots reminded me of a painter's easel. Their size rivaled that of the trees from which they tear leaves with great appetite. They are some of the most beautiful creatures of the wilderness, and I was about to stop to contemplate them with peace and awe, but fear of a nearby band of boars prevented me, even if the grazing giraffes themselves could not have been bothered. Though they may graze, I saw in them a fierce and fearful look that only made the band of boars more menacing to me. My fear of the boars quickly transformed into panic, as I had always been told boars were very dangerous. I decided to hide in a bush to let the horde pass, and I breathed again. Then, getting used to spontaneous danger and not being fazed like in the beginning of my journey, I continued pedaling on my way.

I spent a single night in Garissa, a very small village without any particular interest. Beyond, on my way to Somalia the next day, the trees thinned out, becoming scarcer. Under a beating sun, the vegetation was meager, and buildings give way to areas of hot sand that burned the feet, despite good soles. The people of Garissa warned me about conflict near the border. As I got closer, I could feel the war weigh on my soul; it was a feeling unlike any other. An unusual tension was noticeable in this great Kenyan territory claimed by Somalia. The few travelers that I ran into told me worrisome stories of quick executions and militias that appeared out of nowhere, and they all told me to be careful. I heard the slightest rumble of an engine and jumped; ridiculous, I know, but fear was an uncontrollable animal that made you go wild and lose your head!

Outside Garissa and toward Somalia, there was an extreme change of climate: the heat became suffocating under the scorching sun. Optimism was my only source of energy, and it was quickly waning. A few times, I had to stop and carry my bicycle off the road as military trucks and cars sped past or soldiers marched by, looking for rebels. The further I went, the more the vegetation yellowed, faded, then disappeared completely. All that was left was sun beating down on me from above and sand, reflecting the sun on me from below; my entire body sweated heavy beads. My T-shirt and shorts clung to my skin. With this heat, I had to work like two devils to make any headway in the sand. My bicycle blew its inner tubes out four times. And then, when I thought I was almost out of the straits, a great letdown was waiting for me on the road. I could not get to Somalia. People told me not to even try, that weapons were popping off on the other side of the border. A war without mercy had erupted between Somalia and Ethiopia, and the borders were closed. It was at this point that I had no choice but to venture to the nearest town, Wajir. From there, I would have to go back to Nairobi, because both Somalia and Ethiopia would deny me access entirely, and the journey to South Sudan was impossible due to the lack of roads.

I backtracked, every peddle push a struggle for soles and muscles until reaching Wajir. On the road, hell softened a little, though my inner tubes continued to explode regularly. I could not repair them, as the adhesives did not hold for longer than ten minutes or so, the sun melting the glue like snow. I noticed myself getting only more and more negative, having to continually start over and do useless and sun-harrowing work. I decide to try to invent a solution. I tore a few pages out of my notebook and stuffed them in between the inner tube and in the tire, hoping they would protect the glue from the heat. It helped a little bit, but only a little. The need to drink was more frequent under the brutal sun. But my water supply was too minimal for my body's needs. The quantity I could carry on my bicycle was clearly insufficient, especially in this extreme heat. To make it last all while deceiving my parched throat, I was forced to take a sip in my mouth and hold it there as long as possible. But oh, what water! It seems to be straight out of a boiler. All water, be it boiling or otherwise, puts out fire. But to put out the fire that burned in me with water so hot was just another spiral down into negativity.

When I finally reached Wajir, I stopped to trade for water and search for something to eat. A local culinary specialty preceded the place's reputation: goat skewers. It is a type of barbecue seasoned with African spices, and it is delicious. It felt like I ate half a goat, and at the time, it was the single most savory thing in the world. That is what hunger does to a person. I did not know what greater challenges the desert could bring that I had not already faced, and I realized for the first time that I was not looking forward to finding out. What compounded the depression I felt was knowing that I had to go all the way back to Nairobi. I wasn't making progress; I was going backward. The worst part was that the only decent way to Nairobi meant going further north, then east until I hit the good roads, and then I could finally go back down south and west. It would bring me very close to the Ethiopian border, which meant potential dangers. But it was the only choice I had in front of me. It was at this point that negativity and despair began to attack me from all sides.

On the way out from Wajir I encountered fewer bike troubles, and overall, the journey was more pleasant. But I would never call the journey itself pleasant at this point. There were little moments I found joy in, like seeing my first ostrich. The huge creatures always looked so strange. But it was on the way from Wajir that I made the acquaintance of some of my least favorite animals: vultures. They descended on me. The first to dive down on me almost knocked me over, all the more as I was not expecting such aggression from these giant birds. I did not even know that vultures would attack anything that was not dead. I continued to fight off this unexpected assault without realizing that the danger was coming from carrying a red backpack, attracting them to me. I would only understand it later, while telling the story to friends who knew everything about vulture behavior. It was only then, in the safety of a closed room, that I found that story funny.

## CHAPTER 12

# Kenya: A Break in the Journey

FAUSTIN'S BELATED CHRISTMAS CARD WITH HIS
BICYCLE, JANUARY 1978, IN NAIROBI. KENYA

I took the road that would eventually lead to the center of Kenya, the shortest and highest-quality road to Nairobi, where I hoped to take a rest. Finally, I was off the sand and dirt and found myself on pavement. I felt like I was flying, and by the distance I was able to travel, it might've looked like I was. All around me, fields of cotton and tea spread out far into the mountains like tailored gardens. It was on this road that I met another one of the great beauties of the world, Mount Kenya. I was fortunate enough to circle the mountain and see it from a few angles. On the roadside were pineapples, maize, strawberries, anything I could have ever wanted. A land of bounty! This spectacle helped me to forget the tracts of the past desert, which I had been in for days, but felt like months.

I arrived in the town of Nyeli, just a day or two from my destination of Nairobi. There was an immense crowd on the side of the road. Men, women, and children especially, flown in from everywhere! All came my direction in the middle of an indescribable pandemonium. All I could hear was the word "German" from every direction, from all these mouths.

"It's the German! It's the German!"

Confused, I look in all directions, searching for a German, only to finally understand that they were talking about me. That's it! Now I was German. More insanity! I had tried and done many things in my life, and I had even occasionally reached my own personal limits. But it had never occurred to me to change the color of my skin. For, in my mind, there is no doubt that a German is inevitably white.

The crowd swarmed me, submerging me. People touched me and choked me. My breathing was labored. I tried to pass through the swirling mess, but it was impossible! I struggled to beat back the determined crowd, finally resorting to violence, using elbows and feet, head, and body. I used up all my tricks without success to deal with the crowd. My face was drenched in sweat, flooding my already drained body.

Dazed, I try to find an answer to the mystery. I was bewildered to learn that the day before, the Kenyan media mentioned that a German was doing a tour of Kenya on a bicycle and was expected to pass through this place. Some people in the crowd were just as confused as I, since I certainly did not look German. I wanted to get out of there. I was dead set on getting to Nairobi, and these people were dead set on stopping me. After a while, though, I finally made my escape and pedaled onward, past that strange town.

Nairobi approached! I could detect this from the traffic that again intensified. I did not know how long my rim could hold in this irresponsible traffic. The rims on my bicycle were not the only things that were tired. My bike itself was tired. I could feel it. It did not roll at the same speed. The tires were completely worn, and my brake cable had snapped. It was my foot that took care of the task, despite the risk of wearing down my new shoes, but I had no choice. Still, I rolled on the best I could toward Nairobi.

In early 1978, I was finally in Nairobi. I was flat broke, and my needs were great. I needed food, clothing, and bicycle parts. I must find work, any work, as long as it made me a little money. I finally found employment as a loader and unloader for large trucks, requiring me to unload several tons of merchandise at great speed, but they had me start the same day. It was like hard labor in prison. Foodstuffs, piping, cement, everything went through here. One advantage of this type of work is that you were paid for each truck unloaded, meaning if you were sturdy and quick, you could make a decent amount. The salary was certainly not luxurious, but survival was possible. As the adage goes in our land: *"Ubusa buruta ubusabusa."* A little is better than nothing!

My visit to Nairobi turned into a living; I end up in the Kenyan city for nearly half a year. My employer was kind enough to house me for a just a little bit of my wage. At the start, I was terrible at my job. I did not realize how weak my journey had made me. All the times I did not have access to good food or overworked myself on the road finally reared their ugly head at this job. But after two months of eating well, sleeping well, and doing this backbreaking work every day, I adjusted. After I made some money, I felt much healthier. I had already bought myself new clothes and shoes, and thank the Lord, my bicycle was fixed with new mix-and-match parts where I could not find the original manufacturer parts; it took on its own international character. I replaced the rim, the chain, the spokes, and the brakes, and I armed myself with spare inner tubes and a road map that I had already started to read. I no longer had to be this blind man launching down roads without sight of the goal.

I also took advantage of this stay to discover this attractive Kenya, its many tribes, and varied fauna. When I met with the Masaai tribe, they told me that I came from their tribe, that all Tutsi people came from the Masaai, but more than that, we both came from the Horn of Africa, from what is now Ethiopia. That countless tribes all came from the same original tribe and migrated down and broke off into their own. It was a fascinating experience, to learn about not just the history of other people, but to learn about my own ethnic history as well. It endeared me to all the people in the world and confirmed in me that people are all the same. Hutu, Tutsi, Masaai—that mattered little. But I spent a great deal of time at the discos; Starlight and Choromo were their names. I've always been a dancer, and the disco was a perfect place to blow off steam after a long day of work. I made many friends and learned a good amount of Swahili along the way. In the end, though, my adventurer's disease took over my life again. So when I had enough to leave, I took the first opportunity I could, and that meant going to Uganda. I was back on the road again.

# CHAPTER 13
# Uganda: The Ugandan Turtle

B efore I left for Uganda, people assaulted me with their unsolicited opinions. "Why not go from Kenya to Sudan? Over there," my friends told me, "it's more human." In everyone's mind, Uganda—"the Pearl of Africa," as the English called it—had become the country of the bloody dictator Idi Amin, before whom nature itself seemed frozen with fear.

As was my custom, I ignored all sound advice. Uganda was on my original list of countries to visit, and I insisted on going. It wasn't any more simple or difficult than that. My friends resigned themselves to the inevitable and wished me a pleasant journey. I was still apprehensive, though, as all information filtering out of Uganda, which were just bits gathered here and there, were unanimously negative. It was not encouraging, but I gritted my teeth and remained stubborn. The chief reason I chose Uganda was that it was on my original list of countries I wanted to visit. My original path was to go from Uganda, to the DRC, and then back to Burundi. This time I had no strict plan; I just knew that Uganda was where I would go. From there, it was either the DRC or Sudan, and that decision was not in front of me yet, so I paid it little mind.

The next day, I left very early from Nairobi, heading to the city of Kampala, and pedaled hard until early afternoon. That was when, without warning, a tropical storm crashed down on me with its usual violence. I was not prepared to face the rain.

I had no poncho, nor anything else I could substitute for one—another mistake due to my youth and negligence. Once the rain went, I realize my provisions are spoiled. The biscuits and bread had become a formless mess. I immediately reached for my entry pass and found that, thankfully, it was dry and protected. I had the foresight to take care of the one document that could allow me to travel and had placed it in a small plastic bag. When I took it out to check on it, I was relieved to find it completely intact. I could do nothing about the food situation in that moment, so I simply pedaled on until I arrived at Malaba, the city straddling the Kenyan-Ugandan border around noon on August 16, 1978. I entered Uganda without difficulties, as those immigration agents, like the ones before, spoke only English and did not realize that my pass had expired many months and borders ago. My three-month travel pass had gotten me so much further than it was originally worth; I was thankful. All the better for me. Reassured, I renewed my provisions in food and water in the village and continued on.

My first impressions of Uganda, walking this new soil, were favorable. There was so much greenery and so many signs of fertility, and the soil was obviously rich in everything plants needed; banana groves, nuts, and fruits of all kinds dotted the landscape. The country exuded wealth. I arrived in Tororo, the first town after the border. The local population looked radiant and healthy. I was a bit disconcerted, as I had expected a country ravaged by the dictatorial Idi Amin Dada, a sterile land, with sad and miserable faces. It was only later that I realize the Ugandan people worked hard; that, and the fertile land and plentiful rain, was the secret of their abundance spread before me.

The people in Tororo welcomed me kindly. They greeted me, offering me a glass of water, and of course wanted to know my story, but I couldn't stop for long. Some of them knew me already from an interview I did with a Kenyan newspaper, but they still wanted to hear me tell my story. Still, it was quite early, and I wanted to push on to Jinja, the next town. The distance was roughly 130 kilometers, but that kind of distance I could make in two days without much trouble.

At Jinja, I meet fellow Rwandans, escaped refugees from the cyclical violence that our country had known. I stayed with a Rwandan family, an aging couple with no children at home, probably grown and off to earn their living elsewhere. Whenever I ran into other Rwandans, it brought down my mood. Besides the fact that I was reminded of my family, whose fate I did not know, I was reminded of François, who could have been any-where. But this couple reminded me most of all of Pierre. Staying with this couple took me back to a time in my life that I did not want to relive, but like Pierre and his wife, this couple was kind, if not a little harsh. It was clear that they were worried about me, but when they asked questions like, "Why are you doing this?" or told me I was throwing away my life, it hurt. But I had gone through hurt already; a little more did not destroy my mood. I understood their fear; I knew their pain. But more than that, I understood their disbelief; there was a reason I was interviewed by the Kenyan newspaper.

What I was doing was not something Rwandans really did, traveling around Africa without a goal on a bike. After growing up in Rwanda, death was not something that I feared overly. I was surrounded by it, death and misfortune; they were always close as a Tutsi in that country. So whenever people told what I was crazy for going on my adventure, I recalled all the young peo-ple in Rwanda who died before ever getting to leave their village, and all the grandparents who died never having seen the world.

It was in this family that I learned of an impossible story circulating Uganda that my hosts made me a party to. It was the story of the speaking turtle, a terrifying tale, completely insane. Farmers and even civil servants easily believed rumors, legends, and superstitions of all kinds. Tongues thus kept on running, the whole country under the spell of this fable:

A man comes from Tororo alone on a bicycle, toward Jinja, when he hears a voice calling for his attention.

"Hey! Man! Take me on your bicycle!"

The man, eyes wide, looks around but sees no one, despite hearing the fluted voice.

"I would like to arrive in Jinja before the end of the day."

The man follows the direction of the voice and finds nothing more than a turtle with its head out of its shell.

"Don't be an idiot! Yes, it's me talking," continues the turtle, approaching with its hesitant gait.

The man backs up.

"Have you not heard what I need? Come on! Pull me up!"

The man, hands trembling, pulls up the little creature onto the luggage rack of the bicycle, as carefully as though he were lifting up his sick mother. When he tries to tie the turtle down to prevent its fall, he is rebuked roughly.

"I am not an animal to be tied down!"

The man is in shock. Without saying anything, he pedals, spurred on by the voice of this pest of a turtle that ceaselessly tells him to go faster. He pedals and pedals as fast as he can. At Jinja, the turtle orders him to take them to the police headquarters. The man does as he is told. He is thought to be foolish, as one doesn't willingly show themselves in front of the armed men of Idi Amin Dada's Ugandan forces. At the headquarters, he tells the story. The military men double over with laughter. But not for long. The turtle stops the laughter on the spot.

"I want to see Idi Amin Dada, the president!"

Terror ensues! Amid the total chaos, the general commander is alerted and condemns the man who brought the turtle to be executed on the spot. Despite vehement protests, the man is tied up and bound to a post. The firing squad is formed. The salvo cracks, and the squad goes into shock. All those who touched a trigger have burned fingers, and some of them fall to the ground unconscious. However, the man attached to the post is unscathed. Not one bullet has struck him. The turtle's face makes a disdainful smirk.

"Is this how you thank do-gooders in this country? Now, free this man, and let him go in peace."

The turtle's voice is more authoritative than that of the general commander. Fearful, the soldiers follow these orders quickly. And in the general confusion, those men who had passed out recover and stand, dumbfounded.

"Now take me to Idi Amin, or let me speak to someone who has access to the president," said the turtle. In the latter case, it would not be necessary to see the president in person, so the soldiers take the turtle to the general, covered in medals and full garb. The turtle, however, is suddenly not very talkative.

"I demand the unconditional resignation of Idi Amin Dada, no more, no less. Eight rainless years should he refuse."

The commander retires to phone the president but is worried the president will ask him to fight the turtle. The commander is instead asked to ensure the turtle's protection.

I was not told the end of the turtle's story, but apparently the turtle spoke three Ugandan languages. The stir it caused in the country was great, as everyone spoke of it under their breath. Security services were on alert. Cartoon illustrators were under surveillance. As a foreigner on a bicycle, I didn't know how I should feel about the story. I could have easily been the person bringing the turtle in, and with the Ugandan military on high alert, I did not want to risk my chances. After already being mistaken for a German on my trip, being suspected of turtle smuggling now was not out of the range of possibilities!

The next day, after thanking the Rwandan family, I continued on my way to Kampala, the Ugandan capital. With each pedal push, I expected security agents to burst from a bush to arrest me, or for the local populace to lynch me under the pretext that my bicycle was used to carry the turtle into the country. My heart was palpitating the entire length between Jinja and Kampala. However, nothing negative occurred, and I arrive in Kampala after three and a half day's journey. Contrary to what I feared, each time I was hailed on the road, it was by a benevolent populace that wanted to greet me and satisfy their curiosity. The story of the talking turtle that mostly bothered official tyrants is just a hoax, but one that made quite a few panic. These fictional stories are frequent in Africa and are only meant to provoke an emotional and fearful reaction but can often become much more than just a story. I cannot remember how many times a story had popped up, or a doomsayer entered Jabana to spread superstition. But clearly, this superstition is not limited to Africa. I remember when the Y2K scare was on; I could not even buy a flashlight.

# CHAPTER 14
# Kampala: Kigeli V, The Last King of Rwanda

It was approximately three o'clock in the afternoon when I reached Kampala. I was starving and exhausted after my 650-kilometer journey from Nairobi. Not too far off the road, I was able to find a small restaurant where I stopped to break bread. I enjoyed katogo, a traditional Ugandan dish which consisted of a hearty portion of fried plantains served with soup, beef, beans, vegetables, and peanut sauce. On leaving the restaurant, I ran into a Rwandan who recognized me, as my fame was now established, thanks to my interview in *The Standard*, following my return from the desert. He offered to take me right away to King Kigeli V, the monarch who was dethroned during the early events of Rwanda in the 1960s, and I accepted with both enthusiasm and awe. It was an exceptional favor, taking me to see with my own eyes this king, a living legend for Rwandans, and particularly exiles. To be invited to meet the king just after arriving in this town, and just after hearing the insane turtle story, felt all like a whirlwind. One moment, I was fearing for my life; the next, I was being welcomed by a king. The king himself was a kind of refugee; he had lived in several countries, from Congo to Tanzania, but like myself, he could not return to Rwanda.

A king without a kingdom who had practically no time to reign, as he refused to reclaim his throne, waiting for calmer times. A year and a half later, he was already in exile. He was one of the most controversial kings in the tumultuous history of our poor Rwanda. Even now, I have a clear image in my mind of this king, who stood tall, taller than anyone else in the room. He was exactly how I imagined a king should be. In Rwandan refugee circles, his prestige was even greater, as he shared our struggle on some level. All the depictions passed through my head on my way to meet him. In the interior court of the palace (the residence looked every bit like one), the crowd was teeming with agitated courtiers.

For some of these courtiers, I was an adventurer, capable of anything. They had clearly read the interview and thought highly of me as a result. These people were the kindest to me. The meanest were trying to sell the idea that I was a spy paid by Rwanda, that the Hutu supremacist regime of Habyarimana sent me to collect information on the king's plans relating to the attack he had in the works. Or even to assassinate him!

Thank the Lord, they were not unanimous in their opinion about me. In the meantime, a messenger went to the king's quarters to alert him of my presence. When he appeared, his gaze fell upon us from his great two-meter height. The hands of the courtiers clapped three times to salute him, in accordance with Rwandan tradition. I could not believe my eyes. He was tall and handsome, Lord! His gaze was marvelous, as was his warm handshake. It seemed like he was the one who ought to preside over his people's destiny, but in this loaned palace? It felt wrong; the king had missed his rendezvous with history and now was forced to watch from afar.

I could not bring myself to join the chorus giving words of welcome, as I had lost my voice out of sheer humility: "May his reign be long!" they all said together, accompanied by much clapping. I just stood there in awe, which got me pinches, some more forceful than others, as the courtiers thought that I lacked respect for the king. When Kigeli asked me to tell my story, the courtiers sat in a circle around me, the king on his throne in front of me. I told them everything. At the end, he stood to give me a long handshake.

"You! You are a soldier! A soldier like these I have so few of. You deserve a medal of encouragement, as you are just starting out." All applauded. The king asked me then how far I wanted to go, and I admitted to him, almost inaudibly, that my desire was to tour Africa. He approved. I remembered actually asking myself whether I might be dreaming. I couldn't believe I was staring into the eyes of the king of Rwanda. He talked to me, understood me, and congratulated me in front of his court. In my mind, he was reconnecting with the history of great deeds and the generosity of Rwandan kings. I would have liked to kiss his ring, but I did not dare. Filled with joy and gratitude, I spoke up to thank our *mwami*, our king.

After my speech, the king rose amid a concert of applause and did something that still shocks me to my core. He hugged me! I did not expect a king to ever hug one of his subjects, but this king, a true king, embraced me like a brother. After this, he made it clear that I was welcome in his court as long as I wished and retired to his apartments, accompanied by the bowing of courtiers on his path. Among these, a man of a ripe old age approached me. He asked me multiple questions to determine if I was really my father's son, as I mentioned his name during my audience with the king. It was the first question he asked me, as it seemed he asked all those who came into contact with him. Feeling reassured, the elder told me he was part of my family. I didn't believe him immediately, as his colleagues teased him, telling him it was a strategy to win the good graces of the monarch. He, however, calmly told me he was named Cyubahiro and was the first cousin of Camille Buyenge, my father. At first I was in shock; then that shock turned to joy. To be met with a family member in such a strange place—it was unbelievable. Emotion welled up in me, but he did not stop the shock there.

He promised to take me to my maternal grandmother, who, since her exile, had been living in a refugee camp in Kyangwali, Bunyoro. When he named this grandmother whom we had all lost track of, I immediately believed his story. He gave details that any stranger to the family could not have known. I was told to stay and spend my time in this city at the king's residence. During my stay, I spent some time to reflect on just how strange my journey had become. I remembered all the naysayers in Nairobi, and the ones who told me to go to Sudan instead. If I had listened to them, what joys would I have missed out on? A talking turtle, an audience with a king, and now my long-lost grandmother. This could be nothing but divine providence.

Two days after my audience with the king, under the direction of Cyubahiro, I was already popular in Kampala, and then with no warning, Ugandan television came to schedule a televised interview with me to tell my story, yet again. I was truly honored to share my story with so many people, though the questions were much the same as the newspaper. But the one question that amused to no end was always when they asked, "Why?" My answer was always, "Why not?"

After this meeting, I decided to go see my grandmother Susanne, who I found out was living in a refugee camp in Cyangwali. I was very young when she vanished, so young that I no longer remembered her face, and I was eager to see her, to throw myself in her arms, as any grandson would for his grandmother. With my heart pounding at the thought of being the first child of my family to reunite with my mother's mother since her exile, I arrived in Cyangwali. The last time I saw her, in 1959, she was a woman in her prime who seemed to be able to withstand any-thing. Seventeen years later, I saw an old, thin, and frail woman. She bore a wrinkled face marked by the passage of time and by the misery of exile. She last saw me as a child of seven years. It is a man she sees now.

As soon as Cyubahiro presented me to this elderly relative, she turned into a torrent of tears and got up and brought me into her chest, all the while shaking like a leaf. Moved, all I could do was repeat, "Nyogokuru, Nyogokuru," the word in Kinyarwanda for "Grandmother." Once our intense emotions wound down a little bit, she told me her tale of misery, of solitude and nostalgia. She still had a little sister, more or less in the same state, but with just as few resources. Her disappearance in 1959, during the first events in Rwanda, had brought sadness to my entire family. Hutus had stormed her village and during the attack, my grandfather Michael guarded the back door and had my grandmother wait inside to be safe. When the commotion was over, she could not find him. She fled to the nearby Catholic mission and waited for any sign of him. He never arrived and she believed he had been killed. Heartbroken, she exiled to Uganda with other distraught refugees. Nobody could find any trace of her, and my grandfather had been forced back into celibacy with their children at an or-phanage, as no one knew whether she was alive or dead.

I was glad to finally see her, but her story plunged me back into sadness. Without strength or money, without a husband or children. Oh, how great her suffering! I refused to devolve into morbid imaginings—Jews, Armenians, Native Americans, Cambodians, victims of the slave trade, all the tragic history of the world because of the ferocity of men!

We spent the day visiting the refugee camp, inviting ourselves into friends' homes, joking and lazing about. They had done well, these refugees of Cyangwali. I admired them, their energy, the hard work of my compatriots, exiles from Rwanda. They had planted banana plots, and their fields were full of nuts, beans, cassava, and all varieties of food-producing tropical plants. Some even had sizable herds of large cattle. You could not tell them apart from the region's natives. Being a refugee is an enormous difficulty, as the emotional loss is compounded by the loss of all your property and belongings. To lament, to content oneself with this status and live a life of begging, is not a solution. Starting a small business, a new life, from nothing, is the best strategy for self-worth and the one most often chosen by refugees to rebuild their lives. They live in harmony and organize themselves as best they can to support each other and survive.

In the evening, the dancers among the camp came out. They had amazing abilities. For them, it was a way not only of putting warmth back into their lives, but also to keep their traditions alive, to share them.

After a week near my kin, I was ready to get back on the road to the capital. Bent by age and privations, my grandmother said her goodbyes in a quavering voice.

"My child, be strong and courageous! I don't know if I will see you again. I doubt it. You have lightened our load of misery. Bless you. And may my blessing accompany you on your journey. And if you see your parents again, greet them on my behalf, and that of my sister. Tell them we never forgot them."

The emotions ran high. It took all my willpower not to shed a tear in front of her, knowing it would have done nothing to help. An invisible force kept my feet rooted in front of her house, as though an unseen magnet were placed under my shoes. Leaving the remnants of home that I had found in King Kigeli V and my grandmother was no easy decision. Courage won in the end though. Even still, it was with a heavy heart that I arrived in Kampala. It weighed on me that I did not take the opportunity to thank the king as I should have. My journey continued the next day.

After Uganda, my next destination was Sudan, to the north, as I had decided to tour Africa. The old plan would not do; all the people I had met had changed me. From Nairobi to Mombasa, I was not Faustin of Rwanda anymore, and there was nothing for me in Burundi. What Sudan, and the rest of Africa, held for me was unknown. But it was something I had to know. Otherwise, I would have headed south to return to Burundi, passing through Zaire, now the Democratic Republic of Congo. The decision to carry on was not an easy one. Several factors pushed me to abandon the project: fatigue, hunger, thirst, problems I encountered with the bicycle, illness, and lack of money, among others. There were also the dangers of the forests, deserts, and wars. But I made my decision, irrevocably, so I must go.

I continued toward Gulu in the north of Uganda, pedaling as always. Just before this town, there was a national park called Falls National Park. I passed by it without entering, even though the road was paved and was very smooth. Not expecting any surprises, I was startled, when, after a bend in the road, something drew my eye to the base of the mountain. Everything seemed to move in front of me. The mountain itself seemed to be moving. Was it a hallucination? I stopped. No, my mind was still intact. In front of me at forty meters, there was a whole troupe of monkeys, macaque. They blocked the road. Very near, there was a small water hole formed by a stream pouring into it. The monkeys probably went there to quench their thirst. The macaque are not intimidated by my presence. They played, ate fruit, ran, climbed on a nearby tree, and squealed with joy. Some even mated. I approached them, afraid to get too close, but they let me pass. After leaving the monkeys, I crossed into an immense savanna filled with tall grass, so beautiful, so smooth, and so empty, you would think it was a garden tended by a ghost. I felt a peace that comes with watching bending and bowing grass. Ah, gardens, my old love! A serenity that touched my heart. I felt untouchable in this flat land, as though admitted to a corner of paradise.

# CHAPTER 15
# Sudan: The Land of Hospitality

FAUSTIN'S BICYCLE ADVENTURE IN SUDANESE MEDIA IN 1978

I arrived at Nimule at the Sudanese border on the evening of September 18, 1978. The border guards were at their post. One told me to come forward with a wave of his hand. Before I handed him my papers, he told me something in an unknown language, and I did not understand him. This soldier was drunk; I could smell the alcohol clear on his breath. Suddenly, his rifle

93

was pointed at me, and everything had turned dire. I could tell he would not hesitate to kill me and paint the landscape with my blood. I touched my necklace and made a silent prayer to Saint Christopher, my guardian. I prayed that he may send me a protector quickly, or else all would be lost. Almost instantly, my prayers were answered, and a guardian angel emerged from the building in front of us. He was thankfully sober. When he reached us, he spoke quickly in a strange dialect that seemed to me to contain as many threats as the barrel of a rifle. Thankfully, those threats were not aimed at me, but his comrade. This new soldier signaled me to move forward. The other, strangely, continued to point his rifle at me. Stumbling on obstacles, he got frustrated and gave me a hit on the head with his carbine. In that moment, I felt death hanging over me, and I did not even know why.

There was clearly a communication problem between these Sudanese guards and me. Swahili wasn't used here, so I could not even plead my case. I felt like I was from another world, completely lost, looking wide eyed at all the gestures of each agent that spoke. A third agent was finally called that spoke a little Swahili. He asked me the routine questions: "Where are you coming from? Where are you going? Why?" and others. It was an incredible relief to even hear the broken Swahili, and after a bit, the first soldier lowered his weapon. The Swahili-speaking soldier then asked for my travel documents. He took my pass and gave it to an immigration agent. They ask me what gibberish it was written in, and when I tell them it was French, they hurried to stamp it, not even glancing at it, and bade me welcome to Sudan. I breathed a sigh of relief. It was again my expired pass that allowed me entry into this new country. I wondered what would have happened if the agent had known French and if they had discovered my technically false documents. Whenever I remember that moment and the overwhelming fear of it all, my heart still beats as fast it did then, a mile a minute. But it was not an unfamiliar fear, just an amplified one, one that I felt every time I presented this expired pass. Every time I was met with this fear, I was forced to realize that I would have to fix the problem as soon as I possibly could.

Juba was one the most famous cities of Sudan, before the country separated and it became the capitol of South Sudan. At this time, the country was vast. The north was mostly Arab and Muslim; the south was mostly inhabited by Catholic blacks. My first crossing was through a peripheral region, with typical dwellings of the suburbs of African towns, covered in sheet metal or thatch. This was a poor area. Here the common languages were Arabic, Kidinka, Kishiruki, and many others. I was lost, both culturally and linguistically. Since my departure, it was the first time that I am without a shared language. From the first day I arrived, I knew that this leg of the journey would be uniquely difficult, though this difficult journey was not without its joys. Sudan has an incredible diversity of tribes, and I was fortunate enough to meet many of them.

I continue to Khartoum in the north. This time, I wanted to experience another mode of transportation: the boat. I had never been on a boat that size before, and when I saw the port, I thought, *Why not?* I took one that went up the Le Bahr el Jebel, one of the branches of the White Nile. My destination was Kosti via Malakal. The station was dark with crowds. After difficulties getting a ticket, probably because the boat was overcrowded, I was all packed up, on board, and headed to Malakal. It only made one trip per week, and no one wanted to miss it and be forced to wait another seven days. The fact that I happened to make it just before the boat left was incredible luck. Though I did not feel comfortable on the boat, the densely packed passengers and luggage made me uneasy deep inside. It did not help that this was my first time on an actual boat. Doubts swirled my mind. *Will the weight make the boat sink? Will I make it Kosti?* When it seemed like the boat was about to burst, we finally departed for Juba. On the river, the close quarters did not seem to be a source of tension; rather, it seemed they were a positive influence on the ambience of the boat. It was surprisingly perfect, with music and small chats between neighbors. Some shared diverse food. As for me, I contemplated the water, the nature. And quickly my fears melted away. In one spot, hippos attracted everyone's curiosity. But it was still lonely; I really felt the need to talk. Through gestures, I established communication with soldiers sitting next to me, likely headed for Kosti. We did not talk much, as we could not, but thankfully these soldiers were far kinder than the ones I encountered before. The voyage as a whole was beautiful but long, lasting a few days before tying up in port at Malakal. I was relieved to be done with the cramped and heated quarters of the boat, only to discover that the boat was broken down, which made clear the reason for stopping. We would apparently spend three days here awaiting repairs, a time I decided use to explore the town.

Malakal was a small town in what is now South Sudan. These South Sudanese were very lanky and tall, taller than the tallest Rwandan I had ever known. Still, legends peddled mainly in the West say that the *Watutsi* are actually the tallest humans in the world. The town was full of joy. In town, I saw a sort of boutique where I bought a special beverage, a homemade juice of guava, well iced. This was a shopkeeper that must have made a fortune, thanks to his mixer. His shop was constantly full, and I expected, his wallet even fuller. It was here that I met a strange young man, quite a bit taller than me. I approached him, thinking he might speak Swahili, as he seemed like one of those city boys you can find anywhere who knows how to handle a passerby. Sadly, he did not speak Swahili, but he was a problem solver. So after a bit, we figured out how to communicate with gestures. I pointed at things and made big motions. I smiled for happiness, frowned for sadness, and furrowed my eyebrows for concern and confusion. Sometimes my attempts to communicate with body language and facial expressions were so ridiculous that I would explode into laughter, which led to a variety of reactions from the people I was communicating with.

When I learned, years later, that there exists a language for the deaf, I wondered why the language wasn't spread to all people as a common language. If I had the power to decide, I would make it a staple of every educational system in the world. Communication proved to be the greatest handicap for me during this trip.

In short, this young Sudanese man gestured that I should follow him, and I acquiesced. We walked to his home, and I ended up staying with him there during my few restful days awaiting the boat repairs. I never learned his name, but he was my constant companion those couple of days. My guide helped me to discover his village and his friends. Among these, I met Rebecca, a beautiful young girl who ended up being of great help in communication.

Rebecca was eighteen years old and set herself apart from her peers. The first time I saw her, I thought immediately of a queen. She had very dark skin, like all her people, and her features were symmetrical, including her lovely dimples. With stark, beautiful eyes, well-drawn lips, and a sensual, supple waist, she was a true girl of Africa. Her life was radiant in the sun, and seeing her was like feeling a cool breeze in the desert. I learned later that she was a student. But when I first saw her, she was with her group of girlfriends. My guide took me to what must have been Rebecca's house, but when we arrived, we found the group sitting outside.

Immediately, Rebecca walked up to introduce herself to me. I must have had my mouth open, searching for breath! What a pleasant surprise, but what great tragedy as well, to have no ability to say anything in the local language. I gave her signs that I did not understand and then loudly said, "Swahili, French." What a joy when she responded in French: "Bonjour!" Divine beauty and divine surprise! As if in a dream, I responded, "Bonjour!" We talked a bit. Her French was not impressive, but it was more than enough for me. She quickly introduced her friends to me, but I only had eyes for her.

A star in the darkness! Since Uganda, my mouth had virtually always stayed closed, to the point it was now pasty. I had nobody to talk to, and I loved talking. But now this child, a gift of God, extracted me from my involuntary mutism. We ended up talking for a long time, a very long time. I learned from her that she was a student at the University of Khartoum, that she was a member of the Dinka tribe as well, and that her parents lived in Malakal. She told me of her people, whom I found fascinating. She taught me that the Dinka were divided into clans, or subtribes, and that she belonged to the Agar group. The Dinka have kept their culture and traditions and are a great tribe of nomadic cattlemen. Their herds, numbering in the thousands, are evidence of their wealth. You can find more in Malakal and Bor, than in Juba. They are tall, strong, and elegant. They eat mostly dairy products and the meat and blood of their cows. They are great warriors, like the Intore, those dancer-warriors of precolonial Rwanda, the bravery of whom my parents always told me stories of.

Each teenage Intore had to be part of a war militia. I learn that the young Dinka did the same. They are trained in the art of war, from a very young age, in order to defend against potential aggressors when they guard their cattle in faraway lands.

The Dinka live off the cow, their only sign of wealth. Their women prefer bracelets and necklaces on their bodies to clothing. It is exotic, beautiful to see, and original. A pleasant and real world! An Eden of the world. One day I fear that they may also be submerged by globalization, something I saw rampant in my travels,economic, political, cultural. That is unfortunately in progress across Africa and destroys the beauty, diversity, and originality of African cultures. It will be another Eden destroyed by contact with foreigners, very unfortunate for Africans who seem content and satisfied with their lifestyle. The world draws its beauty from cultural diversity; seeking to standardize the world would make it boring and deprive it of all joy.

She spread my story all around and made me into a local star. Our friendship quickly escalated into something more, and we embraced each other as lovers did. One afternoon, as I went to see her, I found her in the company of her other girlfriends, whom she introduced me to. Sitting on a kilt, she was having her hair braided, as beautiful and resplendent as ever. She stood to greet me, wrapping her arms around my shoulders, and I adored her even more. In turn, I wrapped my arms around her waist, noticing that my skin was not as soft as hers. For our intense minute of communion, my troubles fell away, and I forgot the other people and their hostile looks. Apart from her beauty, Rebecca was my only source of communication in the village. Was that not more precious than anything else?

Rebecca's friends seem amused by this little love, but as always, I had to continue on and unfortunately leave her. The repairs on the boat were finished, and it was time to ship out. As we parted, Rebecca embraced me strongly and looked at me intensely, and, as always upon leaving a love, my throat was knotted. I saw tears on her cheeks, which poured down her face and filled her dimples. My eyes watered too. I closed them and forced them shut, as everything in me tightened to push back tears that only wanted to escape and flow. But men don't cry. In my country, they say, "You cannot cry; you are a man." Then, silence. Goodbyes to my guide and then back in the direction of the port. Each time I separated from someone who mattered, I felt a pain like that of leaving my family once again. And every time, it reminded me of my family, and that broke my heart just a little. I still knew nothing of them, how they were doing, if they were alive or not. But there was no choice but to go forward; there was no time for tears or sentimentality.

Back on the boat, I renewed my vow of silence and noticed that everyone seemed better off after the three days of rest. I also saw new faces, on their way to Kosti, no doubt. These people we had picked up in Malakal. This final leg of the boat trip would take another four days. This half week was incredibly lonely. I still had nobody to talk to, so all I could do was watch nature and try to observe other people's conversations. It was deadly boring.

From Kosti, I took to the road on my bicycle again, my destination being Khartoum, the capital of Sudan. Here, the roads were good and well paved, but the sun was brutal, worse than in the south. My bicycle, thankfully, held up, and I was at peace and able to enjoy my ride and the sights. As I progressed, the conditions worsened. The roads were still good, but noticeably unmaintained. The greenery disappeared and made way for large sandy expanses. I was suddenly in a desert, nature and the temperature leading me to conclude the obvious. I encountered donkeys and horses, not fine, luxurious animals, but those used for the transport of planks, carts, men, and goods. It was here I also encountered camels for the first time. It is a strong animal with a small head carrying large eyes and a long snout, as well as an air of laziness. This beast has no hope of winning a beauty contest, and I find nothing to like in them.

Food was becoming scarce, so I ate anything at all that nature offered me. I grilled birds that I downed with a slingshot made from pieces of inner tubes, and whatever fruits I could find. This inadequate diet made me sick, and I was constantly miserable and had no medicinal solution, none of the medicinal plants being familiar to me.

The people may have been materially poor but were rich in heart, as always. On my route, every village welcomed and sheltered me; these people had true humanity. Cups of tea appeared out of thin air, and it was hard to turn them down. Often, people's generosity made me uncomfortable. To me, their legendary kindness is without equal in Africa, these people surrounded by desert giving me their most precious resource. The poor have nothing but embody the spirit of sharing, whereas those that have plenty are rarely generous. What can we do to change the world and its paradoxes?

On my way to Khartoum, I faced a nasty surprise: I saw from afar the sand fly as though it were rain. Large black clouds also appeared. I quickly wrapped my belongings and continued on, as the wind was headed my way. I was on my own and must find a way. I was afraid that this sand and wind might bury me alive, but it only lasted about thirty minutes, and then everything became dark around me. Sand clouds descended on me and suddenly hit me with astounding force. The sand entered my ears, my eyes, nostrils, and my mouth, even though everything was fully closed and compressed. Once it passed, as quickly as it started, I tried to get it out of everything, but to no avail. So, I gave up and just got used to the grinding of sand against skin. The storm had even damaged my eyes, and I could not fully see. To top it off, the wind continued and picked up the sand, turning it into floating art creations.

After much travail, I arrived in Khartoum, the capital of Sudan, in early October 1978. Khartoum, situated at the confluence of the Blue Nile and White Nile at Tuti, is a small town divided into three parts, Khartoum, Omdurman, and Bahari, by an arm of the river.

Here, my problem was again communication. They spoke Arabic and English in Khartoum. I knew neither. I arrived with a distended stomach; my throat was choked and dry. I asked a passerby where I could find lodging, and of course, he did not understand, so I gestured a sign for lying down. He nodded in understanding, a crowd now joining him. I heard them say, "Lokonda." "Lokonda Hostel," they all echoed. They asked me many questions—at least, I think they did—but I made it clear that I understood nothing. They took a paper and drew streets on it, then gave me directions with hand signs. Africans, always ready to do anything to help a stranger.

In the hostel's garden, there were whites, Arabs, blacks, but I was no longer surprised by the same curious scene I got each time I entered a crowd somewhere. All got up, surrounded me, and wanted to know something. The same questions were fired off from all sides in all kinds of languages, questions I didn't understand but could guess the meaning of. A thirty-year-old giant with a debonair look, who told me his name is Toto, said something in French. I woke up immediately, reached out, grabbed him, and hung on to him. His French was not great, like mine, which meant there were as many misunderstandings as understandings, but he saw my relief and took care of me.

Toto worked for the hostel's check-in desk, and I was grateful to be so taken care of by the world around me. He asked me where I was coming from, and I told him; the incredulous look on his face helped me feel how far I had gone. Sometimes I forgot how impossible this trip had been, and how unbelievable it was from an outside perspective. He even made me repeat it three times before believing me, making sure that he understood through our broken French. I would have liked to stop myself, to tell him it was a joke, that I was coming from Juba, for example. It took him days to come around to the truth of my story, and when he did, it was painful for me; he gave me a congratulatory slap on the back hard enough to fell a bull. With extreme force, he ground my hands, massaged my shoulders, and slapped my back over and over again. To him, I was Ulysses!

In Khartoum, this scorching town, thirst was pervasive, with temperatures of 115 degrees Fahrenheit, and I did nothing but drink. I bought excellent fresh guava, lemon, and grapefruit juices prepared by street vendors, pleasant ways to quench one's thirst. I also got myself a gift of tea, sold on street corners here. And I, of course, drank the water stored in enormous gourds on the street, put there for public use, made available to quench sunburned travelers. It was Ramadan, the holy month of strict fasting for Muslims, and I took part in the practice as a way to embrace the culture while I was there. It was not a difficult task as I had experienced going without food many times in my life; on my journey as well as when I was home in Rwanda. At home, it was due to the recurring decimation of our livelihoods by the Hutus. We Tutsis often had to rebuild from nothing.

However, even with Toto, communication remained my greatest problem. In restaurants, not knowing the names of dishes or their ingredients, I was guided to the kitchen so I could decide what I wanted to eat. I did not know the country's money, so at the market, I was forced to hand all my money to the vendors, and it was up to them to take whatever the goods I was buying were worth and give me the appropriate change. I did not worry about getting robbed. The Sudanese had proven to be both trustworthy and generous. By the end, I knew that I had not been robbed, but instead was occasionally given too much of something, not knowing how to express that I would only like half that quantity. I knew this experience was rare in many societies, where there is such inflexibility and surrender to help people who need it.

Incited by Toto, my guide and counselor, I decided one day to tell my adventures to the government authority. I selected the ministry of youth and sports. It was Toto who got me in to see the minister easily, as if he were the man's chief of staff. He made the authorities believe that my three-month pass that I'd had since the start was still valid. In a sales pitch I barely follow, he gave me praise with a panache that opened the road to Egypt easier than all the immigration stamps of all countries combined. In his poor and incomprehensible French, the minister told me it was unthinkable that I would go to Egypt on a bicycle, at least a thousand kilometers away. The hot desert sand would certainly be my last resting place, and I agreed with him on this; Egypt was too far from home, and I was not ready to die on the way there. But did I have any other way?

Returning to his normal decorum, the minister sat back down behind his massive desk and said, "Let's see, let's see." He was like all our ministers in his dramatic nature. He consulted a few files that a secretary brought, and I watched him sign them. His face had gone cold. I started to regret having come to see him. He told me, "Here is what we can do for you. In one week, I will get you on a train to Wadi Halfa and on a boat up to Aswan."

Though, I would have to wait to continue my journey, I never let something like a delay get me down and appreciated the generosity of the minister. Toto had to work much of the time, so I was left to my own devices. Instead of sitting in the hostel all day, I went about the town and found myself drawn to the Nile. Here, at the meeting place between the White and the Blue Nile,

I swam endlessly. I was astonished to find that not many people were swimming with me; certainly, there were a few, but in the heat, I was amazed that anybody could work at all. Though I suppose if I were raised in a desert, perhaps I would adjust to it as well. The majority of my wait was spent in the Nile, and right in the middle of the two rivers was a beautiful island called Tuti. There was a small population inhabiting and farming the island. They grew limes, vegetables, and alfalfa for donkeys. I spent a day and took a ferry out to the island just so I could swim in new places, and several other times during the week, I went to Tuti again and again. It was a gorgeous place, perfect for escaping the heat. The trees shaded me while I swam, and for a moment, it felt like I was living in paradise. When I was not swimming, I traveled Khartoum. It was a magnificent city that was on every side of the Nile. The different districts of Khartoum were not terribly different. The one that stuck out the most was the one I stayed in. Omdurman and Bahri were very similar, but that did not mean I was bored by them.

The week passed quickly, and soon I returned to the minister's office. He welcomed me as he did the first time and gave me tickets and money, which Toto told me was fifteen Sudanese pounds. "That race, all the same, cheapskates of a man," he said with disgust. I asked him of which race he spoke. "Of ministers," he replied. Why this disgust toward Khartoum, which I so liked? I certainly thought I liked Sudan, and it smiled upon me. What Toto saw as greed, I saw as generosity. The minister also organized interviews with journalists for me, and the next day, my bicycle and I were on the front page of every newspaper. On the eve of my departure, I said goodbye to Toto and thanked him for helping me out so much. Without him, my journey to Egypt would have been nearly impossible.

I had a lot of repairs to make on my bicycle and a lot of down-time to complete them. I got to work on my old companion after loading it on the transport to the Khartoum station, where the train left at dawn. I struggled to enter this place, as the crowd was so dense, especially along the railway. Small children ran and shouted, "*Chai sod, chai sod, chai leben.*" *Chai sod* is black tea. *Chai leben* is a tea with milk. This way, I learned a few bits of Arabic language and culture. On the train, if I leaned casually against the side of the train during a stop and shouted, "Chai leben!" kids would elbow and push through to bring me some. I did this often during my ride, to my great amusement.

The train was busier than an anthill. No one could move. For the duration of the trip, everyone on board was stiff and groaning. It was my second train since my journey to Mombasa, and even as uncomfortable as this one was, it was still more comfortable than that awful, rickety coastal train. I sat near an open window to try to catch a bit of air, but the air was still. Contemplating this hellscape that was the Sahara desert, I reflected on the creation of the world and wondered why such regional disparities exist. I pitied life in the desert with the heat and sand, where elsewhere there is vegetation and a livable climate. The hell of the Bible was here.

The Muslim population packed in the wagons ceaselessly thanked Allah for all they were given by him, and each time the train stopped, everyone got off and prostrated toward Mecca, so the train was emptied. Being the only African not praying on the train, I started to get suspicious looks from the other passengers. I am a Catholic, but to avoid being judged, I decided to follow them, to put myself behind them and imitate what they do after seeing their ritual a few times. I respect all religions. And is it not the same God that Christians and Muslims pray to? Only the method and practices of prayer vary. There were five prayer sessions per day for my traveling companions. Day and night, we rolled along, only stopping in some stations, the names of which were shouted: "Shendi, Atbara, Abu Ahmed!" In the train, it was like overheated iron. I remembered the counsel of the minister: "Do not travel by bicycle because of how hot the desert gets." I wonder how this compared to the desert he spoke of. We arrived at Wadi Halfa at sunset, and the next day we transferred from the train to the boat.

Wadi Halfa—a town resurrected from the dead. The port of Wadi Halfa straddles the Egyptian-Sudanese border. While exiting the train, the Sudanese stamped my old pass from Burundi. Before getting onto the boat, Egyptian immigration officers applied their stamp on my paper. Saint Christopher was decidedly protecting me, as yet again, border agents did not even give my document a second look.

All along the train journey, my greatest worry was for my bicycle. My God! What if it wasn't in the train car? What if, by a stroke of misfortune, it was unloaded in the wrong place by a railroad employee? I could only relax when, showing my ticket, I saw them extracting my bicycle from its resting position in the railcar. I felt its parts, felt its heft. It seemed to have held up, unlike some of the passengers who exited the train still groaning! Countless goods coming from Sudan were transferred from the train to the Egypt-bound boat. When we boarded the boat, we found it, too, was not all that comfortable, but at least it was easier to breathe. At around eleven in the morning, we left Wadi Halfa, headed for Egypt, the land of the pyramids.

# CHAPTER 16
# Egypt: Pharaoh

On November 2, 1978, our boat finally entered Egypt, the land of the pharaohs. I pushed my bicycle without any idea where I was going and found myself on the edge of Lake Nasser, where I sat for a while. I spent some time in deep reflection on the shore of this gorgeous lake. I remembered the bodies of water I had seen so far—Lake Victoria, the Nile—and that made me think of all the people I had met, all the people who had helped me along my journey. Much of my time there was devoted to discovering what I was hoping to find on this adventure. All this time, and I had allocated little time or concern to a *why*. My reason was because I wanted to, and because I wanted to it was something I had to do. By this point, travel had become an imperative. A life without it would be no life at all. While I was deep in reflection, someone touched my shoulder. It was a young man overloaded with luggage. "My name is Jaffar," he told me. Thankfully, he spoke a bit of Swahili. He saw instantly that I was a foreigner, a lost foreigner, and invited me to follow him, introducing me to the town along the way. We visited several families, and he introduced me to everyone and told them my story, each new family requiring a new retelling. It's not something I ever tired of, though, because every time I told my story, I gained a little insight or reflected on something new I did not think of before.

On our little journey, I learned that Jaffar was a young businessman selling bolts of cloth. Spontaneously, he decided to offer me a job carrying his merchandise. We hear the voice of the Most High through messengers, and Jaffar was a messenger with a gift for me at just the right time. Everywhere we went, we were served tea and beignets. Even if we did not sell the goods, we could certainly live this way, going door to door, eating the free food. But Jaffar often made sales; I quickly saw that he was an excellent entrepreneur. As I watched him work, I saw how amusing he is, that people like him, and that he is not only well known, but also well liked and well respected. Every piece of merchandise he pitched, he sold successfully.

Aswan is a sprawling, beautiful town with a dense population and countless mosques. In front of the grand hotels, superb horses pulled luxury cars with two or four seats adorned with drapes of shimmering colors, all for rich tourists visiting the city. After two days of working with Jaffar, I shared my intent to continue my journey. He protested fervently. "Impossible to let you go! You have not even met my direct family that lives forty-five kilometers from Aswan, not to mention, there will be a wedding in my family today. You must join!" It was not just the people who ended up liking him; I did as well. I was sold. Who could pass up a wedding?

Without a second thought, we got in a taxi and set out toward the wedding. It would be my first time attending a Muslim wedding, and I would discover many marvelous things. The family's festive atmosphere was on display, and we were surrounded by Arabic music, an incredible variety of instruments, and good ambiance. There was not much time to gape at the spectacle, though, as the bride arrived with shouts from her entourage, echoed by the family and guests. In the confusion, a rain of perfume and grains of rice scattered about the crowd. I later learned that apparently a wedding must smell good, and the rice represents wealth. To spread tenderness and happiness, we distributed little sugar cakes. Scents emanated from every direction, and Jaffar ceaselessly complimented the bride's beauty. There were fine dishes all around. Every guest consumed with fervor. Everything was perfectly arranged to ensure that the merriment would reign for many hours.

Two days after the wedding, I finally said my goodbyes to Jaffar, and my bicycle started eating up miles of the asphalt on the main road to Cairo. On this route, traffic was very dense, and there were plenty of villages to stop and quench my thirst before carrying on. And in each village, I was met with more kindness and generosity from the fine people of Egypt.

Despite being in a desert, Egypt had developed the most marvelous agriculture. It owes this to the Nile, which reaches the country's length from south to north. The Egyptians who live along the Nile's length from Aswan to Alexandria practice a type of intensive agriculture, to which the country owes its survival. They grow onions, tomatoes, beans, melons, oranges, lemons, wheat, rice, and countless other crops. Even the alfalfa that feeds their livestock. The surrounding region is mostly desert so this fertile land is the only place where such agriculture can exist. The Nile is the second longest river in the world and at over 30 million years old, the oldest. It remains the backbone of one of the world's earliest civilizations. Many of the country's greatest cities lie along the Nile, and on my bike, I found myself in all of them.

I rode through Luxor, one of the largest towns between Aswan and Cairo. I got scared by the blazing speed of the passing vehicles and lost the peace of mind that I was able to enjoy on the less-traversed roads; this stress would only get worse, as I would have to navigate through the dense throngs and crowds, cars, trucks, camels, and horse-drawn carts in Cairo. The city was a string of settlements. Upon entering the city, I felt like I was joining a never-ending street festival. I didn't know where to stand, let alone ride, as everywhere around me, there were people pushing through, vehicles honking, trucks squeezing all through the crowds. The people were in a hurry, and the buses passed without stopping, merely slowing down, not stopping, for the passengers to exit through the bus windows. I pushed my bicycle with some difficulty but got overwhelmed very quickly, losing sight of what to do next. More than once, I found myself stuck in a traffic jam of cars, everyone honking and yelling at me to move. But move where? This city was not designed for bicycles, nor the easily overwhelmed.

Situated at the heart of Cairo was Taharir, a gigantic three-level roundabout, where I observed a ridiculous song and dance. Here at the exact center of the city, it was insanity: cars, bikes, people on foot all in the same place, only separated by a bridge or a sidewalk. I did not know this at the time, but Cairo had a population of more than seven million. It seemed like every single one of those people congregated at Taharir, and why shouldn't they? It was the center of the city, after all, and it was beautiful in a kind of chaotic way. On the top level, there was a bridge for foot traffic that seemed to go around in circles, on the middle, an immense garden suspended above the ground, and on the ground level, the roundabout for vehicles. What madness! After all this, I felt the intense need to rest at a hotel, a quiet place. Thankfully, hotels were everywhere in a city the size of Cairo, which receives so many visitors. After checking in, I went up to my room on the fifth floor and rested, enjoying the quiet.

Much like Sudan, navigating the culture and language of Egypt was difficult. The people of Egypt whom I met did not speak any of the languages I knew, so I had to use signs to desperately gesture to what I wanted. The Egyptian people were also much lighter than I was; it came as a great surprise. And my skin, dark as night, made it clear that I was a foreigner. Sometimes my gestures worked; sometimes they did not. But eventually, I discovered where the Burundian Embassy was—finally, a place where I could talk to someone! The next day, I made it my first stop and in French asked to see the ambassador.

"And introduce you to the ambassador as whom?"

What should I tell him? Oh, my Saint Christopher! At the same moment that I was desperately searching for a way to introduce myself, the ambassador himself came out of his office, and the secretary introduced me spontaneously. He looked at me curiously and then said, "Enter." He returned to his office, and I followed him. He sat, and I stayed standing until he ordered me to sit in the chair in front of his desk.

I sat and launched into my story in my native language of Kirundi. When I told him I was a Rwandan refugee in Burundi since 1973 and that I had come from Burundi on a bicycle, he yelped! He did not want to believe me, like everyone else, but after I assured him many times of my story, he called the secretary and had the whole embassy staff called. In front of this distinguished audience, I retold everything: the departure from Burundi, the countries traversed, the difficulties encountered, and the indescribable joy experienced every day. Happiness, sadness, highs and lows, beginnings and endings. I told the whole story—or nearly all of it. Fearful whispers, happy murmurs, approval, indignation, compassion, sympathy all accompanied my storytelling. Gradually, as my story progressed, the face of the ambassador changed from incredulity to shock.

"It is the greatest journey that I have ever heard," he told me. The ambassador was an elegant man. He had shown himself to be very open, and after the others had left, we chatted at length.

All the pleasure was mine; having the opportunity to speak a language close to my own for the first time since Uganda was the sweetest relief in the world. I confided in this man and shared my plans to go to Libya, Tunisia, Algeria, Morocco, Mauritania, and then on to Senegal. On the train, I'd had little to do but think, and my mind often wandered to what my next journey would be. It was on that hot, cramped train that I decided to further my adventure. To take myself to see all that Africa had to offer. Sticking in the east and the north was not enough; I had to go west eventually. Libya was the natural and only choice, and from there, it made perfect sense to keep going on to the west. But after Senegal, I would traverse western Africa, central Africa, and then journey back down to Burundi. Perhaps that would be the end of my journey. But my adventurer's heart did not know; I could not know where my bike would take me. The ambassador found my plan audacious and equally impossible. But how could he doubt me, considering what I had already accomplished since Bujumbura?

Having made three calls to God only knows who, the news was not good. "It is not possible for you to go to Libya," he told me. "There are tensions between that country and Egypt. The border is closed, and there are no diplomatic relations between the two countries."

The ambassador ended up giving me some financial assistance, and I was impressed by the grandeur of his heart. I decided to return to Sudan, but before doing so, I felt that it was necessary to take a week's worth of well-deserved rest to explore Cairo, which at this point had cemented itself in my mind as one of the greatest cities of the world.

Out in Cairo, the skyscrapers and mosques dominated the scene. From afar, I saw the valley of kings, the tombs of Misri, and the pyramids of ancient pharaohs—crown jewels not just for Egypt but for the entire world. The crowds around the pyramids were also impressive: men, women, children, poor, rich, walking, wounded, hooligans, vendors of all kinds. Different races, different languages. The diversity of this bustling city was startling and beautiful. The imposing pyramids felt like living stones, stones brought up on the backs of men they say, up on the backs of slaves—which I do not believe—assembled and cut entirely by hand! I felt a kinship with these past builders; they were like me in a way. If it was the Israelites of the past who built this, they were exiles from their country as well. Forced to work and live in a strange and unknown land. Seeing it all, I found it unimaginable.

Of course, I had to visit the pyramids and devoted a day to doing so. Right from the entrance, a guide took us under his wing. In some places, we had to walk with hunched backs under the low ceilings, especially in the corridors. But not in the great halls! They truly earned their name. At some points, I could not see their end or even imagine what they could have been used for. There were several, perhaps for the pharaoh's slaves, or rooms to hold court. Who knows? I was transfixed. I smiled and nodded my head in contentment at every word from the guide's mouth, though I understood little of it. He switched from French to English often, and I did not need him to appreciate the mysteries of the pyramids, though I did appreciate having someone to lead me through this labyrinth. Even if I could, there was no way I could ever grasp all there is to know of the deep mysteries of the pyramids.

We continued to go up and down. The mazes were tiring to walk, and I found myself constantly wiping the sweat from my brow, breathing with difficulty in these close corridors. Climbing and lumbering through these hallways was not easy. We saw flat rocks at waist height. What were they for? I did not know; perhaps they served as the king's bed, maybe as a table, or some forgotten funeral ritual. The problem was knowing how all the rocks made it in through the one small door that I saw! We were shown the room reserved for wakes and viewing of the dead, then bedrooms where the king's treasures were watched over, to the last corner and cavity. I heard tall tales of these ancient times. I was told that all these things dated back to before Jesus Christ, as though men from these early times could know how to put together such things. There is a mystery, and those that know, know, and are no longer among us. Maybe one day, upon my death, I will finally have the answer to all these mysteries that I discover.

This visit to the pyramids pulled me up to the ranks of a privileged few in this world who have had the opportunity in their lifetime to come into contact with these historical and cultural marvels of Egypt: the pyramids, mosques, and the monument of Abu Simbell. I saw with my own eyes these things that people talk about all over the world. Coming back from it was like waking from a great dream!

After witnessing the majesty of the pyramids, I returned to the bustling city. Cairo was unlike any place I had ever been in; not only was the city itself gigantic, but the culture and customs fascinated me to no end. In my entire visit to the city, I did not once see anybody drinking alcohol. For such a large city, that was bizarre. I expected to see at least one drunkard or group of partiers while in the city, but it seemed that Cairo was sober. Any alcohol consumption was replaced with other vices. The one that I found the most interesting being *shisha*. Shisha would be what Americans call hookah, and in Cairo, there were countless shisha lounges, each one attached to a café. Though I did not participate, I saw those who did having fun, enjoying time with friends and family. To me, it was a beautiful practice. What worried me about it, and why I did not participate, was because these pipes were public. I did not know whose mouth had touched those pipes, or where they had been. Not to mention that being in an unfamiliar city while heavily intoxicated did not seem like a good idea. And so, for those reasons, I refrained from shisha, even though I usually like to try everything I can. That is the beauty of traveling. But I did enjoy the other vices of Cairo: coffee and tea. The people of Cairo must have drunk enough coffee to supply all of Burundi and Rwanda. I imagined that every person in this city must have been fired up on coffee and tea all day, every day. I preferred tea, of course, being raised on it. Cairo also offered me new foods that I had never tried before. This was one of the greatest joys of my travels, getting to try the foods of the world. The market was abundant with all varieties of goods. Street-side, there were tables as well as donkey and horse trailers teeming with anything one could desire. I could not get enough of a delightful dish called Falafel. It was a concoction of fried and seasoned chickpeas, feta cheese, vegetables, and yogurt sauce wrapped in pita bread. The mixture of all the foods in that wonderful bun nearly drove me to madness, and it was served with more familiar foods like beignets, which certainly helped.

My tourist journey through Egypt rekindled in me a sentiment of pride and satisfaction, and I left Egypt the way I came, traveling back to Aswan, but with my spirit rejuvenated. At the Egyptian border, I had problems with immigration, and the agentrefused to let me leave the country without paying a fine. Apparently, I went over the length of stay authorized in Egypt. Because the visa was written in Arabic, I had no idea, but I also had to keep a low profile, as I knew that I was illegal in every possible way. My long-expired pass already included papers I added myself to be able to include additional stamps. My excuse was that I couldn't read Arabic, and I told the border agent that I didn't have the money to pay for the fine. He thankfully accepted my story and let me go. It was on the boat bringing me back to Waldi Halfa that I celebrated the New Year, 1979, which was not celebrated in Muslim countries.

# CHAPTER 17
# Sudan: Red Tape

FAUSTIN AMONG FRIENDS ELIAS AND JUSTIN CELEBRATING
HIS AWARD OF A TRAVEL PERMIT UNDER A BEATING SUN.

At the Sudanese border the next day, there were thankfully no problems. But for reasons unknown to me, my mind was plagued with negative thoughts. I endlessly pondered the problems of Africa and the problems of my own country—specifically, the problems that drove me to become a man without a country. Then I thought of the Somali-Ethiopian war that was fought over land. My mind wandered to Egypt and Israel's battles over the Sinai, and further conflict between Chad and Libya. Once again, I faced failure due to the animosity between Egypt and Libya. As I visited more and more of Africa, I would learn more about countries at war, wars I was unaware of, tearing apart Angola, South Africa, Chad, Uganda, and Burundi. My heart bled and still bleeds to see beautiful Africa on fire, to see the blood of innocents flow, to see Africans destroy their future. There are better things to be done! Rather than thinking about the development of the continent and improving education, health, and showcasing the great cultural wealth of its countries, Africa launches useless wars that impoverish the populations and destroy infrastructure. And for what? For power? For diamonds or land? Over tribal differences? It would have been better to build roads between countries, East to west and north to south, to facilitate exchanges and promote fraternity between the people. This would be a good example for future generations.

I took the same train back that brought me to Egypt, and it was once again full of people. As this was the only means of transportation and it only operated once a week, this was everyone's chance to ride. I had to be clever to get around and weave a path through the throng of passengers. The train cars were overburdened to the point of bursting, with passengers even on the roof of the train. I joined those on the roof, lifting my bicycle first and then climbing aboard myself. I noticed that there were as many people on top of the train as inside it. The roof seemed to be the place to be, as there was at least a breeze.

Just before the train stopped at the next station, I saw my neighbors both right and left run and jump. I first thought that they were off to buy chai or food, but no! They were running from the police! I saw their uniforms among the massive crowd coming toward me. It was a mad stampede, everyone for themselves. Why? I had no idea and stayed on the train. When the police reached me, they ordered me to come down. My crime, as it turned out, was traveling on the roof of the train car. The police took me to the police station with the rest of the crowd that was caught. Some fugitives explained themselves, receiving baton hits from the policemen and paying fines. The police officer asked for my explanation, but because I did not speak the language, he released me. I was horrified to find that when I got back to the station, I had been left behind! The train took everything I had to my name: my bicycle, my papers, and my bag. I started panicking. After pacing around the station frantically, I hopped on the evening train bound for Khartoum and miraculously found my baggage at the train station there. I know just how lucky I was to find that I had anything left.

In Khartoum again, my first undertaking was to find the High Commission for Refugees (HCR) office to request new and legal papers, which would hopefully allow me to travel without fear. It was something I had put off for a while; I never liked dealing with the bureaucracy. I was young, but my youthful, wild mind finally got tired of all the red tape for travel. As a refugee, I felt the HCR would prove to be my only hope. In the courtyard, filled to the brim with men, women, children, and elders, a true reflection of a whole population, the United Nations flag floated in the air, and emotions flooded me. I saw in this symbol my whole being, my whole soul, my whole existence. The office of the HCR was a building that received hundreds of refugees every day, the majority of which in Khartoum were Eritrean, fleeing the war between their native country and Ethiopia. In this place, all were refugees, but I wondered how many stories I could hear just by going through the line. Perhaps I could find one just like my own. Long lines of people stood patiently under a merciless sun. Thankfully the UN had the good sense put out large water gourds to spare all these people the pain of dehydration. On all the faces, there was a clear sadness, nostalgia, and any number of other feelings that animated any person forced to live away from their native land. The life of a refugee was one I was accustomed to now; for these people, it was new as a fresh rain. Like everyone else, I settled obediently into the waiting line. To pass the time, we talked in small groups, each expounding on the causes that plunged their country into war, the suffering they had endured, the ordeal of the voyage that brought them here. The tears could not be held back by many. I could not blame them; their pain is a familiar one. The atmosphere was dark, heavy with the emotional burden of the crowd, unbearable. When I finally arrived at the head of the line, hours later, I was introduced to the person who would take care of my case.

His name was Jean-François Durieux, and he had himself a modest office, behind piles of files carefully organized on the table. Monsieur Durieux turned out to be a French-speaking Belgian. Finally, someone who spoke a language that I could understand a bit. He was also the first to be able to read my passport. Durieux was always a serious man, honest, jovial, and direct. Without him, I would never have been able to continue my adventure—at least, what I accomplished after Sudan. I laid out my problem to him and presented my papers. He turned it over and back, again and again, in utter disbelief at all the stamps.

His expression was pure shock. "But it is expired by over two years, this pass of yours!"

"Yes, I know, and that is why I am in front of you now," I told him.

"And you traveled that far? What is your secret?"

"Becoming a refugee." I told him that leaving my family in Rwanda changed me. Since then, I had been restless, eager to move forward in whatever way I could, wanting to go far, as far as possible. My biggest problem had been traveling without valid papers. It meant a lot of disdain; a lot of time spent justifying, offering excuses, and explaining. I thought the world belonged to everyone, but I had learned I was mistaken. I was fortunate that these countries I traveled through were largely Arab and English-speaking and could not realize the expiration date of my papers. It was an experiment I decided not to repeat again; it was a risk I could no longer take, especially as my travels took me through more war-torn countries.

I asked my new companion to help me obtain a travel document that would at least let me travel for some time. I told him everything about myself, past, present, future. Durieux listened with great attention, and at the end came a barrage of questions. I answered each of them the best that I could. He told me my case was extraordinary because not only was I registered as a refugee from Rwanda in Burundi, but that I was also the first Rwandan refugee he had met in Sudan. The others came from Chad, Ethiopia, Eritrea, Zaire, and Uganda. What had me worried before now had me optimistic as I slowly learned that Durieux was interested in my story, and that he genuinely wanted to help me, to become a part of my story. He promised to call the necessary people in Burundi to get my documents, and we left it at that.

I went back to the youth hostel in the city with a spring in my step. It was only when I reached my bed that I realized getting my papers would take some time. Here I was, met with financial difficulties again. Staying at the hostel in such a city would cost me dearly, money I didn't really have. I decided to do what I could by leaving town to visit the north of the country. Besides experiencing more of this country I enjoyed, I also planned to learn a little Arabic, as in the capital it gets mixed with English, a language I was able to speak a bit of at this point. Being the largest country in Africa, Sudan has 597 tribes speaking more than 400 different dialects and languages. Arabic was the common thread that tied all these people together.

After leaving my bike with Toto in the youth hostel, I caught a ride with a truck headed east to Suakin, a town to the south of Port Sudan so that I could visit the Red Sea, just over a thousand kilometers from Khartoum. Suakin is a historical site, and we entered under an impressive arch built entirely from brick. It sat on a little peninsula where the Arabian style houses were halfway to complete ruin. I heard it said later that it must have been an old salt trading and export outpost, long since abandoned.

In my imagination, I expected to see a sea of blood—it was the Red Sea, after all—but it was nowhere the color I expected. We were often told of it during religious education. God had drawn into it and drowned the entire Egyptian Army and the pharaoh while they were chasing the Israelites, attempting to stop them from reaching the prophesied country. When I arrived at the Red Sea, I was sorely disappointed. *What a letdown!* This supposed Red Sea had not an inkling of the color in its name.

During my stay, I made a few friends, who invited me to swim with them. By this point, I had swum in so many bodies of water that I thought myself a professional. Swimming was my trade, and I was a master. When I dove in to this sea, though, I opened my eyes and saw shiny objects all over. Whatever these things were, I did not stay to find out. They scared me so much that I raced back to the shore, so out of breath that I could barely tell my friends about my misadventure. They scoffed and laughed. I insisted and told them to go check it out for themselves. The more insistent my tone became, the more they laughed, tears reaching their eyes. Finally, one told me through tears: "Those are plankton that the fish feed on. When it is dark, they fluoresce. They're not dangerous at all!" I felt embarrassed and humiliated, but despite their explanation, when it came time to swim again, I still felt a bit wary. Eventually, though, the oppressive heat persuaded me to take up my craft again.

After the Indian Ocean, the two Niles, and having added the Red Sea to the list of places I've swum in, I wonder just how many more waters can I experience? It is a very beautiful life, with very nice friends. In the evenings, I would pass the time with others my age, drinking tea, sharing camel meat, and learning Arabic. The camel meat was something I ate for the first time. For an animal that I had come to despise in many ways, I was thankful that my hatred did not extend to its flavor. It was pleasantly surprising.

After a few days, I set out for Khartoum again, hitchhiking along the way. I missed my bike quite a bit; it was strange not having my bike with me. It was my only constant companion on the road; on this brief trip, I had to make new ones. Although the road was paved, potholes slowed down traffic considerably. Having to sit in the sweltering heat, jostling at every pothole made the journey a bit miserable. None of my rides were going all the way to Khartoum, so I had to break my journey into stages, going a bit out of my way here and there, traveling through a region alternating between mountains and desert. Here, agriculture was nearly nonexistent; it was a true desert extending as far as the eye could see.

After four days of travel, I arrived in the city and went straight to Durieux's office to hear what news there was of my new papers. He explained to me that this would surely take time, more than I had already waited, and that I should arm myself with patience. It was not what I had been hoping to hear; my financial means were lacking, to say the least. His kindness, generosity, and understanding of how long it could potentially take for Burundi to respond to my case caused him to extend an incredible kindness to me. Durieux decided to invite me to stay with him in his place, only under the condition that I find other accommodations when his family visited from Belgium. I was ecstatic and accepted immediately; of course, I did not have much of a choice. But I knew at this point that Durieux was a good man.

While staying with my caseworker, time quickly got away from me, and thanks to Durieux, I made fast friends with other refugees, largely Eritreans. I was very happy to meet them; I did my best to listen to their stories, which they shared with great candor. They told me the history of their country, and of course I told them the history of mine. They were surprised, as they had not heard anything about Rwandan refugees. I told them this was normal, as Rwandans typically suffer in anonymity. To be a refugee is always a tragedy. One is always different from the next; as all families are happy in their own way, the unhappy families, are, like those of refugees, each unhappy in their own unique way. This experience must be shared with others, as each only knows their own misery and ignores that of others.

There is nothing worse in the world than to be a forgotten refugee. The international community and the great organizations fight as best they can for us, but considering the growing number of refugees, they cannot satisfy all our needs. They also cannot explore every region, every community, to relieve those suffering in anonymity because of war. I hope that our sentiments of gratitude are heard by the UN, UNICEF, OMS, the Red Cross, and others too numerous to mention. These groups that apply pressure, give support, and defend human rights must continue their righteous work and do even more in the defense of the innocents.

A few days later, Durieux announced to me that a response from Burundi had finally arrived that morning at HCR. I had to go in person to Burundi for the renewal of my document. I slumped into my seat. Returning again to Burundi, my starting point? More than two thousand kilometers away? I was not ready to head home yet, I wanted to continue across all of Africa. I closed my eyes and remembered the whole journey: the desert and its sun, hunger, fatigue, thirst, suffering, and the gun barrels pointed at me. All that for nothing? I did not know what to do; all I felt was despair.

A few days following this episode, while I moped around the town, Durieux greeted me with good news. There was a way around going back to Burundi. According to the law, it would be possible for me to obtain a travel document from the Sudanese government that would accept me on its soil as a refugee. I would have to fill out a form, add to it my passport photo, and sign the documents at the HCR office. But if it meant getting to travel more, it was not a problem for me at all. Two weeks later, I returned there to receive my travel permit. The agent handed me a little blue booklet and told me that, going forward, my host country would be Sudan. It was a small blue notebook, and it was as beautiful to me as the pyramids. August 6, 1979 was the day I became a Sudanese; it had been two years already since I left Burundi. I did not know how to thank Durieux, as truly there were no words that could properly express the joy, safety, and confidence that this man had brought me. While I may have been able to hold back the tears of goodbyes to loves, I was unable to do that when saying farewell to Durieux. Through the tears, I managed to express to him my profound gratitude, to him and the Sudanese government. A day of joy, with the pretty little blue booklet that I could not stop contemplating from every angle. For the first time since my departure from Burundi, I was legal! Sudan had adopted me! Relieved and sure of myself, I sensed the rebirth of my wanderer's spirit.

My wish was to visit Western Chad; it was the natural choice, being a neighbor to Sudan and an easy pathway to several other countries. But Chad was at war again! Tensions were tearing apart our beautiful Africa. War continued to deprive me of the possibility of visiting some countries. I had to find a less dangerous region. Perhaps Southern Chad instead? No, the conflict in Chad reached there, too, as I learned. The Central African Empire would have to do. With my destination now decided, I had to obtain a visa for the Central African Empire. I went down to their embassy in Khartoum with Durieux. He spoke directly with the consul and gave me the visa in minutes. Durieux again! *I don't know what I'd do without him!* I thought to myself. Every refugee who met him was better off afterward in some way.

It was time to say adieu to the beautiful and immense Sudan, welcoming and adoptive! The Sudanese quenched my thirst with their tea. They served as my interpreters. How many helped me overcome all the barriers in my path? How many helped me pass over mountains and through valleys, saved me from summary shootings of military guns ready to take my life? When I got to this country, I was lost, but now I could speak some Arabic, and, more importantly, people understood it. I felt Sudanese, and my new travel permit was all the evidence I needed to prove that I was.

# CHAPTER 18

# Central African Republic: The End of An Empire/ Cameroon: The Good Life

O n September 7, 1979, I finally walked upon Emperor Bokassa I's Central African soil. This was the first French speaking country that I encountered on my journey. At customs, all was still. There was only a man stretched out on a mat, listening to the radio, attempting to beat back boredom. I approached him slowly and greeted him. With my dirty clothes, a bicycle, and backpack, strange necklaces like those of a sorcerer around my neck, I must have looked every bit the madman to him. In fact, each necklace was a souvenir of a culture I visited. He did not bother to inquire about any of that; all he asked me for was my passport.

With pride, I showed him my brand-new travel permit. The customs agent examined it, put his stamp on it, and handed it back to me. I made it! I mounted my bicycle but noticed that my legs had become weak with fear and fatigue. I pedaled quicker than normal to help unwind them, but within just a few minutes, I found myself in a forest. My legs clearly sensed what was to come. The road was terrible and shrank with every rotation of my wheel. The forest became so dense that the road disappeared and reappeared without warning. Where there was road, there were countless potholes that tested my courage to continue. Not a soul lived in this forsaken place. It reminded me of Tanzania, and when I got lost in the immense forest, I stopped to think a bit. Should I turn around or continue on? What a dilemma! Whether it once again was my stubborn nature or my dedication, I continued on, walking my bicycle on the treacherous road.

Bit by bit, I made progress, but tsetse flies swarmed in this forest and were a constant troublesome nuisance. They bit me so much that I had to put on a thick jacket; it worked, but only a bit. It was worth it, but I had to bear not just the flies but now the heat. Suddenly, in the distance, I saw a man. It was hard to make out, but he was clearly holding a spear in my direction. No doubt, we were both scared. I looked like a mad shaman, dirty and adorned, walking my bike. When I got to him, I was truly surprised when I discovered that he was white. Upon noticing his skin tone, I could do nothing but stop and stare so intrigued I was to find a white man here in the middle of nowhere. As I approached, I recognized the face as familiar, as apparently did he. He exclaimed that we were both at the youth hostel of Khartoum. So that is where I knew him from! He reminded me of his name: Enrico I met a lot of people at the hostel, but I briefly recalled Enrico; he was an Italian man who was trafficking in ivory in this region full of elephants. It seemed like a dangerous business! At any moment, he could be attacked or even killed by brigands. He was quite courageous, this Enrico! Or mad perhaps? I noted he had a side bag containing pieces of ivory. When he noticed that I was looking at it, he encouraged me to get on my way and continue on my adventure. Knowing the region well, he told me that I was almost through the most dangerous spots.

I continued following the road and spent the night in an uninhabited village. Obviously, there was nothing to do in this ghost town, where the only attraction was abandoned houses.

I spent some time wondering what had happened. The people must have left because of the isolation of the place. I encountered one lone soul in a house where I sought shelter. He seemed to be a native to the village, around 40 years old and very wary of my presence. He spoke Sango, the other official language of The Central African Republic, a beautiful tongue but one I could not understand. Despite our limited communication, I was able to secure a place to sleep. Unfortunately, it was far from a restful night. Every time one of us shifted to get comfortable, the other shifted too. Sleep was impossible due to us being inherently suspicious of each other. When the sun finally rose, we both were relieved. I was glad to survive the night. I quietly thanked Saint Christopher and was on my way.

Nature here was bountiful with fruit, but no one was there to enjoy it except for birds. That, coupled with the fact that I doubted any goods would ever reach this place; survival would have had to have been by their own will. It would have been difficult to survive out in this place, and the corruption endemic in the country would have made things more difficult. They had no road, hospitals or schools, so it made sense that they would eventually leave this village in search of something better. I figured that this village had no road connection with the other towns around it as the path disappeared, overgrown with wild grass. Finally, I got through the grass, only to be met with a roaring river that would be impossible to cross, as it was the rainy season and the river was high and full with bubbling and muddy water.

I spotted two canoes, one on each side of the river; these were probably used as ferries to get passengers across. I called out, but no one responded, nor did I hear any rustling of people hiding or avoiding me. Instead of stealing the canoes, I decided to camp for the night and see if people would show up tomorrow. As I was waiting, I decided to take advantage of the water. Although the river was dirty, it was sufficient to clean my clothes and bathe. Thankfully, now clean of dirt, I looked slightly less mad.

The next morning, there was still not a soul to take me across. At this point, I had to try my luck with the canoe, despite the fear of crossing on my own. To make matters worse, there was no oar. The owners knew that no one could take their canoe without one. My only thought was that this canoe must have been Enrico's; with no people here, it only made sense. Upon this realization, I had no idea what to do, so I decided to relax for a while longer. I spent the day by the river bathing and watching the river flow, vaguely hoping that someone would come to help me across. No luck. I went to sleep worried. The next day, I took charge and decided that I would not spend a third night at this river. I emptied the water out of the canoe and put my bicycle and belongings in. A long stick I found next to the boat would be my best makeshift oar, though it was only used to get off the shore. I paddled with all my heart. After a few moments, my improvised paddle fell apart and disappeared into the current. By this point, I could neither turn back nor go forward. I desperately tried to paddle with my hands. Impossible. The current was too strong, the speed of the water too great. My canoe was quickly swept up by the current. At first, I was terrified; I was lost in the middle of the river without a way out. My mind raced and quickly went to the worst scenario: that there might be a waterfall. My shirt was soaked in sweat. I told myself that this might be the end, and for once, I forgot to invoke Saint Christopher. I threw my hands in the air and gave myself up to fate. Wherever the river took me was where I would go. After three hours of pure fear tinged with a certain acceptance, the canoe slowed down, and the current became gentler. I started rowing again with my hands and finally made it across.

I walked up the riverbank, trying to meet with the original path I aimed to follow. I pushed the bicycle uphill. At one point, I saw a crested crane in an open area in front of me. It was about three feet tall, with gray feathers and a golden crown. It cried and beat its broad white wings three times. It was beautiful. I followed it and it froze. Something was wrong; this crane was giving me a warning. At first, I believed the bird was distressed by my presence because it was trying to protect its young. That is when I saw something unusual in the grass. At first, I did not know what it was. But as I got closer, I saw the pattern and the great coil it made. It was a sleeping python, and an enormous one at that. Perhaps it had eaten the crane's babies. I did not stay long enough to make its acquaintance or find out. As quietly as I could, I ran off with my bicycle on my shoulder. The ground was uneven, and I had to hop where I could not run. I don't know where I find the energy to run, being beaten by fatigue. Had it not been for the crane, I might have stumbled right onto the python. I shivered at the thought.

Sometime later, I found myself back on the path. I arrived, tired and exhausted, in the village of Kéré in the afternoon. All strangers in Central Africa must report to the village chief. Here, I spent the night at the chief's residence. He warmly welcomed me in the African tradition. During the night, we were all outside, around the fire; there was an incredible sense of community between these people, though the greatest blessing was that we could communicate perfectly in French. Sitting under the crescent moon, we talked the night away. I discussed my voyage, the river, the monstrous python in the forest, and the long list of problems encountered since I left Burundi. All the time, there were children playing music and happily playing games among themselves. I talked of the various wars that had, time and time again, made me change my journey, the poor state of roads, and the countless language problems that had dogged me through my journey. The villagers listened to my story with eyes wide; they were flabbergasted to hear my tale, much like the others I had told. They wanted to know the cause of these great travels that exposed me to all these risks; that was their main concern. For these people, it was insanity that I would embark on a journey like the one I was on.

The answer to the question was tied to the history of my country. I told them about the war of one people divided in Rwanda, about all the killing and harassment from my early childhood that made my country unlivable, which pushed me out onto the road. After being forced to flee my country, I felt that taking risks was no longer scary; in short, the problems created in me an audacity that I couldn't describe in words but that had been proven in my actions. I did not know where all this would lead. In those days, I was like a leaf detached from its tree that goes where the wind blows it. I went where the wind took me. The chief listened the most attentively. At the end, he cleared his knotted throat and told me I was lucky to have arrived in one piece, as a few young tourists had just been devoured by an old lion. Their luggage was found at the site of the tragedy. Their passports indicated they were French. He told me to be very cautious on the abandoned roads. These villagers taught me something as well: a peculiar way of making wine. They would climb a palm tree, bringing a canteen, poke a hole in the tree, and connect it to the canteen. Then, the tree would drip out liquid for hours. When it was done, they would climb the tree again, which was no small feat, and you had palm wine. I found the process beautiful. Nothing was needed to be done for the palm wine to be alcoholic. It wasn't a strong wine, but it was very enjoyable and endeared me to these people. It felt pure, unlike anything else I had ever tasted. After the wine was gathered, we had a wonderful evening at the house of the Chief. We dined on smoked elephant meat, a first and only time for me. I found it satiating enough, but the ambience of the evening was what I enjoyed the most.

The following day, I was back out on the road. I did not know, however, that as I pedaled, there were monumental events happening in the country: the fall of Emperor Bokassa. Along the way, I learned this from frightened people, and in turn, I became scared as well. I pedaled in this atmosphere of instability and arrived at Bangui, the capital of Central Africa. It felt deserted, like the first village I encountered, but this was not some small village. Frantic cars and mopeds passed me. Bangui was geared for war. Armored cars, jeeps, military trucks rolled along, filled with French and Central African soldiers, all in battle fatigues with helmets covered in green grasses and camouflage. There were roadblocks and identity checkpoints everywhere. The windows of shops were broken, and merchandise pilfered. I took note of all the vandalism that had taken place since the fall of Bokassa. The people on the streets justified their ransacking and destroying by claiming their loot belonged to Bokassa. The thought of this injustice hurt my heart during my walk through the city. But, despite the damage, the city still lived. Some quarters less affected by the violence were animated, and the shops and restaurants were open, workers at their posts.

I needed to rest; I had vertigo after my long trek through the forest. I pitched my tent in a campground, lay down, and immediately fell into slumber. The warmth did not affect me one bit, but still a great weakness weighed on me. It was at this point I realized that I was falling ill. My suspicion was that it was malaria. Surely, those tsetse flies and stagnant water that I drank had something to do with it. I swallowed nivaquine that I had been carrying since Tanzania. Bit by bit, I got better, and during my recuperation, I went out from time to time to explore the town of Bangui. The town was still bustling of the French and Central African military men who came to depose Bokassa and put in his place the new president, David Dacko. September 21, 1979, marked the date when the Bokassa monarchy was abolished through a military coup, ending the emperor's reign and ushering in the Central African Republic.

My trips into town were not only as a tourist. I witnessed the problems from all sides of this coup d'état and collateral effects left me in total consternation. I needed money to repair my bicycle and something to eat before I could even think about continuing my journey. The town did not make me feel safe at all, but I had to brave all the obstacles to search for work. Luckily, I found a job at the market in the center of town, at a bike repair shop. The owner was a man named Jean Baptiste. I told him that I was very good at fixing bicycles. Furthermore, after hearing about my bicycle adventures, he hired me on the spot. I worked for a week, and during that time, my bicycle was kindly repaired at a low cost.

When I returned to the campsite, I discovered that white tourists had settled in next to me. We got to know each other, and after I got back from work, we cooked and chatted the evenings away around the fire. Among them were English, Dutch, and Australians traveling with tour companies. They took a plane in London down to South Africa, and from there, they wound their way up Africa by truck, and they would eventually end up in back in England. At Bangui, they were about halfway through their journey. The next destination for these tourists was Cameroon. After they told me their story, I told them mine. All of them seemed impressed with my journey, especially that I had trekked a distance similar to them on just a bike. Within minutes, they offered to take me along in their tourist truck. Of course, I gladly accepted the offer.

On the eve of our departure, all my thoughts were thankful for the kind Central Africans who had helped me, and these tourists who were going to take me along my crossing of their country. Ah! Central African Empire. Oh, Bokassa the First! What a waste! Rich country, green and human, but poorly run, poorly governed, and exploited! We left Central Africa through the border at Belokole.

My time in Bangui taught me a lot about this country—about its people, too, about Bokassa, about colonization. The realities of this country are consistent across almost all of Africa. The dictatorial leaders like Bokassa did not work for their people. They worked only to enrich themselves at the expense of their populace. They also worked for their master colonizers who helped elevate them to a position of power. Poor, assimilated people having come to renounce their African heritage and their race to become whiter than the whites.

In Africa, only a small percentage of children reach secondary school. It is a major problem for the whole continent. Education does not seem to be a major priority for our leaders. Health care is also insufficient. Infrastructure is relegated below the bottom of the list. How can one dream of development if African leaders do not invest in education and health, the foundations of a thriving society? Ignoring future generations by sacrificing their education is to sacrifice the future of the country; it is heading headlong into a wall. However, these people allow themselves revolting luxuries. Since my arrival in Central Africa, I had noticed the deep coma that the road infrastructure as well as health care and scholastic infrastructure is mired in here. The people here had good reasons to rid themselves of their emperor.

The tourists and I crossed the border into Cameroon on the fourteenth of October, 1979, through a checkpoint at G'Boulai. Thankfully, we had no problems crossing. The only thing I knew about Cameroon was that their people enjoyed football and the music of Manou Dibango. These two things made the country an artistic and sports celebrity. In the back of the truck, I could see fields of green: coffee, corn, bananas, and potatoes. On the side of the road, the fruit plants were colorful and advertised the people's self-sufficiency. The whole scene reminded me of Rwanda, but many things did, and they always made me sad.

After a while, we got to Yaounde, the capital of Cameroon. We passed through markets that looked more like art galleries. The African clothing next to the fruit stands of pineapple, yams, and bananas were bursting with color. It was a whole multitude of natural products that gave joy at their sight. The cacophony was musical as vendors and customers negotiated prices. Really, art seemed to be everywhere in Cameroon. The evening was good, temperate, and relaxing. After my trying journey through the forest, I felt I deserved a rest and welcomed what Cameroon was offering me. My ride through Cameroon was certainly relaxing; the mountains, fields, flora, and fauna were all breathtaking. It was one of the greenest places I had ever seen. Not to mention the fact that I got to enjoy it from the comfort of a bus.

The luck did not last forever though. After we left town, our bus got a flat tire. A young man of around eighteen years old came to offer us assistance, but my friends declined. Despite this, I still talked to the man; he told me that his role was to help travelers. I found his story touching: "My parents tasked me with this mission—search around for travelers in distress." Rather than stay to assist the driver who was working alone on the bus, I encouraged the group to go exploring a bit in the village of this young man with him as a guide. According to our new guide, all the huts in the village belonged to one single family, his. "We are polygamous here," he said. His grandfather had five wives, the eldest son had four, the second had three. Each of the wives had children of their own. The family organization was such that every two weeks, each woman was allowed two nights with her husband. During these two weeks, she would be the one who prepared the food for the extended family. The others got to relax and did not have to help out. It was up to each to prove themselves when their turn arrived!

In this village, it looked like the men had no trouble making a living for their families. The women were productive ones here, as they were the ones in charge of cultivation. This explained the large numbers of women. The anger of our European friends was great when they were met with this polygamous family. Though even to me, this tradition is outdated, I was taught that such practices in my society were part of the olden days.

Our conversation about feminine emancipation continued throughout our journey, long after we said goodbye to our young guide. The women opposed to this tradition were passionate the whole time. The men said, "If only I could stay in the village to take several wives!" The women were outraged. "What an injustice!" they cried. "Why could the women not also have several men? Me too—I could stay here and marry five men." Then everyone burst out laughing. It was all friendly. My European friends told me that polygamy was a criminally punishable offense where they are from.

Polygamy in some African cultures is a secular tradition; the main reason for its existence was to provide labor for the field work and livestock. For survival in the past, a group needed more than just one woman and several children to help with these tasks, and it was this resource that was considered the greatest economic wealth for families. Even the women were cooperative; they didn't hesitate to suggest another young girl that they liked to their man. Sometimes the girl was even related. Relatives were supportive as the more members there were in a family to assist in work meant greater wealth and power for them all. The concept of mass labor towards wealth has often been seen as a means toward economic prosperity, as exampled by the slave trade in America. Polygamy developed through the centuries but died out in the developing world, as developed countries found another solution to the problems of labor scarcity: technology. A single machine can do the work for several laborers, making the human burden lighter. Technology is indeed a positive force for man, but it does also constitute one of the great causes of joblessness and poverty.

# CHAPTER 19

# Nigeria, Niger, and Algeria: To My Forbidden Country

We continued down the road and entered Nigeria on October 24, by the border at Kerawa. We passed through Maiduguri, a rich town with beautiful houses and countless high-end cars that surrounded us on all sides.

Nigeria is the richest country in Africa due to its large oil reserves, comparable to the industry titans of the Middle East. It is the giant of the West African zone. I've heard this place holds a quarter of the African population. I wonder if it's true—it certainly seems possible. Everything was bigger here: the motorcycles, radios, even the houses. Everything was huge here. This country is a former British colony with several beautiful towns like Kano and Lagos, though we only stopped in Kano. Its food was as varied as its people and culture. At night we relaxed and cooked our own food. The nights were always more interesting; they were when I got to know my traveling companions. During the day, there was too much to do. But when the sun went down, I got to talk, that activity I loved so much, which I could not live without. These companions became compatriots overnight as I listened to their stories.

On the road to Kano, I wished that I could have gotten out and biked it because the roads were some of the finest I had ever seen. This was proof enough of Nigeria's wealth; a country that could keep their roads well maintained was an excellent place in my book. Kano itself was not much for me except beautiful. My traveling companions did a lot of shopping in preparation for the desert that we would soon cross. Having little to no funds, though, I did not buy much. We did not stay long in this country, it was just a quick stop on our way to the next one: Niger.

We entered Niger on the thirtieth of October. Once again, we passed the border without issues; part of that was certainly the company I traveled with. I was also incredibly thankful that I had my new travel papers with me just in case. The first night we spent in Zinder, the first town in the south of the country. The next day, as we proceeded north, the climate changed, and the more we moved away from greenery, the hotter it became. It is the Sahara Desert, they told me. I thanked the Almighty to be in a car rather than on my bicycle. Having lived through the desert in Sudan, I knew it was not something I ever wished to go through again.

After a day's journey, we entered the city of Agadez through a pockmarked road. Upon our arrival, there was a great festival of sheep for Muslims. All around us, there was good meat, traditional dances, a whole wonderful ambiance that made the rest of the tourists and myself jovial, though I felt deep embarrassment for my dirty appearance in such a clean place. All these Muslims dressed in white. I stopped by the campsite to take a shower so I could make myself more presentable. I came back and participated in the ceremonies with my traveling companions. We had all been invited to discover local culture and traditions of their religion. We enjoyed ourselves, relaxed, and ate well. At this point, I realized that along my journey, my mood often reflected the location. That when one enters a morose place, one becomes it too. And if one lands among a happier population, then they can become as relaxed as they are.

Algeria was our destination for the next day, and we left Agadez with the appropriate provisions to traverse the desert: much water, fruit, bread, and so forth. The sun was unbearable, and there was not a single oasis, nor a single person in sight in this desert. The good road ended at Airlit. From then on, we saw no road, and there was nothing before us but immense sand dunes. The heat of the desert burned and made all of us desperately thirsty. The water gourds we carried rarely left our lips. *How much more time remained in this sunny hell?* I asked myself dozens of time before we reached Assanka, at the Niger-Algeria border. Eventually, though, the hellish desert relented for a moment, and we found ourselves in Algeria.

Once again, we entered this new country without any trouble through Guezzam. We were still in the middle of the desert, but at least there was a momentary reprieve. We passed countless decommissioned vehicles that had been abandoned after breaking down. Rather than spending time trying to repair them, at their own risk and peril, their owners preferred to leave them there. In this heat, I did not blame them.

The more we advanced into the desert, the greater the silence. The heat was suffocating. It weighed on us all and suffocated conversation and positive feelings. More surprising for me was the change in the color of the skin of my white companions. They quickly started reddening, then started to burn, then finally bronzed and darkened like me. Over time, they became hard to recognize. I, on the other hand, did not see any change to my skin tone. To see this process happen in real time was interesting and very strange.

We went a bit further, and we met the nomadic Touaregs: men, women, and children on their camels. They approached the driver and talked to him. These people were suffering from a lack of water! The driver, charitable, of course, gave them some,

and we were on our way again. Water is not only a vital necessity for any living being in this sandy hell, but the most valuable
commodity. In the desert, humans tend to be sociable and understanding, and help each other as best they can.

We arrived at our next destination, Tamanrasset, on the afternoon of November 2. Here, there was a customs and immigration checkpoint. It was here that my luck ran out. I learned that
I could not continue to travel into Algeria without a visa. The
agent confiscated my travel permit and promised to study my case
the following morning. Unfortunately, here I had to part with my
companions, who were able to continue, as they had the proper
papers. Unlike me, they were not without a country. Again, my
journey was to be continued alone, but I was not terribly sad by
this. I was sad to say goodbye, but I knew that neither my own
adventures nor theirs would be ending. It was a quick goodbye,
and they certainly felt sorry for me, but we did not even exchange
information! They had to go, and I had to stay. I reflected on the
wonderful time spent with them and did not let myself get bitter
over the goodbye. The next morning, I found myself at the police
station before the flag there had even been raised. This time, the
official sent me to the chief of police, to whom he had given my
case. There, an interminable interrogation awaited me, and soon
afterward, I was locked up.

I was behind bars because of a simple visa problem. Their
stated goal was to deport me. The officer told me that the police
must send me back to Niger. It was strange that they were not
sending me back to Sudan, my "home" country. Clearly, he just
wanted me out of Algeria. I asked him to give me at least ten
minutes to eat and stock up on food. I knew how long the journey would be. And I did not have a drop of water in my gourd.
The desert is the least practical, most dangerous place on earth

for a cyclist or a pedestrian. The officer refused to lose a second on this; the truck was already waiting to take me away.

Like cattle, I was loaded up. It was a truck transporting dates. My travel document was given to the driver, who was to give it back to me upon reaching our destination. They told me to climb onto the roof of the truck, with my bicycle. Thank goodness it was carrying dates. At least I could steal a few of those and not die from hunger or thirst. On the road, I could not stop eating them for one moment. The further away we got from Algeria, the more my hatred for this police chief grew, this man who deprived me of a visit to Algeria, who threw a gigantic wrench into all of my plans, who sent me into the desert without a second thought. After hours of raging deep within myself, I fell into a deep slumber. I woke later to see the driver struggling to start up his truck. The issue was that the radiator is broken. We were not yet at the border with Niger, the driver's destination. I asked him to let me continue alone down to Niger. We had no idea how long we would be stuck in this spot. The driver kindly gave me back my travel document, as he had been instructed. He also gave me some dates and a good quantity of water. On top of all this, he also provided advice. He told me to be careful, as a desert crossing on bike was not one many were likely to survive. Still, I was stubborn and determined. I thanked him and wished him good luck. That is where the driver and I parted. Even though the driver had warned me, I had no idea of the risk I was running on this crossing. Indeed, I knew the road, having already traveled it, but the thought of traversing this desert alone rekindled my hatred for the police officer who sent me back. I wanted to see Algeria.

I started into the Saharan Desert. For a bit, the only problem I had was pedaling in the sand. Even car tires had trouble rolling on this sand without sinking. So how is a racing bicycle to manage with its thin tires? It required an incredible amount of physical effort. The sand was deep. This desert was nothing like that which I knew in Kenya or Sudan.

The heat was unbearable and murderous. Moving forward was impossible, and there was not even an appropriate place to sit. Putting my feet on the sand would burn them, so staying still was also difficult. My only choice was to sit on my backpack, cover myself with the tent, and wrap my feet with T-shirts. Then I tried to drink and eat the best I could. Already, I was starting to realize that I would run out of water very soon. I took with me two gallons, but with the heat as it was, I could drink all of that in half a day. I knew I had to ration my water, but I desperately wanted to drink it all at once. Before protecting myself, I first covered the tires of my bicycle with pants and a T-shirt, but it did not do much. By the end of my first day on the bike, the rubber of the tires had melted, and the inner tubes exploded. I flipped the bicycle to try and do anything to keep going. But here, in the middle of nowhere, it was impossible to fill the holes of the inner tubes. The bands and glue did not hold for even a minute. As a result, each time there was a puncture, I had to replace the inner tube with a new one, and after just a few hours, I was running low.

The different shapes mixed up in the desert gave it the look of an immense sea. It was the sun shining on the sand; it was the reflection of the sun's rays that made the desert so hot. That day as I was walking, a dark cloud formed in the sky, as if it were going to rain. But it wasn't water that was coming for me. It was a huge storm of dust, which covered every inch of my open skin, entering my ears and nose and eyes. My eyes stung. In about ten minutes, the storm had passed, leaving a few dying winds blowing dust near my feet. I opened my sand-battered eyes and was struck with one of the most beautiful things I'd ever seen. I looked down and saw little stones with the shape of roses carved out into them. When the wind died down, I saw that the sand had turned into a different color and had left incredible designs across the desert. To this day, it is one of the most beautiful things I had ever seen, comparable to the beautiful lakes of Rwanda. It was like an artist had come in and painted the desert while my eyes were closed. This fascinated me and gave me joy, despite the obvious danger of my situation. Despite the beauty of the situation, the sand-storm threw me about in such a way that I no longer knew where I was going. I was wandering without a direction in mind, and as my water supplies died down, I knew I was in trouble.

The later it got, the more the heat intensified, and the more impossible life became. It was unlivable. I tried then to dig two holes in the sand. As I dug, the sand slid back into the hole, washing away any progress I had made. My goal was to hide in the hole to escape the heat, but I decided to change my plan after meeting this obstacle. I knew the temperature at night would be pleasant. At the very least, it would be more manageable than the heat. From then on, I would try to travel part of the night; the rest of the time I would rest and lie down. Then in the morning, I would move forward until the heat was no longer tenable. Then, I would stop and cover with my tent and all I had.

The night contrasted the day in the most amazing way; it was beautiful in the desert. It was not dark, to my surprise. It was mostly light, as the moon reflected well on the sand. The sky was covered with thousands of stars, and on the horizon, just as many shooting stars. The custom where I am from says that you have to make a wish each time you see this rare mystery, but here, I was unsure how many wishes I needed to make. I could not tell whether I was seeing shooting stars or desert dust flying through the air. Either way, it was both challenging and beautiful.

This paradise of night morphed back into an uninhabitable hell during the day. I decided to wrap my head, my face, and neck with my sweater. Only my eyes remained uncovered. My skin cracked and became multicolored. The water levels in my container dipped. I did not know how much more of this expanse I had to cross. I feared death like nothing else.

On the third day, I ran out of water and food. My energy and my spirits were low as I tried to combat the vertigo caused by dehydration. I was almost unable to keep going. I did not know how much longer I could resist. I was barely conscious, but I kept walking. What else was I to do?

I walked without water for two more days. I don't remember much from that time, except that I had accepted my fate. Whatever would happen next was not up to me. I was praying to Saint Christopher, who, according to legend, carried a child in the form of Christ across a river. The child became as heavy as lead in Christopher's arms, but the saint managed to carry him across. I put my trust in the saint as I walked, but my hope was almost gone.

After two or three days of struggling along, I saw a man approaching me. Then I saw another with him. Was it a dream or a mirage? I opened my eyes wide, and miraculously, it seemed that I was actually conscious. The two men laid me down under a meager bush, as dry as the earth on which it grew. They made me swallow, drop by drop, some camel milk. Normally, I think I would have found the milk foul and distasteful, but I was not even aware enough to have conscious objections. They forbade me to drink a large quantity at a time. They also covered my skin in this milk. In the meantime, they prepared some bread in a manner that impressed me. They dug a hole in the sand and lit a small fire in it with twigs they had with them. They kneaded flour dough that they then covered with heated sand after having cleared the whole area of ash. In very short time, about a half hour, they pulled out of the hole a fresh loaf of bread, surprisingly clean, as if it had come out of a modern oven. Then we ate. It is no exaggeration to say that it was the best meal of my life. It is impressive, the way man uses what nature offers him.

Little by little, I came back to life, and after a few hours of nursing, I was relatively normal. The freshness of the night helped me regain my strength. I looked upon my saviors, tears falling from my eyes, and wondered how to possibly thank them. They were two Touaregs, these nomads with their five camels. I assumed that they often saw people in danger like myself. They saw the tracks left by my feet, and those of my bicycle. Intrigued by these, they had never yet seen anyone venture on a bicycle into the Sahara! They must have considered me crazy or ignorant! I was both.

Before leaving, they gave me as provisions, water, camel milk, a piece of bread, and dried camel meat. They told me that I was almost at the end of the desert and pointed me back on the right path to finally escape this hot hell. My Touaregs promised to look over me. I thought hard but could not find any gestures to thank them.

I speak here of gestures, as they are part of the language of the deaf that we try to invent to communicate. I would have loved to have covered them with gratitude, in a more expressive language. Not only was I eternally grateful to these men who saved me from death, but I was also very impressed by their limitless generosity. I could see they were offering me the last bits of their provisions. It confirmed to me that strange fact of life: that it is the poorest people who are most willing to share what little they have. My Touareg saviors knew the suffering of others. Suffering is one of those things best seen by eyes that have shed tears. I threw myself in turn on both of these men, hugging them for a long time, as we do where I am from, to express my profound gratitude. I realized, happily, that they comprehended the emotional reach of my gesture. It pained me to think that I likely would never see them again, these poor people with hearts of gold. I believe two grains of sand of the desert cannot be eternally separated; sooner or later, the vagaries of the wind will make us meet again, and my two guardian angels and I will likely meet because of this law of nature. I would also have liked to hug these five camels that contributed to saving my life, but did not want to be taken for a lunatic! In Sudan, I had seen a camel for the first time. I thought it was one of the ugliest animals, and I had no love for it. That day it saved my life, and I saw it differently. That beauty does not always come from the physical, but mostly from the heart.

# CHAPTER 20

# Niger, Upper Volta, and Mali: The General Strike

At the border between Algeria and Niger, my luck finally changed. I encountered no problems getting in, and I spent the night at customs, where the agents treated me well, unlike the police chief I had previously encountered. They recommended that I practice prudence on this route after recovering from the shock of seeing me. I imagine seeing a sand-battered figure emerge from the desert with a busted bike was not something terribly common. "The desert is hell itself, but the end of the tunnel is not far from here," they told me. They told me many people lost their lives there. Seven young Nigerians going to Libya had just lost their lives trying to cross on foot. They were picked up one after the other, dehydrated. One Frenchman died there. He was trying to cross, pushing a wheelbarrow containing his provisions of water and food. Add to that the numerous vehicles that ran aground here, the passengers of which often lost their lives under the intense heat. The dangers of the desert were communication problems, losing one's way, vehicle breakdowns, lack of water, and absence of help and rescue services. I was afraid, but I had no choice. I had another solid week that I had to push through this hell.

I continued on my way in the direction of Niamey, capital of Niger. The place was a beautiful modern city, very lively, with a great view over the Niger River. It was a wonderful break from the desert. I entered it in the middle of the day and crossed the river, and turned to the right in the direction of Upper Volta, which is now Burkina Faso. I pedaled. Thankfully, the road was good, with many branches leading to smaller paths. I passed people coming from the closest Volta market. I biked a little bit more and entered without issue into Upper Volta.

I entered Upper Volta through the frontier town of Kantchari on November 23, 1979. On my way, I encountered a couple of French tourists; Didier Futel and Josiane were their names. Their little bus was broken down after having made it through France, Spain, Morocco, Algeria, and Niger. We spent the evening together; it was good to chat with other travelers. It was an excellent opportunity to trade ideas and travel strategies. They were much like me, having trekked across several countries. And also like myself, they were encountering some troubles, though their method of travel was much nicer than mine. One thing that travelers all have in common is a sense of generosity, and the next day, they offered to take me up to Bobo-Dioulasso.

Bobo, the second largest city in the country, was tumultuous, to say the least. The schools were closed and government offices too. It seemed at every corner, there were people crying due to deaths. In effect, the country was in the midst of a general strike. The sick no longer received care from doctors and nurses as a result. It was total desolation. The streets were dark with crowds; people were in a rush to get their provisions from the shops that were still open. In the beginning, I felt like I was in Peking. I've heard that everyone in that city travels on bicycle. Here, too, men, women, and children were all on bicycles. The great streets all had cycling lanes. A woman cyclist passed me, transporting her two children, one on the luggage carrier, and the other on the handlebars. It was fantastic! I was not used to seeing women on bicycles at all. In Rwanda and in Burundi, as in most African countries, women on bicycles were rare sights, even taboo ones. I did not know whether or not the women on bikes were doing it out of necessity though. The strife within the city disturbed me greatly, but I hope that it would resolve itself well. I did not linger long in this city; I said farewell to my brief traveling companions and once again mounted my bike.

Photo of Faustin on the front page of the newspapers in Upper Volta in November 1979.

After our goodbyes, I hunched over the handlebars of my Peugeot, thankful that it was in good shape. I biked up the paved road up to the border at Kouri. It was December 7, 1979. I passed Segou, a beautiful town of artists, and reflected on what it meant to have a town of artists. The creativity of one seemed to inspire the next. I saw weavers working on looms and creating fabrics by hand. It was time consuming but worth it as the outcomes were beautiful. Artisans carved intricate wooden masks and jewelry makers ornately displayed their wares.

I quickly passed through the town and rested at Bamako, the capital of Mali. I did not want to stay in Mali long. I had to go but quickly encountered a problem. It was not easy to go to Senegal. There was no road network between Bamako and Tambacounda. The only way to go was by train.

The ticket read: "Punctuality is enforced; the train leaves at 6 o'clock in the morning exactly." The next day at 5:30 a.m., I was at the station. Though the ticket proved to be a liar—the train did not get started until noon. Punctuality be damned! While waiting, people hopped off the train, unable to bear the heat. We never learned the reason of this delay, though it did not bother me too much. I was not personally in a hurry, but I cannot imagine the anxiety of those who were! Once we got going, the train made a stop at Kita. This city was still in Mali. Many businessmen and salespeople were headed to Senegal to sell their wares. They all looked like soldiers off to war. They constantly pushed and insulted each other. One of them knocked over a basket filled with tomatoes on me in the bustle. Thankfully they were not my tomatoes.

# CHAPTER 21

# Senegal: Meeting the Ocean

The train arrived after what felt like forever in Tambacounda, its destination in Senegal, on the evening of December 16. This town was at a crossroads. From this place, one could go to the interior of Senegal, or to Mali, Guinea, or even Gambia. The town itself sat on a savanna full of baobabs. The baobab is a large tree of average height. It grows in the savanna of West Africa. It is very important for the inhabitants of these dry countries. The inhabitants of the country built large holes into it as a type of well that stored water. In the rainy season, water would be conserved there and then used during the dry season for any number of uses: washing clothes, washing dishes, feeding animals, or keeping themselves hydrated. The incredible thing about the baobab is that it is a very watertight tree. The holes in these trees were like the street gourds of Eastern Africa.

My road took me in the direction of Dakar, the capital. The road was gray, desolate, and straight. I passed several small villages as I moved forward. My biking speed was no longer something I controlled. My time biking in Rwanda and Burundi had somewhat prepared me for where I was now, but the journey this far had turned my legs hard and my will harder. Speed was just something I felt on the bike; it was intuitive. I stopped from time to time to take a drink of water; it felt as if I was constantly dying of thirst, though it was nothing compared to the desert. It was here that I first saw the Atlantic Ocean. I took long swim breaks to refresh my mind. Seeing another of the oceans of Africa brought me many gifts at once: calmness, harmony, and open-mindedness. This made it official; I had crossed Africa from coast to coast. Of course, I thanked Saint Christopher for this success, for seeing me through all of the struggles and securing the triumphs.

The first indication that I was nearing the capital was when human traffic increased. It was late, and instead of finishing my current journey, I stopped briefly at Kaolac, a modern city, quite large and populous, bustling with well-built houses. I passed in front of a great market, so large and spread out that it boggled my mind. After this little run through the town, I continued without stopping all the way to Dakar.

Dakar, the Senegalese capital, was a town that truly dazzled me. Its tall buildings, immense traffic, and the crowds left me dumbfounded. Its position next to the ocean made it an excellent spot for a holiday. Upon my arrival, there were two events of great importance that I found myself caught up in the crowds with. First was the incredible Dakar Rally, the cross-continental automobile race that began in Paris and ended 6,200 miles away in Dakar, Senegal. The other momentous event was the visit of the world boxing champion, Muhammad Ali. He was touring Africa on behalf of the American government to implore African nations to boycott the 1980 Olympics in Moscow as a response to Russian aggressions in Afghanistan. As a result of the huge affairs, there was a great deal of traffic and many of the roads were closed to drivers and cyclists.

I was looking for a place to stay, and a young Senegalese student approached me and introduced himself as Babaka. He knew I was a foreigner and after talking for a bit, he mentioned that he could take me to the international school at the local university, where I might meet some fellow Rwandans. He was a nice guy and perhaps felt sorry for me. Sure enough, he introduced me to some Rwandan students, who welcomed me warmly. Their names were André, Masikini, Charlotte, and Jean Nyilinkwaya. André housed me for the night. I couldn't express my appreciation for these kind strangers enough! That evening, while we were chatting, the topic moved to our fears and stresses linked to the situation in Rwanda. Like me, they had worries as well. It seemed that we all knew where our country was heading, but we could do nothing about it. When the topic changed to how I arrived in Senegal, they could not believe that I came from Burundi on a bicycle! They asked me a million questions. How did I survive? How was the road? Was I afraid of dying? How did I deal with strangers? I told them the truth. Some parts of the journey were hard, some were sad, others were educational. But no answers sufficed. Their curiosity had no end.

The next morning, I wandered through the town and soon enough found myself in the heart of the town, its beating center, the Kermel market and its beautiful, modern architectural style. Then I visited the Sandaga market, where I saw all kinds of typical African products; after that came the cathedral and the international exchange center. Dakar was not just its markets; the town could also claim pride for its universities and tourist sites. I even went up to the isle of Gorée.

Located around three kilometers from Dakar, the isle of Gorée has a long and sad history. Jean François Durieux's sister, Crea, lived on the island, and I visited her. She gave me a tour, telling me Gorée was a strategic island, a slave collection center and starting point for transit to America up until the late 1700s. There, slave traders awaited buyers and their ships. We visited the jails in which the slaves were kept. There were tourists from many different countries, all engrossed by the evident wickedness of mankind.

At sunset one night, André told me, "Get ready. We are going out tonight. There is a dance soiree for Christmas Eve." At 11:00 p.m., we whisked over there in a whirlwind. We ended up in a vast house, with multicolored lights everywhere. The event was organized in large part by students of Rwandan origin but hosted students of all different African countries. It was a divine evening to be with people of my own country, especially on Christmas. To speak my native tongue, eat familiar foods, and dance with my Rwandan brothers and sisters on the holiest of holidays was a priceless gift in itself!

A couple of days after the Christmas party, like clockwork, my wanderlust kicked in. I needed to move again, to travel, to leave the wonderful country of Léopold Sédar Senghor, this great African leader, a great writer and poet. I told my companions that my next stop was to be Morocco. My compatriots, in unison, discouraged me, as Morocco and Mauritania were at each other's throats. Everywhere I went, it seemed that war was destined to impede my progress. For four days after that, I wandered aimlessly in the town, on the beaches, relaxing. As I stretched out in the sun, a white couple approached me and talked to me.

"Hello, my name is Marc Kap, and here is my wife Anne-Marie Kap. We are Belgian. I work for the World Health Organization, and my wife is a journalist."

I introduced myself, too, and then the man asked me, "Is it you that appeared in *The Sun* newspaper?"

"Yes, it is indeed me."

They were a happy and chatty couple. "When are you planning on leaving again?"

"I do not know yet. I have a problem to resolve first."

"Where are you staying now?"

"I am staying at the university campus."

"We want to help you. If it suits you, you can live with us. It would be a great pleasure for us. We have a very large house; there is room enough for you."

Of course, I accepted their generous offer and went to live with them in the African quarter of Gelta.

Before leaving Dakar, though, Anne-Marie Kap had me meet Camara, a famous South American philosopher, in his hotel room.

Dom Helder Camara was not only a great philosopher and a great writer, but also a great humanist and defender of the disenfranchised. He was a man who truly loved the world and everything good in it. He had come to give a series of conferences on the topic of peace. I was astonished by how humble he was; he spoke to me as an equal. For him, it was peace and charity that counted. This was the message he tried to spread across the world, especially to the poor. I conclude that it is utopian. As he is a priest, he told me, "God will not judge you based on your church attendance, but what you will have done to others." If we had more men like him around, life on earth would be better.

After I met the Dom, my will was strengthened, and I decided that my heart had to lead me to Morocco. Though I left my friends nervous and as always, goodbyes are never happy. I presented myself at the port at 11:00 p.m. *Massalia* was the name of the gigantic boat that I took from Dakar to Marseille, with two classes: first and second. My ultimate destination was Casablanca via the Canary Islands—more specifically, Las Palmas and Gran Canaria. On February 16, 1980, at midnight exactly, the boat left the harbor.

Faustin in the company of Anne-Marie Kap and Bishop Camara

# CHAPTER 22

# Morocco: All of Africa

On the fourth day, February 20, 1980, at midnight, we landed at Casablanca. It was my first time on a huge cruise liner. This was nothing like that boat I took up the Nile. It was an incredible experience; there was even a swimming pool on the boat! Since it was my first time out at sea, I experienced the horrors of seasickness. I was not alone in this either; it felt like everyone on the boat was sick alongside me. The formalities in Casablanca took some time, and by the time we finished, I was dead tired. But thankfully, there was a youth hostel not far away. It would only take four minutes by bicycle, they told me.

After being given directions, I hopped on my bicycle. For ten minutes, I pedaled without seeing the hostel. Suddenly, the beam of a flashlight blinded me. I braked just in time when a voice told me, "Stop!" That was when I noticed the long, bright blade of a knife in the light of the flashlight. The knife's blade pointed at me. I stopped dead in my tracks, in front of two strangers. My heartbeat was at record speed and sweat flowed in big drops off my face. I almost passed out; I thought I was done for. To die here, after just arriving in Casablanca! They ordered me to give them money. I told them in a shaky voice that I did not have any. Frustrated, they told me, "Go on, then. Go, miserable wretch." I moved away slowly, with a heavy head and heart. *The next time, I may well run into less trusting people.* I took a few more shaky steps; then, by pure feeling alone and an unknown logic that still makes me wonder to this day, I made a 180 degree turn toward the two bandits, still standing in the same spot. I asked them if they could point me toward the youth hostel.

They burst out laughing. The eldest told me, "Come now, you have a lot of courage!"

He was the more tenacious, and his aggression was less than his companion. He and I started chatting, probably to allay my fear. Still trembling, I listened, eyes wide. Despite the tone our conversation took on, I remained on my toes. At the smallest suspect gesture from them, I would run off without a second thought. They asked me where I was coming from and going to. I responded, "Coming from the Burundi region." They gestured to the entrance gate of the hostel and disappeared into the darkness, probably off to try and rob some other poor soul. I was safe and sound though. One does not always have this kind of luck.

The luck I had met moments before ran out when I walked into the hostel; it was full. When I told the doorman about my encounter with the two bandits, I noticed his face soften a bit. He handed me two blankets. I rolled up on the floor and fell into a deep sleep.

Casablanca was a large cosmopolitan town with extraordinarily tall buildings, but I saw it as an overpopulated industrial town. The buildings were magnificent, yes, but the crowds were too large and cramped. I saddled up on my bicycle in the direction of the capital, Rabat, a city that proved to be a very different town from Casablanca: political capital, less populated. The city was quiet, without the deafening noise of industry.

All along the journey, I noticed well-manicured fields and fattened up and fluffy sheep as well. Morocco was a country with a varied climate and topography; one could find, at the same time and place, both heat and snow, arid lands as well as beautiful farmlands, mountains and plateaus, deserts and ocean. Morocco showed itself to be a gorgeous ensemble of pleasant tourist sites. Best of all was that the people of Morocco spoke French.

One of the fondest memories that was left in me as a permanent marker is the national Moroccan dish: couscous. It is goat or sheep meat seasoned with vegetables and raisins. It is an excellent dish. Moroccans also appreciate mint tea. Before leaving Rabat, I was interviewed by journalists from France-Presse and the Spanish El País. The act of recounting my journey had become commonplace at this point and was part of nearly every encounter I have. I still did not mind it.

I went north on my bicycle up to Tangier, a Moroccan town situated at the very tip of Africa, facing Spain. From here, I threw a look toward the continent behind me. Despite having been eaten away by colonization, Africa had lost none of its ethnic and cultural diversity, nor had its people lost their warmth in their customs and joie de vivre, the "joy of living." Here, fraternity and sharing reigned. From Senegal to Burundi, from South Africa to Morocco, its vegetation and varied climates offered an agricultural diversity that could feed the whole planet. Its fauna and flora were a real marvel, its subterranean caves full of treasures. Our continent is rich in all its facets. Unfortunately, wars here and there show an uglier face. In Angola, Ethiopia, Somalia, Uganda, Burundi, Sierra Leone, Liberia, and my home, Rwanda—the war that forced me out the door and made me an errant soul. I had to be on the road to understand that it is all of Africa that is on fire. All these dead, these people crippled for life, these families ripped apart—those tears that have flowed... were they worth it? Who wins in war? Nobody, I would say. The dead will be counted on both sides.

What do we have in store for our children and future generations? The colonizers fragmented Africa into countries to serve their interests, tracing borders that would form the heart of conflicts there today. Colonization has killed our languages, our religion, and our culture. What is a people without a culture? Nothing. Why must we follow someone else? If we did, we'd lose everything we know. We should instead base our development on our own mores and customs, on a beautiful culture we know best.

What's worse is all the difficulties we face at borders that include visa problems. There is an adage in Africa that says union is strength. The colonizers divided Africa and split nations of people into two, for their own benefit. Africans should know today that our old masters divided us to better rule, that it is time to eliminate these imaginary barriers.

There may be still a source of hope, hope that Africa will gain awareness and start moving forward again. Hope that one day the sons of Africa, those who have known Europe and America, who have seen progress thanks to their work and efforts at unity, will return and bring their stone to add to the foundation that will rebuild the African continent. I am confident that one day all these wars and other problems will only be a sad and distant memory. War is expensive; peace is cheap. Every man lost in a pointless war is an insurmountable loss to Africa. I am confident that future generations will push Africa ahead without reaching out constantly for a helping hand from the West. We can do it if the African leaders stop relegating education and research to second-tier priorities. If I could have one wish granted, I'd connect Africa from east to west and north to south with roads. It would improve our education and economic opportunities. No one will make our happiness without us, and that cannot be achieved without sacrifice. Proper investment in agricultural innovation along with cohesive efforts among our many countries would put us in a position to be a world leader in food production as well as sufficiently feed our own population. The corruption that spans our continent must stop; even if a wholly unified Africa is a dream, our continent is rich, and we would all benefit from cooperation rather than selfishness. At the root of this cause are our leaders, who do not look to improve the next generations, but only their own lot in life. How better to create unity among Africans than through a road connecting us all together? Then we could have a million people like myself, easily making a journey through this incredible continent. We should look to open our borders and destroy the barriers between us. Africans should be able to travel their continent; the very concept of a visa disgusts me.

Tangier was my exit door from Africa. I stood on the edge of one continent and held before me a panoramic view of the whole of Africa, and behind me was the start of a new adventure on a new continent. I bought a ticket and got on a boat headed for Spain. It was about time.

Faustin on the road, Rabat, Morocco, February 1980
Photo credit: France-Presse

# Part Three: Life on a New Continent

# CHAPTER 23

# Spain: A New World

Pedaling fatigue disappeared as I watched the African coast disappear. I could only see the edge of Africa. May this country of mountains, desert, ocean, sea, snow, and sun transmit my goodbyes to the rest of the African continent! I arrived in Spain, the port of Algesiras on the third of April 1980.

My first steps in Spain brought forth an event I had never dreamed of: walking on European soil with my constant companion by my side. Princess, my bike, had been through just as much as I had. We were both eager to take on new and unfamiliar challenges and were somewhat surprised by the many similarities. I saw trees, houses, and the soil, the same as Africa. We were still on Earth, I suppose.

I pushed my bicycle in the town of Algesiras, without really knowing where I was going. I mounted my bicycle and rolled onward on a lovely, paved, well-maintained road. Before I knew it, I was in the Seville region. Agriculture in this region was intensive: vast fields of vegetables and all kinds of fruit. Here, I saw more wine fields with thick, juicy grapes than I had ever seen before. My only road companions were the tractors that worked the fields. Where I'm from, the only things working the fields were people who have worked the same beautiful fields for an eternity. I noticed many olive trees on my route up to Madrid. This was a new plant that I discovered for the very first time.

On the way to Madrid, vehicle traffic became more intense, like any approach to a capital. The sun was low in the sky when I got lost in my first European capital. But I didn't mind being lost at all. The scene was something else! More than dazzling! I was surrounded by dream houses with stories that could lead you to the sky. The people who lived on the top floor must have been in contact with God the Father himself! On the road, five cars were aligned driving at speeds of at least one hundred kilometers an hour. God only knows how wide this highway was! As in all large towns, people passed each other without talking. I thought of the proverb from my country: "The worst of clans is that which greets no one." It was like the silent movies that were shown in Bujumbura. To this day I don't know if those movies were silent on purpose or if there was a fault with the equipment. Regardless, it was still representative of this Spanish city.

Here in Madrid, the only noise that could be heard was that of motorized vehicles. I grabbed a cup of coffee, a drink I was slowly getting used to. Afterward I found a public park, where I set up camp. For three days, I explored the other parts of the town. My next destination would be France; it was either there or Portugal, but I preferred France. I attempted to get a visa to that lovely country of wine, but it was refused. However, I was able to get one for Benelux and another for Austria. But if I wanted to go on a bicycle, I had to cross through France. I tried to think of a solution without success. It seemed like the French would impede my progress. One day, while I was exploring and trying to come up with a solution, a young man approached me and stared at me up and down. He was fluent in French, so communication came easy.

"Hello! Your face looks familiar. Was it you who appeared in the newspaper *El País*?"

"Yes," I answered with a little smile.

"Your article, I read it. It is incredible, and I am very moved. And how long have you been here?"

"Three days now."

"I also love bicycling, but for me, it is merely amateurish through town."

We chatted a bit, and of course, we talked about my journey, of its difficulties but also of the nice surprises the roads held. He was a young Spaniard in college, and his name was Julio. I told him I came from Burundi originally, and Julio, like so many others, could not believe what he heard. He had seen my story in the newspaper, true, but now he was faced with the image of the hero the newspaper created. His eyes stayed wide as he listened intently. He asked me where I was staying. I told him I was camping in a public park.

Touched, Julio asked me to follow him. He wanted to ask his parents if they could house me. His mother was French and his father Spanish. When I got to his house, his parents approved. Julio also made a good case for me, which I could see without understanding his argument, which he made in Spanish. His father's face softened, and his sympathy grew as Julio told him my story.

The house was incredibly clean. Julio took me into the room I'd be staying in and showed me the rest of the house. I was most excited about the shower, since it had been two weeks since water had touched my body. After the shower, I felt alive again. When I went out again, I was offered a tasty, steaming soup, which I gulped down in a second. In the meantime, Julio was on the telephone. In fact, he just called his friends and his girlfriend. He told me that they were coming to see the African cyclist who'd come from Burundi all the way to Spain. Soon after the phone call, his friends arrived, and after greeting me, asked me to tell my story. I was so used to telling it that it rolled off my tongue.

Only Julio and one of his friends, Pinto, spoke French, but they translated for the rest of the group. That same evening, my new friends gave me a tour around town. They took me all through Old Madrid, which was lively and filled with cafés. We spent some time in one, drinking beer, and then we continued on to many others. Julio knew the town well, especially the bars. After a wonderful night out, we retired back to Julio's house and rested for the next adventure. The next day he invited me to go to Soria, the university he attended as a graduate student. We traveled by bus about 2 hours into the mountains to get there. The scenery we passed was full of trees and quaint villages. The town of Soria is known for its Romanesque architectural heritage and religious monuments, accentuated by beautiful nature reserves, rivers, and lakes. He showed me around the campus, which at the time was partially covered in steadily melting snow. The trip took the better part of a day. I was in awe of the generosity he showed me even though I was a complete stranger to him such a short time ago.

After a day of exploring the university we went home, where I finally met Julio's mother. As soon as she started talking to me, I got emotional. It seemed all mothers are the same. Their kindness is divine. She pushed me to eat a lot.

"You must have lost weight," she said. "You must regain it. You should also think to return home. It must hurt your mother not to see you. I am sure, every time she thinks of you, she must suffer. Don't waste your youth. Go enjoy it with your people; otherwise, you'll go home old, incapable of anything."

If only she knew how hard it would be for me to reconnect with the woman who gave birth to me, she would have shed tears. Just to comfort her, I promised to go home as soon as possible. I knew I wouldn't take her advice, but I was profoundly touched, to the point of tears. The words of this wise mother made me revisit my conscience and reflect on the madness of my journey. Unfortunately, it was not something I could change. It's not simply that I had developed a taste for adventure; it also seemed that there was no other avenue for a better life. I do indeed remember sad moments where my mother was pushing us, my brother and I, to leave her, so we would not be torn apart by the enemy. I knew the situation hadn't improved since. My stay with Julio and his family was full of life and love, but I had to say goodbye. After about a week, I decided to leave. Julio and friends organized a goodbye party for me. They asked me endless questions about Africa and its inhabitants. One friend told me, "Television is not enough. We are shown on the screen wild animals and the poorest of little African villages." I told him that the media showed them what they want to think of Africa, to accentuate the characteristics of the third world they thought it was. My continent was not just jungle and misery. As anywhere else in the world, there were rich and poor people, uneducated and educated, literate and illiterate. Africa may well be the greatest continent because of the wealth of its culture and social spirit of its people.

The unhesitating nature with which Julio granted me hospitality was beyond my understanding, and I imagined how beautiful and peaceful the world would be if people of this kind were more numerous on the world's streets. Unfortunately, similar hearts to Julio's are not legion. After these goodbyes and the anxiety of separation, I set back out on the road. My feet were itchy to move after a week of not pedaling.

At nightfall, I left Madrid. But soon after leaving that bustling city, I saw a campground and decided to spend the night there. There were plenty of people, music, and dancers. It was like a tiny city of its own. In this crowd, I crossed paths with a couple of young girls, Teresa and Marianne, who immediately proved friendly. I was starting to understand and speak a bit of

Spanish. They were obviously interested in my story. Out of the two, Teresa seemed the most drawn in. Her look and angelic smile spoke volumes. She invited me to dance. With pleasure, I accepted the invitation. What dancing! Her body against mine, her shoulders and arms, her soft gaze with fiery eyes, her perfume—everything about her was incredible, a sight to behold, and a force all herself.

In front of her, I must have looked like a bear in front of a pot of honey. What warmth she gave off in my arms! During the entire night, I danced with these two girls; I did not completely neglect Marianne. But after a while, a type of fear crept in. I was the only black in the middle of whites, dancing with their girls. It was not prudent on my part. Anyone jealous could have tried to hurt me. The idea continued to haunt me, but I tried my best to hide my fear from my two partners. The moment eventually came when each of us went to sleep. But during our dance, I received an invitation from Teresa to go visit her the next day. In my tent all night long, I could think of nothing but what would come.

In the morning, they both came to see me. We went off for a walk and spent the day together. I held hands with Teresa, caressed her fingers, and looked deeply into her eyes. Bit by bit, we got used to each other. In the evening, we returned to the campground. When it was time to return to our respective tents again, Teresa took me by the hand. She took me aside from the rest of the group around us and softy put a warm kiss on my cheek. It was good! I felt my whole body tremble. It was very sensual and full of romance. I went to sleep, or rather, lay down in my tent. In my tent, I was no longer myself; Teresa's love had swallowed me whole. When I closed my eyes, I could not see anything but her. On her side, it was evidently the same. She knew where I pitched my tent. The same night, she came to see me, to keep me busy.

I did not hesitate to invite her into my "castle." Though my tent was small, she entered without hesitation.

It was a moment of intense joy, together. She wanted me as much as I wanted her. On my side, love had been missing for a long time. She filled me with love and joy. I hope that I did the same for her. The love was short, though, as the next day, we parted. She had to go back to school, and I had to go back to my adventure. I have never stopped wishing her a good life.

Reinvigorated by the days of romance, I started back on the path of adventure. Spain is a wonderful country. It surprised me to see all the languages that people spoke—Catalan, Basque, and Galician, just to name a few. My pedaling directed me toward Bilbao. Here I ran into Basque protests, opposing Spain. The former were looking for greater autonomy. I learned that this is an old dispute. At San Sebastian, it got worse. Here, the protesters were more violent. Soldiers passed, their accusing eye on some people. There were even gunshots, but in this case, I was not afraid. My skin alone was witness to my innocence. San Sebastian was a pretty town, if one ignored the violent protests. Its Basque inhabitants were strong, mountainous people, well suited to the violent protests they were engaging in. So far, it was one of the most beautiful places I had seen in Spain. The mingling of mountains and countryside, and the buildings on the ocean's edge, made it a place that I still dream about. It was situated in the north of Spain at the edge of the Atlantic Ocean. Fine sand and clean beaches made it another excellent place to relax. After some time on the beach, I went over to the French consulate in hopes of obtaining an entry visa into France. Their rejection was clear and, admittedly, with good reason; the travel document that I had was not a valid one for a visa request. On top of that, I was a refugee, which made everything more difficult. Without anywhere to go, I was lost and wanted to try to enter illegally. At the border, before I could even give it a real try, I ran into a customs agent who turned me away vigorously.

I turned back toward Pamplona, where, spent with fatigue, I set up camp next to the railway. I got in my sleeping bag, and just before I fell asleep, I felt the presence of a man in the dark, walking slowly toward me, on the tips of his toes. My first thought was that perhaps it was a passenger, or maybe another camper. He was still coming. I let him approach slowly. He had gotten close enough; I quickly got out of the bag. Immediately, hop! He turned around and disappeared. I went back to bed, and around three o'clock in the morning, I dreamed of a human mass in the gutter near me. My heart beat quickly, and I woke up just in time. I saw something moving, in the same gutter as the one in my dreams. I focused all my attention on it. It was a man crawling like a crocodile stalking its prey. Was it the same man that I had just seen flee? Perhaps. With my senses on the alert, I left my sleeping bag quietly and waited, spear in hand. At first sight of this man, I thought he was lost, but on the second attempt on his part, I started to understand that he wished me harm. I was ready to defend myself. The man kept crawling; he still thought I was asleep. I was black, he was white, and we were both in the dark. Five meters away, he saw me! You should have seen him run! To see a man with a spear in the darkness—it is the dark fear of many a person who has never seen Africa! He ran crying out for help. After his disappearance, fear fell upon me. I quickly changed my campsite's location and spent the night.

I plunged into deep reflection after I calmed down and got some sleep. This encounter shook me to my core. Continuing to the north of Europe through France was my dream, but here was an insurmountable wall erected by the visa problem. Could I continue this errant life any longer? I recalled the warnings of my friends in Burundi on the dangers that I would risk running into on this adventure; I recalled, too, the strong words of Julio's mother as to the pain I was causing my parents. When the path to the unknown is inaccessible, we at least know where we came from. Returning to Africa was my decision and my solution. Once in Sudan, I would travel back to Burundi via Uganda and Zaire (now the Democratic Republic of Congo). I would put away my bicycle and finally end my journey.

# CHAPTER 24

# Khartoum: In the Grips of Love

S till in Spain, I got in touch with an old friend named Angela, who had relatives in the country. She herself came to see me though. She gave me some money, which I combined with the little money I made doing odd jobs here and there along my journey to buy myself a plane ticket out of Barcelona. After landing in Khartoum on the morning of August 6, 1980, I went directly to the High Commission for Refugees. I was met with more luck here, as I ran into Jean François Durieux, who I thought had already left Sudan. He once again took up the mantle of my defender, always welcoming, cheerful, and understanding. As a welcome greeting, he looked at me and said, "You are still alive?"

After catching up a little, we went back to his house. I was very happy to meet his family: Anne, his wife; Jules, his two-year-old son; and Emilie, his year-old daughter. To think that Durieux had started a whole family while I was gone! He had a kind of adventure all his own, and to see that one of my dearest friends was happy and had children brought me an indescribable amount of joy. I relished playing with the toddlers, who bore my friend's likeness. That night, we had no time to sleep. There was still a lot to talk about. I told them all about my journey since I left Sudan, in detail. Anne was particularly interested; her kindness was only comparable to her husband's. And after, he told me what had happened in Khartoum since I left.

Everything had changed in the country that adopted me. And I was expecting to come back to my home! A fear gripped me. All my old friends were gone, except for Jean François; Toto, who was still working at the youth hostel; and Marie-Ange and her husband, Jean-Michel. They mentioned that the University of Khartoum was looking to hire a driver in the French department. I jumped at the chance and quickly made myself a chauffeur at the university, where, besides driving cars, I would learn many jobs. Starting with building renovation, painting, plumbing, and even carpeting. Everyone approved of me there; I was in the good graces of the dean and the professors. Among them was a girl from Holland, Neilly, who gave lectures at the history department. Over a very short time, I developed deep feelings for her. Regrettably, there was a barrier between our two social classes. She loved me for my exploits; she told me over and over again. But something hid inside her. When she looked at me with her loving, innocent eyes, I felt like fainting. Within a week, she finally declared her love for me: "Faustin, I love you madly."

One day she invited me over to her place, and I showed up, nervous. We ended up lying together on the couch. It was on that couch that I died for the first time. I lost consciousness as she caressed my chest with her long fingers. An hour of cuddling, full of temptation, and I couldn't handle it any longer. Her eyes weakened, and her skin reddened. Realizing that I was shy, she drew a bath for us, and we both got inside. The moment was special. Afterward, we often went out arm in arm. She was an intelligent girl, fluent in French, English, German, and Arabic. She had done much traveling in Africa, Europe, and America in order to write her thesis. She taught me many things. I called her "Kanyoni Kanjye," which means "my little bird" in my Kinyarwanda. She called me the same.

But beautiful things never last long, and all my youthful loves were beautiful. Four months later, Neilly finished her work as a visiting professor and left Sudan. My bird flew away! She left me without hope of seeing her again. For a whole week before her final departure, a mortal sadness grinded at my heart. Adieu, Kanyoni Kanjye. You had managed to win my heart.

The separation was painful, but some good came out of it. After she left, I was able to rethink my plans. I picked up my initial plans. The desire to discover other horizons never left me; it just had gone dormant for a time. After having tried everything, finally, I managed to obtain a visa for France. That is something at least! Being a fool, I returned to Europe despite all the difficulties I had there. My French friends in Sudan, ashamed at their country's rejection of me, actually encouraged me to continue my journey this time, which was a far cry from the voices I had heard in years past. This time, I thought my journey would continue endlessly. I pictured India, China, but I had no definite plans other than Europe. With the money I had made working for the university, I bought a plane ticket, mounted my bike, and prepared for France.

# CHAPTER 25

# Paris: Lost in Another City

I arrived in Paris in May 1981. As soon as I got off the plane, I was greeted by airport problems due to my travel document. After an intensive interrogation, the immigration agent let me enter the country. I was miraculously admitted into France. Paris is a city that I cannot describe. For a full hour after I left the airport, I stood on the sidewalk, not knowing what to do. I could not move. The city was overwhelming. *Where should I go? What should I do?* The two questions sent me into my thoughts for an eternity.

After a week, I had gotten to know the capital. The Eiffel Tower, Notre-Dame, Pompidou Center Place, the Champs Élysées, the Bois de Boulogne, the Grévin museum and its statues that would leave anyone breathless. The architecture of the buildings was of unimaginable beauty. Paris impressed me very much! The city also had such diverse people living well alongside each other: Spaniards, Germans, but also Africans coming from all over Africa. When I got the chance, I telephoned a couple, Didier and Josiane, whom I had met traveling in Burkina Faso. Didier picked up the phone. He exclaimed, "Impossible, Faustin, here, what a good surprise!" I heard him call out, "Josiane, Josiane, it is Faustin on the phone." They were clearly happy to have news of me and invited me to join them. They lived in Le Havre. I set off on the road on my trusty bicycle once again. The density and speed of traffic became a tough equation for me to solve, but the nature of traffic here was different than the cities I had been in throughout Africa.

I reached Le Havre quickly. I was thrilled to be reunited with Josiane and Didier. We shared our stories of what had happened since we were together the year before. Josiane seemed tired; to my surprise, she was nine months pregnant! We ate and remembered our brief journey in Upper Volta. And Didier told me, "Your courage is exceptional, Faustin! We were at the ends of our strength when we all met."

We toured the town by car in the morning hours, but we did not travel far, as Josiane had to be driven to the maternity ward. I was there in town when she delivered a big baby, a beautiful boy. I was thrilled to have seen my friends and to have seen their newborn, their first child. Despite all the obstacles that popped up in my way to get to France, I was glad I went through with it.

I bypassed Paris to get to the south of France at Montpeyroux, where my old friends Marie-Ange and her husband, Jean-Michel, had been living since their return from Sudan.

Montpeyroux was a pretty little town, sparsely populated, with an aging population. Everyone knew everyone else here. It was a village that was part of the greater wine region of southern France. The grape harvesting season had begun when I arrived. Hired by a farmer, I worked with four Spaniards, a woman, and three other men from different countries like England, Holland, and Denmark as grape pickers. The medley of languages reminded me of villages back in Africa. Nearly every night after the day's work was done, everyone met up in a café. Little parties were organized often. The harvesting was seasonal work that only lasted one or two months, perfect for my needs. My wanderlust kicked in again, and I decided to continue my journey after the season. I said my goodbyes to Jean-Michel and Marie-Ange soon after they had birthed their own little girl, Stella.

I headed back to Paris. On my way, I dreamed of traveling through Europe and Asia. The four months spent working in the countryside had taught me many things. I passed through Limoges, where I saw vast fields of apple trees, cherry trees, and crops that did not exist in my country. When I got back to the French capital, I was interviewed on Radio France Internationale and the newspaper *Young Africa*.

**AVENTURE**

*Un jeune Rwandais parcourt l'Afrique, puis l'Europe, depuis quatre ans. Bientôt ce sera l'Inde. Toujours à vélo.*

# Le monde à la force des mollets

Yann Le Galès

Cinquante mille kilomètres dans les jambes. Telle est la performance de Faustin Rusangawa, un Rwandais de vingt-six ans installé au Burundi. Parti de Bujumbura en 1977 avec une poignée d'*amafranga*, il a depuis sillonné sur son vélo le continent africain d'est en ouest et du nord au sud. L'envie de regarder par-dessus ses collines l'a saisi un jour. Et devant ses yeux « *les horizons se sont mis à reculer* ». Dans un premier temps, Faustin part pour un périple régional : Zaïre, Ouganda, Zambie, Tanzanie, Kenya. « *La première semaine c'était dur*, raconte-t-il. *J'avais le cœur serré. Je quittais ma famille, mon pays. J'étais seul. C'est à Mombasa, au Kenya, que tout a basculé. Là, pour la première fois, j'ai eu envie de connaître tout de l'Afrique, de voir d'autres visages, d'autres paysages.* »

Grand, mince, énergique, il demeure avare de mots comme si son exploit — être le premier Africain à parcourir le continent à bicyclette — le laissait impassible. Taciturne comme tous les montagnards, il lance : « *Je ne compte pas les kilomètres que j'ai avalés. Ce serait idiot.* »

*Étonné*

Vêtu d'une chemise et d'un bermuda kaki, chaussé de tennis blancs, son éternel chapeau cloche délavé sur la pluie et le soleil vissé sur le crâne, ce cycliste pas comme les autres a vagabondé au Soudan, en Egypte, en République centrafricaine, au Cameroun, au Nigeria, au Niger, en Haute-Volta, au Mali, aux Iles Canaries. Et là, il a décidé de franchir la mer, de connaître l'Europe. La France puis, plus au nord, la Hollande, peut-être même la Norvège. « *J'ai l'impression que plus je monte vers le haut de l'Europe, plus la vie est chère. Comment peut-on vivre quand on est fauché ? Ce qui m'intéresse ce ne sont pas les capitales. Ce sont les petits villages. Je suis à Paris pour quelques jours mais j'ai l'impression que ce n'est pas le vrai pays. Ici les gens ne sont pas naturels.* »

Après le nord, ce sera la redescente vers le sud puis vers l'Inde, ultime étape de son errance sur les pistes et les routes du monde. « *Je pense me promener encore deux ans. Six ans de voyage, cela me suffit. Et puis, une fois en Inde, mon périple sera achevé, j'aurai l'impression d'avoir bouclé la boucle. Alors je prendrai le bateau et je retirerai au pays. Là, j'accrocherai mon vélo. J'aurai des souvenirs plein la tête.* »

Car cette odyssée cycliste aura été une formidable école de la vie. Faustin a parcouru des pays en guerre. Il a connu la faim, le froid, la solitude, la soif. Il a vécu des nuits d'encre où la rumeur de la faune l'emplissait de craintes. Il a parcouru les forêts noires d'arbres où il tremblait comme une feuille et où il ne pouvait dormir que juché dans les branches. Il a traversé des déserts dont le sable torride brûlait les pneus de sa bicyclette. « *C'était la première fois que je découvrais une étendue qui fuyait sans cesse devant moi comme si elle ne devait jamais finir. J'ai vécu le même étonnement quand j'ai vu la mer, pour la première fois, à Mombasa.* »

Si ce voyage fut lourd d'épreuves il fut également riche en bonheurs. Partout, les mêmes questions ont fusé : « *Comment fais-tu ? Pourquoi ? Que manges-tu ? Quel est ton but ?* » Et chaque fois Faustin, patient, a raconté son périple.

*Heureux*

Au hasard de ces rencontres certains admirateurs s'étaient offerts de l'accompagner dans son périple. Mais, mal préparés, ne possédant pas les qualités physiques et morales nécessaires, tous ont abandonné. Vagabond devant les hommes, « clochard céleste », muni de son seul baluchon orange, il aura vécu la route pour son plus grand bonheur. Heureux comme un homme qui a accompli un beau voyage. J.L.A.

Faustin Rusangawa dans les jardins de J.A. « Voir d'autres visages, d'autres paysages. »

JEUNE AFRIQUE - N° 1068 - 24 J...

72

ARTICLE FEATURED IN JEUNE AFRIQUE FOLLOWING AN INTERVIEW OF FAUSTIN IN PARIS, FRANCE, WITH HIS BICYCLE

One morning, wanderlust in full force, I went up to the Dutch Embassy on a whim to try my luck. I asked for a visa. And luckily enough, I got one the same day without any complications. A surprise! If only every country admitted people without visas. We would all be better off.

Early in the morning, with my bags packed, I kissed my camel of a bicycle and headed off for Belgium. A penetrating cold slowed me down; this kind of weather was not something I was used to. A European winter is a harsh one! I pedaled quickly to try and warm myself up, but it did nothing. My fingers were frozen onto the handlebars, despite my gloves. I had hit winter!

# CHAPTER 26
# Low Countries: At the End

A t the Franco-Belgian border, I had no problems; there was not even a customs office as I eased myself through this invisible border. I did not really know I was in Belgium until I reached Brussels. It felt like my troubles were centered around France, but I left that all behind in Belgium. I pedaled without stopping up to Brussels. It was special for me; it was the capital of our colonizers. I was glad to be there, but in truth, it was hard to differentiate Belgium from France.

I saw the palace of King Baudouin with its magnificent land and gardens. The town was immense. I visited its Atomium with Martin, my English friend whom I'd met when he was teaching in Kenya years ago. He was now in Brussels to visit his family and I contacted him to get together and reminisce. The Atomium was a marvel to me. The design of the structure mimics the molecular structure of an iron crystal magnified 165 billion times. Within it were five habitable spheres that featured exhibit halls. An elevator opened in front of me, and I flew up at a dizzying speed toward a restaurant with a magnificent panoramic view of the city. The Atomium was even prettier when one saw it from afar, with its dominating height and its voluminous bright balls. The person who conceived it had a very rich imagination.

In Brussels I met many Africans, mostly from ex-Belgian colonies of central Africa. Many of my fellow Rwandans set roots down here. Some were owners of shops selling African products:

clothing, masks, statuettes. Others kept African restaurants. It felt a little like home. I even got to speak Kinyarwanda and ate Rwandan dishes. While in Brussels, I learned where Durieux's generosity came from, as I stayed with his parents. They took me all around Brussels; I was truly blessed to have met such an incredible family. Mrs. Duriex specifically fed me endless food and showed me everything there was to see in Brussels, all while asking me endless questions about my journey. The kindness of mothers showed itself once again, but like every other mother I encountered, she advised me to head home and worried more than she admired. More than myself, though, she was worried about my mother. Mrs. Duriex was living in a situation much like my mother was, with her son halfway across the world. But at least with them they could communicate. As for Rwanda, all I knew about it was what I heard from other Rwandans, and I knew nothing about the fate of my family.

After getting my fill of Brussels, I went back on the deserted road and pedaled in the cold, which, according to the weather forecast, would soon bring snow. To the north, I crossed an industrial part of the country. Communication became impossible, as Flemish, not French, was the primary language spoken here. Thankfully, I arrived in Holland without any issues.

Like crossing into Belgium, when I left it, there were no customs barriers. The Netherlands itself was a flat paradise, easy to bike through. I looked out in front of me, a plain out to infinity with no unused land; either it was inhabited or cultivated. From the start, I noticed Holland was a well-organized country and was made safe for bicyclists. The roadway had three lanes: the car lanes, bicycle lanes, and pedestrian lanes. Each was in their lane, and no one bothered anyone. It was extraordinary. Here the bicycle was dominant. If everyone followed this example, we would surely pollute less of the atmosphere. I saw tandem bikes for the first time in my life. The cultural food of Holland was very different from other countries. Here, the breakfast was the most bountiful in the world. It was rich and heavy, while dinner was light.

Without trouble, I rolled to Sint-Michielsgestel. The season had changed; winter was more and more biting. A glacial cold stopped me from pedaling altogether. I found myself shivering and truly risked freezing to death. It was impossible to ride in this weather, and I had no choice but to take the train. The journey was made through a vast plain dotted with ancient windmills.

I fell in love with this liberal and peaceful country. Every behavior, every philosophy, was accepted. Each was allowed to live as he or she saw fit as long as it did not bother others.

Only one problem bothered me: leaving this beautiful country. A few days from my arrival in Sint-Michielsgestel, my visa would no longer be valid, and the immigration office in Holland denied my extension when I tried for one. I had two reasons to leave now. The climate and the expiration of my visa were both working against me. At the start, my plan was to pass through Germany, Denmark, Sweden, Norway, and the USSR to get to China or India. But winter stopped me. Another idea I considered was going south through Lebanon, Iraq, and Iran, but war had beaten me there! The only option left for me was to return to Burundi. I had crisscrossed several regions and wandered through mountains and valleys. I had spun my wheels everywhere. It was time to go home and finally rest. In the afternoon of December 23, a train took me to Brussels. After two days, I was back on a plane bound for Burundi through Zaire.

# CHAPTER 27

# Bujumbura: Home

Onboard Air Zaire, the national airline of the former Zaire, I made a stopover in Paris, then took a long flight over the Sahara Desert. The next layover would be at Bujumbura, my ultimate destination.

After five years of adventures, I landed safe and sound at Bujumbura, my starting point. It was January 2, 1982. I closed the loop by bicycle in about five years. The emotion choked me as I entered the city. People greeted me, told me they heard about me on Radio France Internationale, told me they read about me in the magazine *Jeune Afrique*. Indeed, several papers and reviews of several countries I had visited had published my story—for example, the *Standard* of Nairobi, a newspaper from Sudan, a paper in Upper Volta (Burkina Faso), *The Sun* of Dakar, the *El País* of Spain, and the *Young Africa* of Paris. I also did radio and television interviews—to just list a few: Ugandan television, the RFI-Radio France Internationale, and the Radio Nationale of Burundi. Among all these media tools, the *Young Africa* and the RFI made the biggest waves in the Great Lakes region around Burundi, Rwanda, and in other francophone countries.

It was a surprise for me; I did not know that the people of my homes had heard of me or read any articles of my trek. Others thought I was a ghost, since they had scratched me off the list of the living.

I arrived at the home of my cousin Marianne, where some members of my family had sought refuge. Among them Innocent; he was doing well for himself. To think that the two of us, who had left Rwanda so many years ago, had made something of ourselves. That both of us had established our lives in our own way. Neither of us wanted to leave our homes, but we made our own homes now. My home was the world, and his was Bujumbura. This was further demonstrated by the fact that he had started a family—I now had a niece! They were all surprised to see me again, and some to meet me. It was pleasant, and immediately I was bombarded with questions. The news of my arrival spread through the town quickly. Marie-Cécile, my girlfriend whom I had left with aching heart so many years ago, received this information. She quickly came to see me. The years that passed had in no way degraded her beauty. She was still ravishing. The most exciting moment was the meeting of our gazes. She immediately threw herself in my arms, with a large smile. "Welcome, Faustin; I am glad to see you, you are still so handsome." She introduced me to her daughter Afi. She informed me she was now married with two children. "Congratulations! As far as I am concerned, it is status quo. I am married to my bicycle and to the roads," I told her, looking at her straight in the eyes.

"I invite you to come meet my husband and daughter in a few days," she said.

She organized a big feast for my arrival. Her house was packed with people, food and African music in abundance, a beautiful decoration made of flowers and candles. Everything was beautiful. The moment had arrived to begin the soiree. Marie-Cécile got up and rang a little bell to get everyone's attention. She spoke up: "Our presence here today is special. I would like to present someone who played an important role in my life." She said my name and had me stand as the crowd of twenty or thirty applauded. She continued her speech. "We have witnessed the dramatic situation that our country has lived through. I have suffered enormously, as you all here have. I was struck. In total despair, I left my country, crossing a distance of more than three hundred kilometers on foot. I was welcomed into a refugee camp, though life was not easy there. My whole body was swollen and bruised; I had lost contact with my family, and my heart was broken. This man, also a refugee in the same camp, armed me with courage, shared with me his meals, massaged my swollen body, and supported me in my emotional ruin. He is full of benevolence and always puts others before himself. Without his assistance, I would not be here today before you with my husband and children. You probably know his story. For those of you that do not already know it, Faustin is the first African to cover two continents on a bicycle. What a challenge! Faustin is my hero; he is our hero. Once more, thank you, Faustin, for all you have done for me; thank you, all who accepted my invitation. Now, let's feast and party."

As Marie-Cécile returned to her seat, soft music played, and five girls gave me bouquets of flowers, candies, and other gifts. Then came all the other guests, each with a gift. It was an emotional evening, an overwhelming one. I was taken aback to be honored so graciously by this wonderful community. It was undeniably heartwarming. I remembered something my parents used to say: "The more you give, the more you get." Your kindness will always come back to you, though not always from the same person you show kindness to. After the gift giving, we all celebrated on the dance floor.

Everyone was happy to see me again, but for me, the most important challenge was to go to Rwanda to see my family whom I had left there more than ten years ago. Friends didn't encourage me to go back, as according to them, the country was still unsafe, and I could lose my life there. In fact, everyone I talked to told me not to go; they all thought I would never return. As for me, I was used to the actions and behavior of men. In Bujumbura, I was discouraged from starting a bicycle adventure. If I had wanted to listen to them, I would never have started. All the advice was given with good intentions, but it didn't apply to me. No one knew what hell I had already gone through. I knew well that there were dangers waiting for me in my country, but I had to go back. I had to see my family, and if I died, it would have been for a good cause. I know that everything happens for a reason; I was merely following my destiny, and I felt that my destiny lay in Rwanda.

The next day, it was just me and my princess, headed toward Rwanda. I found myself riding on an old road that I knew well. I saw the rolling hills and the fields just as I had left them. This means of transport was a monumental error, as I could not move discreetly. Everyone had heard about me and recognized me very quickly. The whole country was informed of my arrival. Great crowds formed around me everywhere I went. The Rwandans were all pleased with me and shouted, "Here is our brother that circled the world on a bicycle. We are proud of you!" The people in my old village, Jabana, were happy. But the joy my family felt at seeing me again, I could not describe. First, I was just the son they had lost. Then I became a hero. I settled in for a long reunion with my family, only to discover that my brother François had made it home! Not long after we left Rwanda, François managed to travel back to Jabana without being caught by Hutus. I was overjoyed to see them all still alive, especially François and my mother. We all kissed and hugged for what was one of the most incredible moments of my life. It was a marvelous moment, reuniting with my family. It was also the last time I would see them.

# CHAPTER 28

# Rwanda: The Interrogation

The news that I was back home spread fast, likely aided by my acceptance of an interview with Radio Rwanda. This seemed to alert the governmental authorities of my return. One day, a man dressed in fine clothes delivered a letter to my home. I had received a summons from the immigration services. I was worried. My entire family was worried. My brother told me, "Faustin, none of those that respond to this summons come back, especially when these people are Tutsis." Several thoughts flashed through my head. Should I flee? No, they could exterminate my family. I needed to show up at the Office of Immigration Services.

In the office, I received a harsh interrogation to determine the reason of my departure from the country and the reason for my return.

"I was born here and grew up here. The Tutsis had always been considered second-class citizens, without representation, rights, education, work for them or their children. There was no reason for this discrimination. Many people were beaten and lost their properties. That is why I left my beautiful country, as many other Rwandans, too, in order to seek refuge. My family stayed here, and my parents thankfully survived. I am thus back in my home. We are several thousand refugees in the neighboring countries and throughout the world. It is a great loss for the development of Rwanda that will not be able to get its head out of water without the common effort of all its sons."

The man shook his head and gave a long sigh. "I understand what you are saying. History is what it is, but if you want to stay here, you have to make a formal request, but that does not guarantee that it will be granted to you."

When I got home that day, I had a somber meeting with my family. They told me I couldn't stay in Rwanda. It was too dangerous for me. They told me about others who were locked away or killed out of nowhere. It would be goodbye again. More painful goodbyes, especially as my father told me, "If I die, I will die in peace, having seen you." He would perish in a traffic accident sometime after I would leave this second time.

The day after the interrogation and subsequent goodbyes to my family, I fled the country. I escaped this bloody regime. However, I thought about my loved ones staying behind. What would become of them? I left them in an uncertain situation. I could only hope I would see them again.

I felt completely powerless under a reign of executioners. How could I be afraid of my Rwandan brothers, when I had not been afraid of strangers that I crossed paths with on my trek? Did my brothers in power in Kigali have something more savage in them than the wildness of tropical forests? More than savage beasts, than ocean currents, seas and rivers? My question remains open.

# CHAPTER 29

# Bujumbura: No Choice but Forward

The bike ride back to Bujumbura in Burundi was sad and miserable. I had decided to settle there. Things had changed. Friends had gone, and others came. The same people who told me not go on my journey had gone, started families, or even died. It felt like a new city to me. I felt like I was starting over. Part of that was nice—new starts can always be nice—but it felt alienating. It felt like I had lost all my friends, like I had lost my home. This very poor country's economy was improving, so setting down roots made sense. It was time to find means of survival, a job. Then I could think about writing a book.

Starting from scratch, I had to get creative in order to sustain even my most basic needs. I began buying and selling clothes at local markets for a small profit. The income was meager, but it put food in my belly; and the nature of the business allowed me to socialize, as well as afford some downtime to begin working on my story. Traveling was a whole education. I learned many things. I had rich experiences that I felt I needed to share with the world, especially with the young. I had lived through great extremes, and I hoped to capture those stories while my memory was still fresh. I just had one issue: I couldn't read or write. My country had taken away my opportunities from me for life, taking away my voice, hurting me even to this day. So, my only option was to find someone to tell my story to in my native tongue, who could transcribe it and write it in French. Telling my story, in this book, would be like reliving my beautiful voyage in another way.

I settled into Bujumbura for a while. I found a steady rhythm to life; I even joined a cycling club. William Grant, an American working for USAID, was in this same cyclist club. Outside the club, we were friends. He spoke to me of an American project named PROBE. It featured American students in geology who had just arrived to prospect on Lake Tanganyika. More precisely, they were searching for petroleum deposits under this lake. They needed an employee to work with them on the *Nyanja*, their boat. The project was attached to Duke University in North Carolina. Bruce Rosendahl, a professor at Duke, led the project. Jim Miguel and Deby Scott were the student researchers from the same university. These researchers had to navigate on lakes Tanganyika, Victoria, Turkana, and Malawi, all in the region of the Great Lakes. I was interested. The date was July 14, 1982. Since Mr. Grant knew me, I was a shoo-in for the job. The Americans hired me that same day.

Lake Tanganyika was an immense body of water, six hundred kilometers long, that connects four countries: Burundi, Tanzania, Congo, and Zambia. It was surrounded by massive mountains as well. It is the second deepest lake in the world. We spent a whole year working on the lake before embarking for lake Turkana, in the north of Kenya. This lake also connects with Ethiopia and Sudan.

# CHAPTER 30
# Turkana: Probing the Lake

There were three of us heading for lake Turkana, as scouts for project PROBE. These years that I spent working with the Americans were among the best of my life. Stable employment, highly enjoyable work, and great coworkers. It was paradise. At Nairobi, we first passed by the museum of Nairobi to meet paleontologist Dr. Richard Leakey, our contact for the project. After touching base there, we left toward Lake Turkana, which was surrounded by horribly arid land. Agriculture in this region was nonexistent. The lake was not as deep as Lake Tanganyika, either, and was certainly more dangerous, as it contained crocodiles. After about a month of boating work, I was on the beach when someone called me to see a crocodile that had been caught in a fishing net meant for tilapia. In order to save the net, the fisherman called over a wildlife service employee to shoot the crocodile. That day, I ate crocodile meat for the first time. It was surprisingly very good. It tastes like fish, but the meat is tougher. The Turkana people love it.

The Turkana, to be specific, are a people who live on the fish they catch in the lake. Their daily life tends to be full of difficulties linked to their geographical situation. They are a people anchored in tradition and form a strong and loving community. Each evening, they gather for traditional dance and very joyous performances. These dances are more impressive, given the fact that they are performed without anyone consuming even a drop of alcohol. These people were incredibly poor, some of the poorest I had ever seen, but they did not seem unhappy. Money meant nothing to these people; they valued family, survival, and above everything their community. Turkana people worked all day and danced every night, I could not imagine living a life like that, but I admired them. But their work was not even work to them; it was living, and they acted as if they lived their happiest lives. To me, living a life like that, where money means nothing, and living without stress and with such energy, is something to truly strive for.

A CROCODILE IN TURKANA IS ACCIDENTALLY CAUGHT
IN A FISHING NET AND KILLED. FAUSTIN WOULD LATER
EAT CROCODILE MEAT FOR THE FIRST TIME.

FAUSTIN WITH FISHERMEN AT TURKANA, NORTHERN
KENYA, CARVING CROCODILE MEAT

FAUSTIN WITH MRS. SIMON AND CHILDREN, TURKANA, KENYA

After about a year, we finished the work at Lake Turkana. The next job was at Lake Victoria, one of the largest lakes in the world. It borders Uganda, Kenya, and Tanzania. Unfortunately, we would not stay there as long as we expected. The lake was too shallow for us to work with it, and the research equipment was faulty by that point.

Lake Malawi was the next lake to prospect. Before going there, I had to take my vacation. I thus left my colleagues at Kisumu while preparing a move. In my new itinerary, I planned to visit the United States, where Liz and Tom Dunkelman, Debbie Scott, and Jimmy Miguel had invited me to stay. They wanted me to visit Duke University, which they talked about nonstop. The three of us—Liz, Tom, and I—had become very close. After working for a while longer, I took my vacation and headed to Nairobi. I booked a flight from there to Cairo, where I would spend a week before carrying on to the New World. It was in Egypt that I had one of the most profound religious experiences of my life. I took a day trip to visit Mount Sinai, the site where the Ten Commandments were delivered from God to Moses. The atmosphere was full of spiritual energy as people were traversing up and down the mountain to see the holy place for themselves. The mountain holds immense cultural significance for Christians, Jews, and Muslims alike. I felt like it was a gift of life to bear witness to such majesty; I could do nothing but stare at this place where God, the Almighty, had delivered his word. But I also was saddened by the fact that this Sinai area had been plagued by intense wars between Israel and Egypt. That this incredible place, full of such meaning, was being washed with blood. In the following days, I sought to discover more of the region's rich history and found myself in museums which housed venerable biblical artifacts. Being in such holy spaces made one feel the connection between heaven and Earth. After my stay in Cairo, I continued on to the United States of America in the summer of 1985.

# Part Four:
# New Life in the
# New World

# CHAPTER 31

# United States of America: From Durham to Davis

My first destination was New York. The flight was long. We flew over the Atlantic as I thought about America, with a little bit of fear. The United States were not well regarded by Africans. The blacks had suffered too much in this country from slavery. We were told that blacks were not safe, that there are many racists, killing them when they caught them. We were told it was dangerous for blacks to even wander outside after dark. I had mixed feelings about these rumors, since they departed from my own experiences with Americans from the PROBE project. They never seemed racist to me; they were kind and human.

On the other hand, some American films that I saw in movie theaters in Burundi were violent, like *Roots* and *Rambo*. These films also showed horrendous traffic on wide freeways. I wondered how people dared move about in this chaos. What would happen to me in this country, a country that I had never thought to visit years ago? And at that moment, I was on a plane bound for New York. My destiny was filled with surprises. *Oh, well,* I thought. I had already faced many difficulties during my bicycling voyages. I had met many friendly people, and bad people, of course, and had survived it all, to this day. I was confident that I would be welcomed by true friends.

We landed at John F. Kennedy airport, in New York, on the morning of August 13, 1985. I was intimidated by this human mass that writhed about the airport, the passenger searches, and the identity checks at immigration. I presented my travel document, which had a visa I got in Nairobi. Luckily, I passed through without problems. However, I did not rush to get anywhere. I like to take my time and observe when I arrive in a place I do not know. The airport was very busy. Its expanse and its activities impressed me. I strolled calmly, observing these things, the people. Bewildered, I approached a black man, an airport custodian. I felt a sort of kinship because of our shared skin tone in a sea of white and asked him how to get to Manhattan. He very quickly understood that I was a new arrival. On a bit of paper that he took from his pocket, he drew me an itinerary and told me in a singsong accent unlike any I had heard before, "Bus, then subway." This man was so friendly that he completely broke the fear that I had of this country. He pointed to the bus I needed to take. There, I asked around for where I needed to stop to take the metro. In the metro, I also had to ask where I should step off, all the while brandishing the piece of paper that held my itinerary like a badge. I finally exited the metro and found myself out in the open air, in the middle of the city. I had truly arrived in the capital of the world, and it was exactly at it had been described to me. There was incredible diversity here; the whole human race lived together in the city of New York. The media outside the United States taught me to fear this city; now it impressed me. It was bustling, as alive during the day as at night. It was the New York on television, but better! Everything was bigger in this city; the cars, roads, people, buildings were all enormous. It was dazzling! Trying to get around, I had to make my way through a human river that never stopped. Everyone was busy and in a hurry.

The Statue of Liberty though, haunted me from the moment I saw it. She represented liberty that I had not known in my country. Liberty that had been taken from me by colonizers and imperialists, liberty that had been taken from me by own Rwandan brothers and sisters. Here, looking at the massive statue, I felt shivers down my spine. It felt hollow, like it was not real, like it could fade away at any moment. The rest of the city, though, was dazzling; it was as if this city lived and breathed. Every color imaginable was around me; every language I had ever heard was found here. This truly was the city that never slept. Going through Manhattan, I realized that this crowded, cramped city was the grandest place I had ever been in. But more than that, I was in the city where the United Nations is headquartered, the largest and most powerful organization in the world, the nation for nationless people, people like me. The next day, I took a bus bound for Washington, DC, and soon enough, I arrived in the capital of the most powerful country in the world. Yet another one of my dreams had been realized. *Never doubt destiny,* I thought as I walked that gorgeous city.

Soon I was reunited with my cycling club friend from Burundi, William Grant, who was the man who originally got me the job on the PROBE project. He was waiting for me at the bus terminal. We drove through Washington, DC, this city that held the destiny of the world in its hands. William gave me a tour of the White House and the Pentagon and took me all around. The George Washington Monument stood imposing over everything, this general who had commanded the revolutionaries in the eighteenth century to achieve this legendary American liberty. I was the most surprised to see blacks everywhere I went. At a glance, they seemed happy. For giving me the chance to work, and for serving as my tour guide, I thanked William profusely. He opened up a thousand and one opportunities, and that allowed me to discover the United States. After the capital, I took another bus bound for Durham, North Carolina. There, I visited the famous Duke University, a name that came up often in conversation when we were on the African lakes. It certainly lived up to its talk! Countless buildings spread about in a beautiful park. My first stop was the geology department.

I finally got to meet Dr. Bruce Rosendahl, my boss. His news was not good; he told me that the project would come to an end. Funding had been cut. This was devastating; I could barely contain my tears. I had just lost the best job of my life. I had to start over again. Once outside, I sat on a bench and thought. What was to become of me? What was I to do? My belongings were limited to a few items of clothing and hygienic products in my small backpack. I had come here for vacation but found myself in a trap like a rat.

However, I would understand later that in life, nothing is pure chance; all that occurs is grace. The end of the PROBE project had caused me great difficulties of all kinds and made me stay in the United States. Without knowing it at the time, it would be because of the project that I would be able to escape the genocide that would occur in my country nearly ten years later. Today, I strongly believe that all things happen for a reason.

I met many of my student friends from the PROBE project, mainly Tom Dunkelman, who had left Africa after the end of the project. We were very close, and he took good care of me and even tried to help me find solutions to all the difficulties I encountered in this new world, so different from the one in which I had previously lived. He housed me. And almost every night, I was invited to a different home for a barbecue, an incredibly American affair. Tom helped me meet many people; he was like my little brother. Tom was unlike any person I had ever met. He always pushed me to do more, to reach out to the world and take it. Not only that, but he gave me advice along the way. Without him, it would not have been possible for me to navigate the beautiful countryside of the little university town.

The beauty of the landscapes of North Carolina were without equal. In this region, two remarkable realities existed paradoxically alongside one another. Being from Africa, I had never experienced a true change of the seasons. North Carolina had the truest fall I had ever seen. My native Rwanda and Burundi had but two seasons— dry and rainy— but Durham had all four. I saw the leaves turn brown and fall away for the first time in my life; it was astonishingly beautiful, and I was terribly sad that I had missed this sight for all my life. Alongside all of this were the ruins of tobacco plantations, a vestige of slavery that bizarrely coexisted with the three great university towns of Durham, Raleigh, and Chapel Hill. Together, they formed the Research Triangle.

But none of that helped assuage my concerns for the future. Everything was uncertain. Fortunately, I was able to rely on my host and his family, with whom I always felt at home. I drew from this family the first inspiration for my life in the United States. I was particularly impacted by the love of work and the hardworking character of Dr. Ronald Green, another professor I met at Duke. This PhD in Chemistry often left his home around six o'clock in the morning to get to his office attached to the Duke University laboratory. He sometimes returned home at six o'clock in the evening, ate dinner with his family, and then returned to work until 9 o'clock at night. One day, Ronald offered to give me a tour of his lab. He showed me with pride his own creations and his cherished work site. That evening, I thought to myself: *If this gentleman has equals in his attachment to his work, I can understand why the United States is such a great country!* I realized how often work constitutes the first key to development; a country cannot develop if its people do not like their work. Ronald gave me hope that a better tomorrow would come, that simply working hard would be enough in order to grow.

The Green family offered me an English improvement class. This good family was ready to help me get whatever training could help me in this world. I knew it would not be easy for me; my few years of schooling, as well as my age, put me at a disadvantage. I was not able to get beyond the third year of primary school, and I always thought that older people didn't need further education. In Rwanda, school is for the young, and never afterward! Ronald's wife in particular encouraged me to study, and I was determined to take advantage of this heavenly gift. My eagerness for studies had been broken by the madness of men that had thrown me on the path to exile. I thus committed myself to work hard to get back into it. I felt just as much a part of the Green family as their daughters, Liz, Alison, and Nikki. It was Liz who would become my first wife, but our marriage was brief. We had met back in Africa on the PROBE project when were both working on Lake Turkana, and working there with her and all the others remains one of my fondest memories. However, we were always too far apart to ever truly be together. Still, my life continued on.

Two weeks after my arrival at Durham, a friend of Alison's who had a small construction business offered me a job. From there it was off to the races, my first job in this country. The boss of the company, Alison's friend, was wealthy, a real estate developer. He bought houses, fixed them up, and then resold them. I secured a second job at the Sometimes Restaurant, where I was a dishwasher and a cleaner. It was not glorious work, but it was enough.

My daily schedule consisted of English lessons from 8:00 to 10:00 a.m., construction from 10:00 a.m. to 5:00 p.m., and the restaurant from 5:00 p.m. to 1:00 a.m., a plan that changed often based on the needs of my superiors.

At Durham, having a car was more than a necessity. I was forced to buy a vehicle to be able to move about between school and my two jobs. My first car was a Ford Galaxy, for fifty dollars. But what a car! It was Alison's friend who sold me this old, beaten-down car. It was so old that each time I went out, I knew I was taking a risk. It attracted cops like nothing else too. On one encounter with a Durham police officer, I had been pulled over. Before the police officer got to my car, I exited my vehicle. Being a foreigner, I had no idea that you were supposed to stay in the car. I saw him approaching me slowly, his hand on the butt of his gun. I walked toward him with my hand out to greet him so I could shake his hand, as drivers did back home in Rwanda. He then drew his weapon and yelled at me to freeze or he would shoot. Despite my loose grasp of the English language at the time, I understood the intensity of the situation and did my best to try to comply with his commands. He then forced me, gun drawn, to return to my vehicle and sit back down. To this day I do not understand why he reacted this way. Was he drunk or just insane? He did not show any of the usual signs of drunkenness, however. Maybe he was mistaking me for some criminal he was looking for? My whole body was shaking after the gun was drawn though. Finally, after what felt like forever, he let me go, once I had shown him my driver's license from Burundi. I would learn later how lucky I was; he could have shot me in self-defense. I shared this misadventure with my friends. They told me sternly to never get out of the car, touch my pockets, or make any other suspicious moves when a police officer stops me. They could think I want to shoot them, and they would preemptively shoot me.

My first week of classes gave a bad impression of me to the teacher. Indeed, when she was giving us a fifteen-minute break,

I thought it was the end of the school day, and I rushed to my construction job. I also did not do my homework. Not only did I not understand it, but more importantly, I did not have the time. Another difficulty was that I did not have the same level of schooling as the other students in the class. They had all studied at universities in other languages, and most of them had some prior knowledge of English. I think the teacher considered me a druggy or a drunk. I always came to class bleary-eyed from work the night before. But with my loaded schedule, I had no choice. The teacher finally approached me to understand what was happening, and after I explained my situation, she started helping me more in class.

The construction work, however long, was fascinating for me. I had some basics, but quickly managed to learn roofing repair, wall repairs, plumbing, and painting. My bosses were also impressed by the progress I made. I was proud to be worthy of the confidence that Alison's friend had placed in me, hiring me under the table. The restaurant job, however, I got completely legally. I received a temporary work authorization.

I started to feel life turning back my way, things were getting better. I told myself: "I am the owner of a Ford Galaxy. Though she is old, she can get me around. I have two jobs, and I am going to school." In my mind, I had already achieved the American dream.

One day, at the restaurant, there was an impressive reunion. I was doing my job in the kitchen when a colleague called me over: "Faustin, come here, someone is asking for you."

I saw a man, white, whom I did not recognize. I thought that there must have been a mistake; it could not be me he was looking for. He stared at me for a moment and then said hello. I responded timidly; I did not hide my surprise. He then asked, "Do you recognize me?" I told him forwardly that I did not. "You gave me rides in Kenya!" he shouted. I was surprised once again. Then it dawned on me: God loves me so! He kept giving me surprises! I answered, perhaps. I knew that I had given lifts to a ton of people. The man described the journey we had made together, from Lake Turkana to Lodwa in the north of Kenya, a town about sixty miles from the lake. I was traveling with Tom Dunkelman to Nairobi, and we gave him a lift. He then told me he saw me from outside the restaurant, and that he wanted to make sure it was me. After this, he finally reintroduced himself as Peter Cegielci.

We exchanged addresses and were even more surprised to find we lived right next door to each other! Not only did I gain a new friend, but this event was one of the loveliest surprises of my life. Good deeds are never wasted. We stayed up together and shared a meal or a drink every chance we got. I didn't expect something so small like giving a ride to someone would have come back to me like this. I was happy to have another friend in a country where I had few who could truly relate to me. You never know how good deeds will do well for you down the line.

In my search for a better job, I found work at the North Carolina Museum of Life and Science. For a whole year, I returned to my roots and cared for the garden. It was fulfilling work. I found open and friendly minds at the museum. I also learned new professional skills, in gardening and driving tour vehicles.

While living in Durham, I first traveled to Davis, California, for the wedding of Nikki, the daughter of my hosts. California impressed me like nowhere else. It was a huge state where there were definitely more chances of finding work than in North Carolina. But the most important thing that pulled me to the state was being able to meet with a community of native Rwandans and Africans in general around UC Davis.

I was also excited at the idea of getting to live in this great state known for its economic potential and its temperate climate. I had learned that California was the most powerful state in the world when it came to agriculture, and that it had the best climate in the United States. I had also heard of its natural beauty and its marvelous tourist sites, like Lake Tahoe, Yosemite National Park, and the Pacific's beautiful beaches. I had made my decision. I was moving to California.

My journey from North Carolina to California ended up being very long. In effect, I was crossing the United States from east to west—breadth, beauty, and wealth infinite. That is the United States. Though a country; it is as large as a continent. The road trip took me three weeks.

I arrived in Davis, safe and sound, in August 1988. My stay in Davis started with a positive sign. Nikki and her husband, Tim Costello, were there waiting for me; I was well received by the young couple. Soon after settling in, I dug up several jobs in restaurants: with the Marriott Company, which ran the UC Davis cafeteria, at McDonald's, at Caffe Italia, and several other small gigs. The pay was insufficient, but at least I was not destitute. What's more, I could finally have my own place, if I worked up the money. After six months of working in the restaurants, I realized that I would not get far with my salary. Life in California has always been expensive. Still, I was confident in my gardening skills that I perfected while living in North Carolina. I bid adieu to the Marriott Company and all the other employers of mine to try something. I started my own gardening business. Almost all the residents of Davis had gardens. But how to go about this? I did not have the capital to buy the necessary equipment, but I still had to try and improve my lot.

One evening, I asked my flat mate to help me make a sign: FAUSTIN YARD CARE. I made hundreds of copies and distributed it to every residence I could find in Davis. I went door to door. Sometimes, dogs got to me before the owners. But soon after my canvassing journey, phone calls began to trickle in. The first customer told me his lawn needs mowing, but I had to tell him I had no lawnmower. He told me sorry. Same thing for the second. I would hear "Sorry" for at least a month. However, I used some courage and did not give up. One evening, by chance, a wise lady called and asked me the same question, whether I had a lawn mower, and I gave her the usual answer. But instead of sorry, she told me that she had a machine she would let me use. The only thing was that she was not sure if the machine still worked.

I quickly bicycled to her house. When I got to her house, I found out that the lawn mower definitely did not work. When I tried to get the machine started, it sputtered and spat out foul sounds. Then the elderly lady said, "Sorry," and went back inside her house. Not one to give up, I took it home with me to try to repair it. New spark plugs, a filter, a change of oil and gas. It did not take long to get it going again, and after some cleaning, I returned to mow the woman's lawn. She paid me thirty dollars. I was thrilled, and on top of that, she gave me the machine! I thanked her from the bottom of my heart, as she had just laid down the foundation for my company. From then on, I had a lawnmower. This elderly woman would be my first customer and one my best repeat customers. Also, thanks to the Georges of Elfrink's Outdoor Power Equipment, a longstanding family-owned company in nearby Woodland, I was able to get other gardening gear I lacked. Even when I lacked money, Elfrink's repaired my lawnmower, but beyond that, they gave me gardening tools on credit. It was only through the abundant kindness of these helpful people that I was able to get this business off the ground.

My customer list grew with every day. The only problem was transporting the lawnmower. I still had to tow it with my bicycle. My car had broken down a few days after I arrived in Davis, and I did not have the money to repair it. As I was dragging my mower everywhere around town; people often thought that I had just stolen it and weren't shy in letting me know.

While having trouble finding my footing, around the end of 1990, I finally secured some financial safety by finding a part-time job at the University of California, Davis (UC Davis). It was a job that I was particularly interested in due to the evening work schedule; it would not impede my business hours, as I took care of that during the daytime. These two jobs required a lot of physical effort for anywhere from twelve to fourteen hours a day. Combining them was difficult, but it was what I had to do. I was first assigned to the university extension department, where I took care of the movement and setup of furniture and electronic equipment in classrooms. Eventually, Eileen C. Leung, a Contracts and Grants Manager, noticed my work ethic and personally got involved to get me a full-time contract. She was widely respected for her dedication to both her job and the university as a whole. She saw my struggles, got to know me, and rewarded me for my hard work. It was a great leap forward; and granted me medical insurance for myself and my whole family. I am forever grateful to Mrs. Leung for her compassion and recognition of a man who was trying his best to provide a better life for his young family. I would only change departments after this contract, joining the custodial department facilities services. This work mostly involved building and classroom maintenance.

It was with this latest job that I was able to build up some savings again, to the point of even being able to acquire an old truck for five hundred dollars. A lawnmower, a truck to carry it, customers, and a night job; I was well on my way, living a decent life. But despite the material success, nostalgia always lingered for my family, and it began to truly weigh on me. Davis and Rwanda felt so far apart.

# Part Five: Horrors and Tragedies

# CHAPTER 32

# Davis: My Savior, the Telephone

Between 1982 and 1992, I was not able to see my mother, nor any other member of my family, nor even speak to them. 1982 would be the last time I would see my family. The political situation in Rwanda forbade any contact between the Tutsi people inside the country and those exiled from it. This diaspora was not welcome in Rwanda. Those who attempted to return were either kidnapped or simply killed. I therefore could not communicate with my family. The fact that I had survived my original visit to Rwanda was remarkable. But after a great deal of effort, I was able to get in touch with them through the intermediary of a priest from the parish of Kabuye. I could now speak to my family. What joy and good fortune, the day my mother came to speak to me on the telephone! She was there at the church, with my little brother, waiting for my phone call. When I called her, it was the priest himself who picked up the phone and passed it to my mother:

"*Uraho mwana wanjye!*" ("Hello, my child!") It was indeed my mother's voice. I felt reborn. I answered.

"*Uraho Mama!*" ("Hello, Mama!")

The three words of my mother's greeting in our language had the warmth of an entire life. The value too. The warmth and value of a lifetime. And for good reason. The mother tongue was an apt name for the words that I hear. I was so overwhelmed; I started to cry. Those words contained the message of all we had to say. It was more than I could handle. After recovering, I spoke to my brothers and sisters. I would be able to speak to my family from then on, thanks to the priest, to whom I have always been indebted and grateful.

The voices of my family had reawakened my fears for my parents and stoked my desire to visit home, whatever the cost. What's more, my mother would not stop speaking of events in the country that were plunging the people into anxiety and despair. Indeed, there were clear warning signs of what would come. The fears would be both reinforced and confirmed when an event, baffling to me, occurred. In 1990, Rwanda went to war with the Rwandan Patriotic Front Inkotanyi (RPF). The RPF-Inkotanyi was largely composed of Tutsi refugees. In our mother tongue, the term *inkotanyi* means "unbeatable combatant."

The sad souvenirs of the successive Rwandan conflicts, of 1959, 1960, 1962, and 1973, came back to my mind as if they happened yesterday. I imagined all the horrors that had occurred and came to the firm but dangerous decision to go back to my homeland, through Burundi, to try to save my family.

# CHAPTER 33

# Bujumbura: My Lucky City

I returned to Burundi, my host country, in 1993, this time not as a refugee but as an American citizen. The return had saved me a surprise, which would forever rekindle the fires of my life. I boarded the plane in San Francisco, passing through London and Nairobi, landing in Bujumbura. I wanted to help my mother, brother, and sisters escape, but arriving in Bujumbura, I found the project impossible. The risk of getting them killed was too high. My determination was just not enough to get me into that country.

The warning signs of genocide had already been appearing, but they seemed direr when I got closer to the country. It felt as if people were just waiting for the signal. I tried all that I could and tried to make productive use of my time in Bujumbura. I went to visit my extended family members in exile as well as friends that were family in their own way. All of us were exiles. I visited tourist and historic sites, places where I had lived, Lake Tanganyika, the Saint Esprit School, and so forth. Everywhere I went, people received me like a movie star. Again, I ran into Innocent, and we talked endlessly about what was happening in our home country. He knew more about the situation than I did, and he advised me not to even try to get into Rwanda; he knew that it was far too dangerous. The despair that we both felt being unable to do anything just one border away. All we could do was watch as things unfolded.

The rest of the city remembered me well, despite eight years spent abroad. I was still their eternal idol, the famous cyclist. Even the children greeted me by my proper name. I felt at home here. The beautiful little world of Bujumbura had adopted me in 1973, and I adopted it as well. The powers that were in my country had wanted my death, but on my path, I was that country's pride. I had not yet forgotten the words of the Spaniard: "You effectively represent your country. You have the pride of your people. You are their ambassador par excellence." I was, within my abilities, on a quest for knowledge. Knowledge of people, of the fascinating world. Knowledge is power. Everything resides in thought and probably in action. I have been driven by curiosity; I have moved forward despite doubt. I have lived with danger. What does not kill man makes him grow.

At Bujumbura, in the circles I frequented, attention was always on the civil war in Rwanda and the scourge of AIDS. Significant numbers of people were dying of the disease. People of all ages, young children, to the elderly were suffering. There were no exceptions, and the rate was frightening. And it wasn't only AIDS. Other factors contributed to the epidemic. Bad living conditions, poverty, and other maladies, like malaria, plagued our lands. The tragedies themselves were not so terrible as the world's indifference to them. It all broke my heart, to the point where my time in this city that I loved was nothing but sorrow.

Bujumbura, at least, was still my lucky city. I loved Bujumbura. This town gave me back an appetite for life. It was also there that I got a taste for my bicycle, "the queen with two wheels." It was again at Bujumbura that I found my better half, during this nineties summer. With Claudette, I was able to create what is today a full and fulfilled life.

I think it is more a preference than anything, but I had always dreamed of a woman from my culture, one for whom love, respect, and harmony in the home would be paramount. Here, my return to Bujumbura offered me a golden opportunity. The greatest discovery of my life would be meeting one, Claudette. During one of my multiple visits to friends, on one particularly beautiful day, was when it happened. Everyone came to greet me. But as soon as Claudette appeared in front of me, I could not stop admiring her. She was stunning. I felt something unusual in my body: flashes of warmth, mixed with cold snaps. A kind of fever came over me. She was radiant, like the moon surrounded by stars in the sky. Her face gave off a charm that no other girl in the world could touch. She was the perfection of creation itself. Of course, I was immediately drawn to her. I was head over heels, to the very tips of my shoes, from the moment I saw her. Her brilliant teeth mirrored the neat pearls around her neck, which were supple and straight, like a cellist's bow. I felt the urge to sigh with love every time I glanced at her.

To avoid overstaying my welcome, I had to cut my visit short, despite my excitement. I decided that I needed to take a step back in order to jump forward. On my way home, all I could see was her. All night, I only slept in short bursts; her face kept popping in my mind again and again. She approached me in my dreams, to tell me in a very soft voice that she loved me. I did not know by what misfortune the dream stopped there. I would wake up and look around me—no one there except for me.

She was real in the dream; it could not be mistaken for some form of hallucination. It was fantastic. I wanted to see her again. By dawn the next morning, I had already awoken, washed, and dressed. I was impatient to go in search of my newly beloved. Her mother welcomed me with joy, as the last time. Everyone was home this time. We took time to discuss different subjects, but it was much the same as my first visit. I only had eyes for her.

If they could not tell on the first few visits, then upon my fourth visit, my intentions were culturally very clear in the eyes of the entire family. I loved her deeply, and when I looked at her, I told myself this flower would be mine. It was a true love, as true as the earth and the sun! I did not have to tell them anything on the subject. They had no doubt. I lived it, and they knew it as well as I did. My Claudette, my unique flower, had her place in my heart. I wanted her with me in the United States. I wanted to marry her. Such was my desire, and such was my prayer. However, I did not know how to formally declare myself. I was in a quandary. Where was I to begin? My heart was about to give out. Would her family stand my uninterrupted presence? I was no longer able to go a day without seeing her. Thank the Lord, my parents, and kin, strength came back to me. Each passing minute was now just a chance flying away. From thought to action, I buckled down. No more prayers, no more pity. Without saying anything to her parents, I started to search for a passport and visa. I knew that if the marriage proposal were accepted, these two documents would be our greatest obstacles.

In the family, there was one of her elder brothers who was apparently in charge of representing her. One day, he came up to me. I wanted him to intercede on my behalf, and thankfully he accepted. Traditionally, this type of intervention worked better than others. I had a very good reputation in the town in general, and within the family, I was well liked. Having a good reputation is very important in my culture. One more time she accompanied me. While we were coming up on a street corner, we looked at each other. I told her, "You know, I'll take you to my home in America." She stared at me with an inquisitive look without saying a word. I looked at her. Her surprised, bright eyes did not leave mine for at least a minute, as if she were asking the question: "Is it true you love me?" The expression on her face spoke volumes. I said, "Yes, you are the only one I love in this world." She smiled with joy. The evening was unforgettable.

Seeing how serious I was, the family accepted me as their son-in-law. With many friends from Bujumbura, the dowry ceremony was organized and occurred on May 30, 1992, one of the greatest days of my life. The occasion brought together three hundred people, who came to celebrate the traditional marriage of the "American," a nickname that I was given around the neighborhood.

Things had thus far unfolded wonderfully, but the peak of my happiness was when I saw her ease into her seat next to me on the plane. I had come alone, and we were leaving together. I had come to see my mother and family. I was leaving without having had the chance to visit my family in Rwanda, but I went home with Claudette, my spouse. A great relief. My visit in Africa was certainly not done in vain. I promised that I would do everything to make her happy. I told her that I would love her more than any man in the world could. She answered that she would be the woman that I had always wished to have. She was happy to be mine. She laid her head on my chest, and it felt like heaven. My heart, which had been empty for so long after losing connection with my family had been filled up again, as I started a family of my own.

When we finally arrived back home, I went out to buy groceries. I was only gone for a minute, but when I got back, our home had already changed. Claudette had decorated and cleaned the furniture; everything was in its place. The house was simply a palace for princes. A strong emotion rode over me. We fell deeper for each other in that moment. Nothing in this world was as good as coupled life. She made me forget the past of a solitary man; any sorrows I had melted away in her arms. True happiness is in the little things. But there is no perfect happiness. My sorrows washed away, only to bring in a tide of new ones.

# CHAPTER 34

# Rwanda: The Genocide

The war of liberation of the Rwandan Patriotic Front had lasted three and a half years when it turned even worse. One day in April 1994, I went to the store to buy a cell phone. We were making a trip to Los Angeles and needed one. It was about four hundred miles from Davis, and I did not want to rely on pay phones. We had been invited to the wedding of an old Rwandan friend. Claudette and I were to go with our three-month-old baby, Arnell. While I was checking the workings of one of the cell phone models, the vendor told me I could try it. I called the house and spoke to Claudette. With a shaking voice, she told me that a missile had caused an airline catastrophe in Rwanda. The Rwandan president, Juvénal Habyarimana, and Burundian president, Cyprien Ntaryamira, along with the entire crew, had been killed. I was shocked, not because of the deaths of the presidents, but because this threw the future into even more uncertainty than before. I became worried about my family's fate and the fate all the Tutsis in Rwanda. My whole body was shaking. How much did I end up spending to buy the phone? I could not tell you. By which route did I get back home? I don't know either.

I came home to find Claudette's eyes red with tears. Holding her, I rushed to the television. We both watched with fear all around us. The event was all over the news. All the television stations from around the world showed the horror and animosity of the Habyarimana regime. People were killed in front of cameras, and the bodies were littered on the streets and roads. Streams, rivers, lakes—all of them carried Tutsi bodies. I looked carefully at the bodies on the ground, to check if any of them were my family. It felt like the end times, "The Apocalypse", as announced by Colonel Théoneste Bagosora at the Arusha negotiations in Tanzania, where he refused the sharing of Hutu power. He believed that the only solution to Rwanda's problems was to eliminate the Tutsis.

The genocide went beyond any inhumanity in human beings that I could have ever imagined. A man took a machete and cut a baby that was just a few months old to pieces, just because it was born to Tutsi parents. Men and women were hunted down on every street. Some were cut up with machetes or taken by their hands or feet and run over with cars. As for the elderly? Utterly defenseless, they were simply taken from their homes and decapitated. Like animals. All of this done by a rampaging Hutu population brandishing all kinds of weapons, like animals themselves. At least animals did what they did for survival. But these humans, why do they do it? Everywhere, cries for help. All the Tutsi houses were on fire. The smoke reached high into the sky and invaded all the Thousand Hills. I trembled with fear. Where was the Savior God, the God of justice? Why, Lord, did you let this innocent blood flow? In the depths of me were only prayers. The bodies were left to the mercy of flies and dogs. The horror was complete. It was countrywide.

I lost my mind watching the news on the television every day. What could I do? My people were in danger from the genocide. I decided to call the Red Cross. I gave them the address of my family so they could check on them. I also sent a letter to my congressman, begging him to put pressure on the American government to put an end to the extermination of the Tutsis. Finally, I called the headquarters of the UN and even the White

House to ask if anything could be done to save all these innocents. Alas, I was sorely mistaken. The situation was unfortunate, unfortunate for more than a million who were dead, as a
tragedy in front view and well known to all. The United States,
the powerful police of the world, turned its back on my people,
repeating during the duration of the horrors that they could do
nothing. I quickly understood that the great powers only went
to the aid of countries when it was in their financial interest.
The poor were left to their own fate. Not even the neighboring
African countries offered help, this Africa that I had hoped for
so long would pull together sat and watched as hundreds of thousands were killed in cold blood. Where were the superpowers of
the world? All watching from the sidelines as a million died. No
country was innocent in this genocide. All who sat and watched
were, in some part, complicit.

It saddened me even more to see the UN, an organization set
up for the peace and security of the world, come late to the genocide. Like a doctor after a death, or a fireman arriving after all
had been burned. What was the value of a trip to Rwanda after
the genocide? A journey of no more than an hour by the secretary general to say, "I'm sorry." I was sorry that he chose to bring
his compassion to my people rather than his help at the time
they needed it! A million lives lost without anyone's intervention. As for the French and the Belgians, partially responsible,
in my opinion, for the million dead, why did they set the fire and
then retire as if nothing had happened, to sit back and watch the
crackling of the flames in Rwanda? Shame to them all.

My spouse and I went to Los Angeles, as planned. During the
marriage ceremony, people were not happy. All the Rwandans
cried. Each of us had family in Rwanda. The marriage looked
like a funeral. I remember a woman received a phone call during the wedding ceremony. She was told that her parents had

just been killed! After the wedding, we returned to Davis, and I stayed glued to the television, for long hours. To me, the world was collapsing.

At work, I had no concentration, and my morale was through the floor. My colleagues asked me for news on the situation and my knowledge of the country as well. But I had no more information to give them. I did not know any more than them and anything they saw in the media. I could shout for help to all the great powers in the world, but my cries of distress would be lost in the telephone line. Where did these great military powers go? Why did France insist on supporting a portion of the population that is massacring Tutsi innocents? Only Hutus, in the end, were able to save people, all while a genocide was being perpetrated in their name. Some good Hutu souls paid for their resistance with their lives. I salute their courage and humanity. As much as I ask for the identification and condemnation for those responsible for the genocide, I also plead for recognition for those who refused to see their compatriots killed, at the risk of their own lives.

FAUSTIN'S WIFE, CLAUDETTE, AND THEIR CHILDREN
MEET MARTHA, FAUSTIN'S SISTER, FOR THE FIRST TIME,
AND CHILDREN, KIGALI, RWANDA, IN 1996.

FAUSTIN WITH HIS CHILDREN AND SISTER
MARTHA IN KIGALI, RWANDA, IN 1996

FAUSTIN'S NIECE AND NEPHEW (CHILDREN OF HIS ELDER SISTER, SPECIOSE MUKABUZIZI) IN KIGALI, RWANDA, 1996

FAUSTIN'S MOTHER, BROTHER, SISTER-IN-LAW, COUSIN, AND NIECE IN JABANA, RWANDA

Soon enough, news came around that the RPF had won out. But just the thought of going to look for my family who may have survived was an idea that tormented me. It was still dangerous. Despite this, I made firm plans to go, come what may. No airline could land in Rwanda, the airport being closed. I had to pass through Uganda on a small private plane. When I saw Kigali, it was nothing like that city I had seen so many years ago. Nearly all the houses were destroyed. Traffic was stopped in some places by mountains of sandbags propped up by the military. The roads had been blown up by shells. Neither running water nor electricity worked. What's more, one had to drive or walk carefully since some roads were still covered in mines. What stuck out to me the most was what was on the sides of the streets. There were a lot of shoes, all different, here and there, along the avenues. I wondered why these people were abandoning their shoes. But after seeing so many shoes, I realized that people were not abandoning them; they belonged to the victims of the genocide. Out of those million people who died, if they had not died, what difference could that have made in the world? In those shoes walked artists, scientists, writers, presidents, and so many others. I do not speak just of Rwanda; how much potential has been lost because of senseless killing by our fellow people?

Many of the people I encountered carried the scars of war. Handicapped people dragged themselves along the ground or got around with crutches. Some people had horrible scars or even open wounds somewhere on their bodies. There was no age distinction. Everyone paid a price. I started to truly understand what had happened.

Every step toward Jabana filled me with dread. Security was not complete in the whole country, even in the capital, in the days immediately following the genocide. Rare gunshots could still be heard at night. People were kidnapped by strangers. There were still pockets of resistance scattered in some parts of the country. All of this on top of the ordinary banditry that came from war. Theft and robbery were commonplace. Some Hutu people, still agitated, put up surprise barricades for buses headed for the interior of the country. They would ask for identity papers and pull the Tutsis off the bus to execute them. But I had to go to Jabana, even if I was to die there. It was the place, and the people there, that had given me life. It was this land that soaked up every scrape, bruise, and scratch I received as a child. It was this earth on which I made my first steps. Jabana, my lost paradise. This beautiful village where I played as a child. What I saw there was not Jabana. It was unrecognizable, fallen. I ran into people I knew. They told me what I dreaded most. My family had been murdered, they told me bluntly. How many others had they told this same awful truth? Everything had been destroyed. The past in its totality flew past me, on a background of tears—my mother's tears. Where was the mass grave? I had to find them so that they could be buried with dignity.

A Hutu woman, our neighbor, told me everything—how they killed my mother and younger brothers. She told me that the spouse of my younger brother Célestin Kabisa had survived, but she did not know where she may have gone to hide. I learned, too, that one of my sisters, Marthe Mukabazaire, may have survived, but she had no knowledge of that either.

I would learn later that this woman who told me everything about the extermination of my family is the very person who gave my brother up to the executioners. To us, she was more than a neighbor; she was family, how we treated everyone in that village. During a difficult and painful moment, my brother turned to her for refuge, knowing she had a big heart. Hiding him in her backyard, she covered him with banana leaves. She then called two other neighbors, two men, brothers, both Hutus, who grew up with my brother. They took his life. Today, justice has been done, in some sense, and she is in prison for eighteen years with her two accomplices.

My search then took on more meaning. I started to look for my sister everywhere. I finally found her after a few days of frantic searching, in a town outside of Kigali. When she saw me, she couldn't believe her eyes. She thought she was hallucinating. She jumped on me and hugged me very tight, both of us crying. Befuddled, she looked upon me without saying a word. When she opened her mouth, it was to say, "There is just you and me left." She filled me in on what happened. After Juvénal Habyarimana's plane was shot down in April of 1994, war broke out instantly. Hutus became violent, and Tutsis were being massacred by the thousands. My sister told me that the day after the crash, our family was exterminated. Everyone. My mother, brothers, sisters, cousins. Only we two had survived.

She recounted her own exile and the suffering she experienced. The Hutus with whom she traveled toward neighboring Congo told her to turn around. Starved and dying of thirst, her baby died. Alone, she dug a hole in the soil, buried her child, and then continued on her way in sadness and desolation. Emotions had reached their peak for both of us. She spoke with her throat choked and eyes far away. The grief over our lost loved ones filled us both beyond description. She could manage no more. She threw herself in my arms, and we cried bitterly. The sadness never ended, though, and the bitterness never stopped. That hurt we carried—and more pain was piled on top—it never ended. Some years later, a Hutu woman would hold one of my sister's newborn babies, pretending to play with her and then suddenly squeezing her ribs until they had been crushed. The infant screamed and cried all night and died early in the morning. Even after the war, things didn't return to normal.

Hutu and Tutsi both suffered in the war. These twin people shared a country, a language, and a culture—driven to massacre by arbitrary differences. The country's heart was broken. Tutsi and Hutu grew up together. It was unfathomable to think that people could kill someone they had grown up with, struggled with, and shared with. Some families were entirely wiped out. Some children lost all their parents and found themselves alone in an empty country. The effects of this indescribable crime will be felt for generations, and the traumatic memories will never leave the blood-soaked grass of Rwanda. This genocide was the final gift from the colonizers who sowed the differences in the beginning.

I now had to take care of my sister and nephews. She had lost everything. She and her children would go hungry and did not even have a roof over their heads at night. Everything had gone up in smoke. "Africa is solidarity" has always been one of our sayings. If there is enough for one, there is enough for two. In our current situation, if there was enough for one, there was enough for ten. Since returning to the United States, my wife, my child, and I only ate once a day. I sent what was needed for our second meal to my sister and her six children. Having even one meal was enough in these dark times, and the situation in Rwanda did not help our appetite. Lamenting served no purpose. Should we not make it a habit to celebrate each day God creates? No one knows what tomorrow and each day has in store, and each day we draw breath must be treated as a holiday. It is a lesson that war teaches me, this war that has taken all joie de vivre from Rwandans, the women and children being the greatest victims.

FAUSTIN WITH CLAUDETTE AND CHILDREN ARNELL, ARIANE,
ARVIN AND ARCEL IN THEIR BACKYARD IN DAVIS, CALIFORNIA

The TV stations of the world will have shown enough of the atrocities perpetrated against the Tutsis of Rwanda in 1994, but the extent and extreme cruelty inflicted on women and girls during the genocide is indescribable. The stories that I gathered while I was there still trouble me. My nights remain haunted.

Few surviving victims dared share what they went through. Those that did, did so in vain, as there is no form of justice out there that can right the wrongs. Indeed, in most cases, the women did not know the person or people responsible. Few are those who still have the mental fortitude required to properly communicate with those around them. To share one's fate as a rape victim is akin to condemning oneself twice, once as soiled and again as improper for marriage. Rapes were committed on a massive scale. AIDS and other sexually transmitted diseases were a common consequence.

Some women stayed locked in at home, away from the looks of others. A rare few went out, and those who did, did so to let out the overflow of feelings by running in the streets. Madness— that was the general order. My sister Martha was condemned to lifelong mental and physical treatment at the hospital due to the weight of what she endured. Her journey to the hospital was now a part of her daily routine. Nothing can heal the wounds of the unjustifiable loss and traumas that were inflicted upon our people, but to grieve among others who had suffered similar fates was a method of, hopefully, moving forward.

# CHAPTER 35
# Davis: Return and Sadness

My stay in search of surviving family members lasted three long weeks. I would have liked to have stayed as long as possible, to look for the bodies, exhume them, bury them with dignity, and help my country, but it was impossible to find the bodies in such little time. The executioners in prison or those out free kept their mouths sewn shut. I did not have the chance to see my father's or mother's bodies so I could not inter them in the way I wished. I did not see the bodies of my brothers and sisters either, nor those of my cousins, nieces, and nephews. Though my intentions were not realized, my inability to locate the bodies of my loved ones served as a way to keep them "alive" in my minds eye, and not marred by memories of their demise.

So, I returned to Davis, where I had left my wife and child alone. My arrival was a surprise for them. I did not know where to begin to tell them about my journey. I was tired before a word even left my mouth. I looked upon my wife and told her: "I am sorry; you will never know either your mother-in-law or brothers-in-law. They are all dead." My children will never know their grandparents or uncles.

She was certainly anticipating more bad news than good news, but she collapsed all the same under the weight of the emotion. The nights that followed would be punctuated by terrible nightmares. My wife and I took a long time to recover. The residents of Davis did not fail to assist us and give us comfort in these painful moments; they knew our birth home had been taken from us and did everything they could to make this small college town feel like a home where we could raise our family amongst love and compassion. To this day, I thank them from the bottom of my heart, especially local philanthropists Grant and Grace Noda. Grant was an incredible man who had lived through the Japanese internment camps in the United States; he could relate to my experiences and the immeasurable pain they wrought. His heart was generous, and he listened to my pain as only someone who understood it could.

As the former president of Burkina Faso, Thomas Sankara would say, "Woe on he who does not do better than his father." I pray there will be no more genocide in Rwanda through eternity, nor in any other part of the world. It is a new challenge we must all ponder.

After everything my surviving people have seen, everything I have seen, I put forward a challenge—a challenge not just to Rwanda or the United States or any small nation in between, but to the world. We must rediscover our humanity. We have so many free gifts in life that go underappreciated—flowers, the breeze, and so much more. Humanity needs to support each other for life to be without unnecessary pain and hardships. We must make the world whole again, healing it and promising the end of genocide so that our children and grandchildren, and all the generations that follow, will live without fear. When they learn of the events of my lifetime, I hope they will seem much too far from their own realities to be true. Only such a world is worth hoping for. Only such a world is worth living for, even though you will never live to see it in your own day.

# CHAPTER 36
# Epilogue

This cyclist odyssey that I undertook was a wonderful education in my life. I traveled through war-torn countries. I knew hunger, thirst, heat, and solitude. I lived through pitch-black nights, where the noises made by wild animals filled me with fear. I crossed forests dark with trees, where I shook like a leaf and could only sleep perched on branches. I went through deserts whose torrid sands scorched my bicycle's tires.

My bicycle took me through Burundi, Rwanda, Zaire (Congo), Tanzania, Kenya, Uganda, Sudan, Egypt, the Central African Empire (currently the Central African Republic), Cameroon, Niger, Nigeria, Algeria, Upper Volta (Burkina Faso), Mali, Senegal, the Canary Islands, Morocco, Spain, France, Belgium, and the Netherlands. This whirlwind tour of the globe took five good years. I owe much to my bicycle, which I still hold on to, forty years after the start of my adventures. It is carefully hung up at my house in Davis, the little California town in the United States where I live.

My journey was steeped in trials, as well as riches of joy. Through the countless meetings along the road, I always learned something new about this Planet Earth. I constantly think about all the different people I met on my path and about the people, both in the city and in the countryside, who helped me along the way. I would not know how to thank them. Thanks to them, I was fortunate to survive this adventure, and I am glad I got to complete the loop. It's impossible to keep silent about the different romantic encounters that gave me warmth and joie de vivre. Thus, is youth as well. I am glad to have accomplished this beautiful journey. I have no regrets.

What could have possibly motivated my mad adventure? It was nothing less than the evil and animosity of man. Leaving was the only way to save my life. It was difficult for a young kid to see people die in front of his eyes and be forced into exile. God only knew how painful this departure was and the unbearable nostalgia that it created. This lingering wound, would it ever heal? I have no idea if it has healed, even now. But I still had to leave. They say when the going gets tough, the tough get going. In my case, this is true. The flood of refugees that emptied into neighboring Burundi, and the hardships of all kinds—food, hygiene, terrible sanitary conditions—was there a reason for any of this? No one knows what the future holds or the great joys that can spring from great hardships. Life is like waves on the ocean; you don't know where or which way it will take you.

I have crisscrossed Africa. It is full of natural marvels: the great lakes that different birds with beautiful songs fly over; the tropical forest; the Nile, the longest river in Africa, bordered by the desert and a variety of agriculture. In short, our Africa is a wonderful continent. Europe is also a wonder, with its great buildings, views, and climate with real seasons—spring, summer, autumn, and winter—and a beauty of wealth without equal. Not to mention the vast fields of vines and delicious apples. Unfortunately, the paradise that is this earth also contains hells. In truth, this long voyage helped me discover the world and all facets of life.

With little education or qualifications, without great means and without support, I find myself settled in Davis, California.

The United States is a very powerful place and remains full of opportunities, a potent example of the ideal that unity is strength.

It is by no means paradise, but all things have their advantages and disadvantages. Here it is everyone for themselves, and God for all.

What could I do in a country where the language is foreign to me? My integration was not easy, and my path was always filled with hurdles. I took many hits, but determination and the will to move forward made me what I am. For the past few years, I've worked at the University of California Davis as a lead custodian in addition to my small gardening business that I manage myself. Without bragging too much, I make a decent living. I am grateful to have been able to work alongside caring people who have made me feel like a valuable part of this wonderful community and that I am loved again.

I'm glad to have accomplished this adventure, to have settled in the United States, and to have acquired American citizenship. Finally, I have shed this refugee mantle. I now have a country, a real one, where I have, with Claudette, started a happy family with four children: Arnell, Ariane, Arvin, and Arcel. Thank the heavens and the Americans. Were it not for the genocide in Rwanda in 1994 that took away my people, I could have declared victory. May God have their souls. Since the genocide, I have not been able to live normally.

"Hell is other people," and "Man is a wolf to man," said the great philosophers Jean Paul Sartre and Thomas Hobbes, respectively. Coming from a Rwandan, they could not be more right. I'm sure the others who have seen genocide would say the same. However, other people are a necessary evil that must be accepted and taken as such. Following conflicts and difficult experiences, one must strive to forget or at least forgive to be able to make a new start. To get there, may justice be given for the sake of the victims. It is a moral comfort. I sincerely hope these criminals will be punished and justice rendered anywhere in the world where injustice is done. We Rwandans have been witnesses to the inhumanity of man. May the globe reflect on its past!

I conclude without conceding a conclusion. Humanity cannot end this way. Its doors stay open to generations that follow. I have had the good fortune to get to know so many worlds without losing my life. I was glad to be able to write this book with the noble collaboration of people who love me and respect me so much.

I would like this personal story not to be solely mine, but that of all the world's youth.

I would ask to each and every one who reads this to pass on the story of Faustin Rusanganwa, a modest young man, illiterate, but daring nonetheless! Thank you to all those who contributed to my story and who continue to work to make this world a little more habitable with each passing day.

# Special Thanks

This book's writing is a long story that dates back to 1982, from my return to Bujumbura. As I said earlier, not knowing how to write, I had to dictate my adventure so that it might be transcribed. Alas, I ran into several difficulties. The people who were asked did not always prove to be honest. They found in this project a means to enrich themselves at my expense. On several occasions, people asked for money before doing the work for which I hired them. They received this money, but the work was not done.

In the United States, being unable to find someone to tell my story in my language, given my poor level of English and the fact that French is seldom spoken in this country, I wanted to give up. (*No, Faustin, once again, you cannot give up.*) I have since learned to believe that anything is possible as long as there is still breath in my body.

Wanting is power, and my will to share my story burned in me so much that God put Aimable Ruzindana on my path. This amiable man, as his name indicates, gave me much of his time and energy to make this project a reality, putting my spoken French into written French. But man proposes, and God disposes. Aimable was taken away from me too fast by the God who gave him to me. He would never see the end of what he had so well started. He will never enjoy the fruits of his labor. May his soul rest in peace. Aimable Ruzindana, dear brother-in-law and friend, you patiently took down in school notebooks the story of an uneducated young man. It is indeed you in the end that gave shape and life to my mad adventures. I cannot find words strong enough to thank you and your family properly.

Without Axel LaForest, my story would still be limited to French. His patience and attention ensured the English was faithful.

I'd also like to thank Naum Milyavskiy for helping tell my story in my voice and my voice alone.

I could not close this book without addressing my sincere thanks to the people of Rwanda who worked to rebuild the country after a genocide of a million deaths. You spared no effort to come to the aid of the people, especially women, now without children or husbands, so they might have a chance to find a new zest for life. Also, the discriminatory policy of making different identity cards for people of the same country, to better distinguish Tutsi from Hutu, is now in the distant past. You transformed your dwellings into makeshift orphanages by adopting all those children, Hutu and Tutsi alike, who were made parentless far too soon by the war. You recognized that a child is a child, no matter what tribe they are part of or where they come from. God does not do anything randomly, and if he put Hutu and Tutsi on the same earth of Rwanda, it is because together, they can do great and beautiful things. By combining their efforts, Rwanda is reborn today from the ashes, and God alone can reward you.

# Acknowledgments

"Thank you" is, no doubt, the prettiest phrase a person could utter.

At the time of publication of this story, it is important to thank a great number of people. However, will I remember to name them all? Probably not, which is why I think "Pardon me" is maybe the second prettiest phrase.

To all parents, all honor. I think first of my mother and my father, carried away forever by the cyclical extermination of the Rwandan Tutsis since 1959. I owe you more than life: I owe you love, self-sacrifice, courage. You sacrificed everything to ensure my survival. You forged in me an iron will that helped me face all of life's difficulties. You were the last to go to sleep and the first to rise, to work from the cock's first call. May the Almighty grant my prayers, so that descendants honor your memory and erect memorials *indaro, ingore,* as African and Rwandan traditions require.

Claudette, dear wife, mother of all my children! Silence is, they say, the loudest of cries, but perhaps it is also a good analogy for the act of love. Your love and tenderness have rubbed off on our children. They reappear today through the lines of the story of my life, a story that is also yours. To whom, if not to you, do I owe the spark of emotion that no one else would have known how to light? Of course, I must also thank my son Arcel Rusanganwa for helping me to read this project. That is proof enough that Claudette and I did well with you! And, of course, to all my children: Arnell, Ariane, and Arvin, who constantly bring joy into my life; without them, this project would have died years ago.

Many friends helped me with their counsel, their encouragements, and their sympathy. I think notably, with emotional gratitude that the years have never blunted, of the families Amende Jean-Pierre (known at Bujumbura, Burundi); Jean-François Durieux (Khartoum, Sudan); Tom Dunkelman (Turkana, Kenya); François Nyirinkwaya (Senegal); Bruce Rosendahl (Duke University); Debbie Scott (Duke University); Jim Miguel (Duke University); Assumpta Richeux (Bujumbura, Burundi); Liz, Alison, and Nikki Green (North Carolina, United States); Youssouf (Tanzania); Ronald and Christian Green (North Carolina, United States); Benjamin (Kenya); Kimberly Sellon (Davis, California); Hubert Leverne (Morocco); Pierre and Thérèse Masumbuko (Ouagadougou, Upper Volta, Burkina Faso); Julio and his family (Madrid, Spain); Seth Morrison (Davis, California); Martin and Stella Weddel (Mombassa, Kenya); Didier and Josiane Futel (Fada N'Gourma, Upper Volta); Bill and Catherine Ribière (Montpeyroux, France); Bea Talvard (Paris, France); William Grant (Burundi); Jean-Michel and Marie-Ange Allano (Khartoum, Soudan); Mariana Nyirankusi (Bujumbura, Burundi); Marie-Cécile (Bujumbura, Burundi); Marc and Anne-Marie Cap (Dakar, Senegal); Lee Losson.

May the following people also receive my profound gratitude: Ahmed Karadawi (Khartoum, Sudan); Maître Rwagasore (Bujumbura, Burundi); Ndikumagenge Salvator (Bujumbura, Burundi); Mark Stinson (Davis, California); Bill Grant (Bujumbura, Burundi); Jean Claude Aguillaume (Bujumbura,

Burundi); Dan Toole (Bujumbura, Burundi); Eileen C. Leung (Davis, California); Debra Scott (Bujumbura, Burundi); Josepha and Faustin Kagame (Switzerland); Innocent Iyakaremye (Sacramento, California); Innocent Bayijahe (Jabana, Rwanda); Evariste Nimubona (Sacramento, California); Bryanna Reeves and Jay Knickerbocker (Sacramento, California); my companions of the PROBE project of Duke University; the Turkana community on the edges of Lake Turkana. Especially to the Touareg people, who saved my life, these people who, I will never be able to contact again—I pray that someday you will see these words and know how much of the world you have affected by just sharing food with a starving Rwandan in the desert. To all of these as well as numerous other persons who have been helpful in my life but that are not specifically mentioned in this list, I thank you.

Generous souls housed me, fed me, accompanied, and guided me on my long journey across continents. Others opened doors for me that would otherwise have been closed. Some assisted me in various ways in the writing of this significant story of my life. Some will hopefully forgive me for having lost their family name. Each and every one should find here the pride and the badge of honor that is their due, above and beyond the debt of gratitude I owe them. Without all of you, I would not be where I am today; the kindness of strangers brought me across the world from Jabana to Davis. It breaks my heart that I will never see so many of these people again, but I pray that my thanks here will be heard. I hope that the fact that my journey was accomplished is a sort of thanks itself. Know that I never gave up, and that your help bridged rivers, brought down barriers, and flew me over mountains to where I am today.

Cory Golden/Enterprise photo

**A MAN APART:** Faustin Rusanganwa leans against a wall in the back yard of his Davis home, far from his violence-ravaged homeland of Rwanda.

# Only anger and a photo remain

**10 years after genocide in Rwanda, the pain is still fresh**

By Cory Golden
Enterprise staff writer

**Then:** Third from the left in the gold-framed photograph stands Faustin Rusanganwa's mother, Maria, wrapped in gold and green cloth, her head covered.

She looks straight ahead, her wrinkled face expressionless.

### Then & Now

On one side of her is Faustin's brother, Celestin, on the other side a sister-in-law Faustin has never met. Celestin looks tall, lean, his shirttails hanging loose, his eyes looking off to his left somewhere. He smiles a little. His wife, in bright pinks and blues, seems determined, serious.

Farther right: A girl of perhaps 12 or 13 in white dress looks down at the ground.

This is a niece, Faustin says, looking at the photo, and next to her, with his hip cocked, is an un-

cle, Jean, smiling broadly, his shirt open down past his thin chest. In his left hand, a cigarette burns.

There are six people in the photograph — a man in the shadows, on the left, is a stranger — standing evenly spaced, with nothing but green fields and trees and hills behind them in what looks to be evening in a village near Kigali, Rwanda's capital.

On the next day, or the next or the one after, perhaps, everyone in the photograph will die, save Faustin's sister-in-law, whom he will be unable to locate.

Rusanganwa also lost his father and four other siblings, who were among the more than 800,000 peo-

ple slaughtered, most with machetes, between April and June of 1994 when the government called upon the Hutu majority to kill everyone in the Tutsi minority.

In September 1994, Faustin Rusanganwa traveled from his Davis home to the village he had not seen since 1977. He climbed off the bus and into a ravaged place where seemed everywhere.

Where his childhood home once stood, where the only photos he owns of his mother were taken, only grass grew.

"Everything was gone," he says.

See GENOCIDE, Back page

# FAUSTIN RUSANGANWA

## GENOCIDE From Page A1

**Now:** Faustin Rusanganwa, now 49 years old, starts his days around 7:30 a.m. He runs his own landscaping business, then, at night, works as a custodian at UC Davis. He comes home at 1:30 a.m.

In that way he supports his wife, Claudette, a community college student, and their children, Arnell, age 10; Ariane, 8; Arvin, 5; and Arcel, 3.

He also supports the surviving members of his family in Rwanda: his sister, Martha, her four children and two more children whose mother, another of Faustin's siblings, was killed.

Rusanganwa fled from his home to Burundi at age 17, during one of the regular waves of killings in Rwanda since the Hutu uprising in 1959.

He traveled throughout Africa and Europe, painting, driving a truck, cooking, cleaning — whatever anyone would pay him to do — before returning to Burundi in 1982. There he took a job, working for Duke University geologists, as a sort of logistics man, managing local workers, finding fuel, buying shovels.

Three years later, as the project ended, he visited Duke. After attending a wedding in Davis, he decided to relocate here, joining a small, close-knit Rwandan community in the Sacramento area.

In 1992 Rusanganwa traveled to Burundi, in hopes of making his way to see his parents. During his stay, he met his future wife, but because of the danger was unable to travel the final 5 miles into Rwanda.

Two years later he asked a friend in Davis, Suzanne Plopper, who was traveling to Rwanda as a public health contractor for the U.S. Agency for International Development, if she would visit his family.

Plopper did, and took the only photographs Rusanganwa has of his family. She says she's unable to remember what day she took the pictures.

Plopper, who later escaped with the aid of the U.S. Embassy, talked with her friend's family perhaps 30 minutes.

Hours later, the genocide be-

Cory Golden/Enterprise photo

**FAMILY TIES:** Faustin Rusanganwa of Davis poses for a family photograph with his children, from left, Ariane, Arnell, Arcel and Arvin. Rusanganwa operates his own landscaping business and works as a custodian at UC Davis to support his family — his wife, Claudette, is a community college student — and the surviving members of his family in Rwanda.

> *"Animals are not dangerous, humans are dangerous. Dying is OK; everyone dies. But the things these people did, you cannot imagine. These people, they spoke the same language, they grew up together. I ask myself, why did that happen?"*
>
> **Faustin Rusanganwa**

"Every time there was a war, we lost a member of our family," Rusanganwa says.

When he returned home in 1994, after the RPF victory, Hutu neighbors who barely recognized him confirmed his worst fears about his family.

Only his younger sister, Martha, had survived — and just barely.

As she tried to flee, a newborn starved in her arms. She was raped, and when another baby

hurts in my heart, I cannot help it."

### Faith endures

The stories of priests in Rwanda who lured Tutsis to their deaths did not shake Rusanganwa's faith in God. But he recalls standing in a church in Rwanda, seeing the bones of the dead in the shadow of the cross; his sister-in-law survived a grenade explosion in another church where Tutsis had gone to

lies on now, remembering how his father cared for him and his brothers and sisters when they had no food, no water.

On Sunday evening, Rusanganwa sat on his living room couch while his wife studied in another room. Their four children sprawled on the carpet before him, laughing and drawing pictures. One son reminds him of a lost brother, while his daughter is "a photocopy" of his surviving sister, right down to her walk.

His walls are lined with smiling photos of the children and his wife.

Every day, he says, he thinks of his family in Rwanda. Every day, he says a prayer for them.

And often, he picks up the picture of his mother.

Even now, he can only wonder what she and the others beside her were thinking as they stood before the camera.

"Every day it is differ Rusanganwa says. "Some

Community College and works as groundskeeper at the museum.

He would like to make a cross-country bicycle trip here, but not unless he has a traveling companion, said Faustin. There were times during his trip that he was lonely and just wanted to return home, he said.

"But in my country there was lots of tribal problems and not much chance for education. My trip was like a school—a university for me. Every day was different. People everywhere helped me," said Faustin.

"If you want to be (friends) with people, you can, wherever you are. It's when you don't want to, then that's what's bad."

MARTIN WEDDEL WITH FAUSTIN IN BRUSSEL TOURING THE AUDITORIUM

# RWANDA

Continued from Page A-1

in the killing of the families throughout the village.

"By the time I got there, I had the feeling no one would be left," Rusanganwa said. "I caught a bus from Kigali and went as far as I could, then took a bicycle taxi further, and finally walked the rest of the 12 kilometers out to my family's land."

Rusanganwa's only surviving relatives — his sister Marta, her husband and their four children — fled to Zaire in early April when the massacres began. To increase their chances of survival, Marta and her husband separated: She went one way with the baby, while her husband took the four older children. The baby died en route to Zaire. The family did not find each other until a few months ago.

"My sister will rebuild on our family's land," Rusanganwa said. "But it will take a very long time. There is nothing there; they even cut down the coffee plantations."

A short walk away, Rusanganwa discovered that his uncles, aunts, cousins and grandfather had all been killed at their family enclave. Hutu neighbors described armies of Hutu rebel soldiers arriving with machetes, and mutilating and killing all the Tutsis they could find.

"It was unbelievable," he said. "I screamed when they started telling me everything. I feel so sorry — for the children especially."

Rusanganwa described walking through rooms in remaining buildings that serve as makeshift orphanages. "You go in a room, and there are 100 kids lying there. You go into the next room, and there are 75.

**FAUSTIN RUSANGANWA**
Recounts arduous journey

"So many children are there: premature babies, children missing arms and legs, children with no families or homes. They are there, some of them lying in blood."

Rusanganwa spent "a good three days" walking around the country. In town, he saw many scarred and mutilated people in the streets, streets that are filled with scattered shoes.

"They are the dead people's shoes," he said. "I saw no pairs."

Rusanganwa spent days speaking to his family's neighbors, law-abiding Hutus who have always lived in the same houses, just as his mother and brothers had. Hearing him describe growing up in the neighborhood is mind-boggling.

"We shared the same food, the same language, the same color," he said. "But each time there was a change in the government, we were expected to hate each other, and fight. There would be stealing and vandalizing and muggings, in our homes, on the streets, in our churches.

"And then it would be over. The political situation would change, and we'd all be neighborly again. We'd go to their homes for meals, and see things that had belonged to us, things they'd taken and never returned.

"We had to live with our Hutu neighbors because they had the power. We had to try and stay friendly."

Numbed by the senselessness of the massacre, Rusanganwa said goodbye to Marta and her family, and returned to Davis three weeks later.

"I'm glad I went because now I know for sure what happened," he said sadly. "Of course, it was a shock, although I didn't expect my family to have survived."

Rusanganwa is glad to be home with his wife Claudette and their 11-month-old son, Arnell. Arnell had grown two teeth while he was gone, and was much closer to walking without hanging onto the furniture. Although Arnell is an outgoing, friendly toddler, Claudette said it took him a few hours to warm up to his dad.

"And then, all of a sudden, it was OK," she laughed. "He snuggled up to Faustin."

Rusanganwa is appreciative of the people in Davis who made his trip possible. The self-employed gardener and landscaper said that if people want to help the Rwandans rebuild their country, money is the most efficient way to do so. ("It *does* get there," he affirmed.)

Checks can be made payable and sent to the Rwanda Refugees Association of Northern California, P.O. Box 19434, Sacramento, CA 95819.

Rusanganwa also said interested people with questions could call him at home at 758-4816.

"The children need help," he said softly.

# BEYOND THE CHINESE FACE
## INSIGHTS FROM PSYCHOLOGY

# BEYOND THE CHINESE FACE

Insights from Psychology

MICHAEL HARRIS BOND

HONG KONG
OXFORD UNIVERSITY PRESS
OXFORD NEW YORK

Oxford University Press

Oxford   New York
Athens   Auckland   Bangkok   Bombay
Calcutta   Cape Town   Dar es Salaam   Delhi
Florence   Hong Kong   Istanbul   Karachi
Kuala Lumpur   Madras   Madrid   Melbourne
Mexico City   Nairobi   Paris   Singapore
Taipei   Tokyo   Toronto

and associated companies in
Berlin   Ibadan

Oxford is a trade mark of Oxford University Press

First published 1991
Eighth impression 1995

Published in the United States
by Oxford University Press, New York

© Oxford University Press 1991

Library of Congress Cataloging-in-Publication Data

Bond, Michael Harris, 1994–
Beyond the Chinese face: insights from psychology/
Michael Harris Bond.
p.   cm.
Includes bibliographical references and index.
ISBN 0-19-585116-1 (pbk)
1. National characteristics, Chinese. 1. Title.
DS721. B617 1991
951—dc20 91-25802
CIP

British Library Cataloguing in Publication Data
available

Printed in Hong Kong
Published by Oxford University Press (China) Ltd
18/F Warwick House, Taikoo Place, 979 King's Road, Quarry Bay, Hong Kong

# Preface

A people is a mirror in which
each traveller contemplates his own image.

André Maurois

IT IS my fifteenth year in Hong Kong and I still feel like a newcomer, a foreigner surrounded by an ocean of Chinese. Surprises abound in my daily world and even the old stand-bys retain their capacity to amaze, delight, irritate, and perplex. Some examples:

— A woman in her thirties enters the train, a baby strapped to her back, bags of shopping in one hand, a toddler of 3 or 4 clutching the other. The carriage is crowded and I offer her my seat. She thanks me, sits her toddler down, and remains standing.

— I am swimming lengths in our University pool. It is a Sunday and the water is crowded. Three students are racing widths, oblivious to anything but their own excitement. One of them ploughs into me full tilt, stops short, waves, smiles, and churns on. I look to the lifeguard for intervention. He is laughing.

— I stop our car at a toll booth to pay the fee. The attendant refuses my payment, pointing out that the driver of the preceding car has paid for me, and motions me through. The other driver waves as he speeds off and I recognize the dealer who sold us our car five years before.

— A candidate for a job opening in our Department is giving a seminar, so we can learn about his research (and his teaching skills) at first hand. He begins by apologizing for not being adequately prepared. 'It has been a very busy week and I have not had time to give my presentation proper attention. I do hope that you will overlook any shortcomings.'

Of course these events may give you no pause, but I am a 44-year-old, Canadian, male psychologist and they are some of my personal windows into Chinese society. As Edward Hall once put it, 'All cross-cultural exploration begins with the experience of being lost.' And the terrain in which you will find yourself lost will be determined by the terrain with which you are familiar. My youthful neighbourhood in Toronto did not prepare me for my travels in the back alleys and office corridors of Hong Kong, but learning my way around has been fascinating. In the midst of my personal frustrations, I have always tried to ask, 'Under what cultural rule can that puzzling behaviour possibly make sense?'

Such questioning has stimulated the design of many scientific experiments I regard as important. For example, cheerful collisions in the swimming pool have led me to wonder how Chinese might perceive someone they were compelled to compete against. The prediction based on Western theories is straightforward. The sentiment will match the relationship — friendly if co-operative, hostile if competitive. In fact, Chinese rate a future competitor as friendlier (not to mention warmer, kinder, and more capable), a reversal of the prediction based on the social logic that prevailed in the Toronto of my boyhood. As we shall discover, this reversal is eminently sensible in a culture where there are large inequalities of power, where the rule of law is perceived as ineffectual, and where a supportive interpersonal network is often one's only defence.

Indeed, the Chinese puzzle-box is full of many such surprises for us Western-trained social scientists. A sample might include the following:

— The children of immigrants have traditionally shown inferior academic results in their new schools. Recent Australian data, however, indicate that immigrant Chinese students dominate the top positions in their classes.
— The four 'little dragons' of South-east Asia — Hong Kong, Singapore, Taiwan, and South Korea — have averaged annual growth rates in Gross National Product of 9.5 per cent over the last twenty years. By contrast, the figure for the United States is 1.7 per cent, and for Austria, 3.5 per cent.

These examples bring home the challenge of the Chinese experience for non-academics as well. Caucasian Australian parents are worrying about how their children can compete for scarce places in professional colleges dominated by Chinese students; American housewives boycott Taiwanese textiles in an effort to protect their husbands' jobs. These concerns, like mine in the streets of Hong Kong, have led to much fruitful questioning. American educators have begun examining the reasons for the Taiwanese superiority in reading and mathematics; English business men are experimenting with Oriental approaches to labour relations and employee input. *Newsweek* entitled its cover of 22 February 1988, 'The Pacific Century?' Suddenly esoteric fascinations have become public currency.

In June 1986, Oxford University Press published a book I edited, entitled, *The Psychology of the Chinese People*. My intention at the time had been to consolidate the fragmented studies involving Chinese persons into a single academic reference that would provide a point of departure for professional social scientists doing research in this area. My editor at Oxford University Press predicted total sales of 1,750, typical for such academic tomes. By June 1988 over 2,500 copies had already been printed. Sensing a sound bet, the Press proposed that I write 'a layman's version'.

I have enough respect for so-called laymen that I paused before accepting this suggestion. After all, laymen are decidedly indifferent to the obscure language we academics use in writing for one another. Could I write clearly enough, colourfully enough, topically enough, to hold such an audience? Of course, there was only one way to find out and taking risks has always been a part of my Toronto boyhood, so I said, 'Yes!'

I did not want this undertaking to yield merely a more palatable version of *The Psychology of the Chinese People* however. In a generally laudatory review of that earlier work, Arthur Kleinman had lamented the absence of 'chapters that attempt to integrate the very different contributions and reveal the golden thread tying each together'. In the late 1980s I certainly had more data at hand to help me weave this 'golden thread' and I certainly had more faith in my skill to do so. It is by striving to weave this golden thread that I could test whether I had made any academic progress in the intervening years.

This golden thread provides the basis by which the Chinese and Western traditions may be drawn together and compared psychologically. Its various strands become evident as scientists struggle to discover some means of understanding the contrasting types of behaviour of people from different cultural groups. Out of this intellectual struggle new theories and ideas sometimes emerge. These insights would not have been stimulated if the psychologist had been examining people only from his or her culture of origin; it has been teased out of the experience of being culturally lost. As a result of this confrontation with difference, however, a scientific basis for human unity across cultures has been woven. It was in this spirit that Abdu'l-Baha asserted long ago that 'the East and the West must unite to provide one another with what is lacking'. For surely the ultimate value in this scientific exploration across cultures is to discern how 'Within the four seas, all men are brothers'.

MICHAEL HARRIS BOND

# Contents

# Contents

but a human race speaking many tongues, regarding many values, and holding different convictions about the meaning of life sooner or later will have to consult all that is human.

Gardner Murphy

# 1

# Some Warnings about Studying the Chinese Scientifically

> The eye cannot see its own lashes.
> Chinese adage

A COLLEAGUE at the Chinese University recently observed that there are 'hundreds of books like yours, purporting to explain the Chinese'. Being himself Chinese, he added, 'Of course, yours will be better!' Better or not, this book's distinctiveness must lie in its claim to scientific status. I am attempting more than traveller's notes, journalistic impressions, and insider's secrets, however judicious and experienced they may be. Instead, I am attempting to bring together the results of many observations that arise when scientists attempt to translate 'the words of sages' into methods of measuring 'things at hand'.

This short chapter has a philosophical focus and is meant to put the chapters which follow into context. Readers who are more interested in what psychologists know about the Chinese should proceed to the next chapter, giving these reflections a miss.

## We Are Unique!

All groups value their identity and their creations — material, artistic, political, and so forth; indeed, they must do so to keep going — attracting new members, holding old members within their ranks, and generating the motivation to work towards group goals. As Henri Tajfel repeatedly demonstrated, group members derive some of their personal self-esteem from their membership in groups which they value.

A culture or nation is one such grouping. Such groups, especially when they feel under attack (even under scrutiny), are likely to close ranks and assert that they are special, different, or unique from other cultures or nations. This claim of distinctiveness nourishes a group and sustains the pride of its members. Groups avoid making cross-cultural comparisons and challenge any comparisons that are made. They will claim that the investigator did not adequately understand the culture examined, that the measures distorted the real cultural phenomena, or that the interpretations of the results were biased.

The typical response is thus to dismiss the researcher's findings; the scientific response should be to improve the research. Which of these two responses happens depends on the researcher's personality characteristics and cultural background, and on the relationship between the cultural groups being compared. Social scientists are as much the human subject of their study as they are the studiers of their human objects. We can hardly expect their debates to be any less psychologically shaped than any other debate.

But we do. Science promises objectivity, rules of procedure, progress towards consolidated knowledge, and structure. Science can order the physical world, but often threatens our interpersonal world. For those who believe that the scientific journey is worth undertaking, all we can do is to offer up the rules of procedure for scrutiny and hope to reach an agreement. Ultimately each of us must decide what to accept. As St Thomas Aquinas put it, 'No man believes what he does not first believe to be believable.' These are the considerations which underlie the beliefs I present in this book.

## Assumptions of this Book

The procedure of science requires the psychologist to choose a concept which interests him or her, such as interpersonal dominance, linguistic ability, or parental warmth, and then to devise ways to measure this concept reliably. The choice of a single aspect of a culture is selective and so cannot reflect the unique pattern of the whole culture. Any comparison made must be understood within the context of the culture and against the background of other comparisons, but such sympathetic 'packaging' of a comparison depends on the capacities of the psychologist involved.

Nor is there any guarantee that the comparison made will involve a concept which is of equal interest to both groups. American psychologists, for example, seem obsessed with attraction between people, fairness, and the concept of 'self'. Chinese psychologists appear more interested in modernization, leadership, and the early identification of learning ability (or disability). The amount of interest in a particular research topic does not make a comparison any less valid, as long as those involved in the research understand what they are doing.

Figure 1    The Distribution of 'Formality' in Two Countries

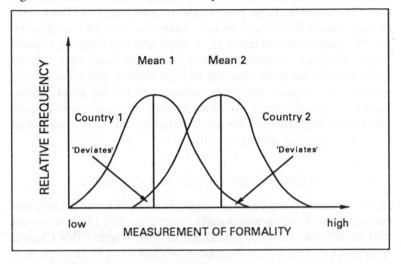

I hope that future cross-cultural comparisons will involve topics of greater interest to Chinese psychologists than those studied in the past. More trained psychologists and support from their educational institutions will help. So will moves to involve more Chinese in studying Chinese psychology, such as that currently led by Yang Kuo-shu in Taiwan. In the meantime, we will have to content ourselves with the comparative work currently available which has generally been initiated by non-Chinese psychologists.

### Statements About Cultural Differences are Generalizations

Statements about cultural differences are based in the simplest case upon results of the sort that are presented graphically in Figure 1. We might conclude that this figure indicates that 'Members of Culture B show more formality than do members of Culture A.' A quick glance will show, however, that this is *not* true for some members of Cultures A and B whose scores fall beyond the average score of the other group. These deviates are more like members of the other group than those of their own. The blunt conclusions of any cross-cultural comparison are thus only more or less accurate.

*How* accurate depends on how much variation there is in the way people in the different cultures carry out the particular behaviour under study. For some types of behaviour the range of variability is narrow; for others, large. As an example, David Buss recently ran a 37-culture study on preference in mate selection. There were strong cultural differences in the importance attached to chastity, but the importance attached to a good earning capacity showed fewer differences between cultures. Although there were cultural differences in the value attached to both chastity and good earning capacity, the relative variability within cultures for good earning capacity was very much smaller. So, not only can cross-cultural conclusions be challenged for particular cases, but some conclusions may be challenged more than others.

## Chinese in Different Countries Are Similar

In the past most cross-cultural comparisons have involved only two cultures, one of which was usually American. Any Chinese sample will be different from an American sample, whether this Chinese sample comes from China, Singapore, or Chinatown in San Francisco. As a result psychologists have developed the questionable habit of talking about 'the Chinese' as if they were all the same and have tended to ignore the possible differences among the Chinese samples.

What is lost in this simplifying process is the answer to two intriguing questions:
1. Are the Chinese in various political, social, and economic settings similar? If so, how similar and for which sorts of behaviour?
2. To which other non-Chinese groups are the Chinese similar? If so, how similar and for which sorts of behaviour?

To answer these questions one needs multicultural, not bicultural, studies and one needs to examine many types of behaviour. Only now are such studies beginning to appear and the results are often surprising. For example, with respect to preferences in the choice of a marriage partner, the results for China are furthest away from those of Spain but closest to those of India; Taiwan is also furthest away from Spain, but closest to Bulgaria. Both China and Taiwan are different from the United States. With studies of other types of behaviour these patterns change and the Chinese groups show more similarity to each other (as with values), or less (as with rates of homicide).

At this stage of our knowledge, judgements about 'the Chinese' are obviously precarious. None the less, I will make them in this book. Some judgements I will make with confidence, especially those involving a contrast with 'Western' groups. Others will be more arbitrary and tentative. We make judgements of similarity (or difference) with the hope that they will make us more effective in the world. If a judgement that a difference exists can help us make a difference in the world, then it is useful.

## Similar Results Increase Confidence

There are many ways to collect data on a given theme. For example, psychologists studying cultural differences in the basic psychological area of collectivism versus individualism have used paper and pencil measures of values, diary records of daily activities, non-verbal responses to insult, and the allocation of money to people who are not group members. The results from these different types of research are similar, that is, they converge. When the results of different tests converge, we believe that what we are measuring is a valid robust phenomenon. I can see considerable similarity between certain themes in Chinese culture, like the fragility of social order, the importance of hierarchy, and the training for group cohesiveness. Such themes may, however, lie in the eye of the imaginative investigator. An organization of scientific facts is very much a creative act. I will draw my conclusions, but encourage you to draw your own.

## Conclusion

We psychologists often believe we are engaged in a value-free enterprise called science and we may attach considerable authority and significance to the results we produce. I submit that we are engaged in a creative enterprise which has a set of public conventions that enable us to draw conclusions. Making sense of the outcomes from cross-cultural psychology is a risky undertaking, given the sketchy data base and the potential for offending some cultural groups. None the less, I choose to go ahead.

A journey of a thousand miles
begins with a single step.
                                        Tzu-ssu

# 2

# Socializing the Chinese Child

A thousand days at home, peace;
A moment abroad, trouble.
Chinese adage

THE CHINESE child is brought up to regard home as a refuge against the indifference, the rigours, and the arbitrariness of life outside. This feat is achieved by indulging the infant, restraining the toddler, disciplining the schoolchild, encouraging the student to value achievement, and suppressing the divisive impulses of aggression and sexuality throughout development. Constantly during this process one is taught to put other family members before oneself, to share their pride and their shame, their sadness and their joy. Family relationships become a lifelong affair, with family activities continuing to absorb the lion's share of one's time and responsibility.

Even after one has married, the obligations continue. Article 15 of China's family law asserts that: 'Children have the duty to support and assist their parents. When children fail to perform the duty of supporting their parents, their parents have the right to demand that their children pay for their support'. This cardinal relationship extends past death, with the tradition of maintaining family shrines to the departed and two major grave-tending holidays every year. Such relationships of mutual succour are not confined to parents and children. Aunts, uncles, elder brothers, and elder sisters are expected to contribute their finances, their dwelling space, their good offices to their junior charges whenever the need arises. Inside the womb of the family, 'you and I are one', as a Chinese proverb puts it.

The foregoing summary is, of course, an ideal. In Chinese culture there is neglect and abuse of children, divorce, alienation of sons from fathers, dereliction of duty by gambling parents, abandonment of grandparents, and so forth. These failures of the family are especially acute in Chinese society, however, precisely because there are fewer personal and institutional supports outside the cradle of the family. Many Chinese learn early to 'swallow anger' and to tolerate the intolerable because they do not see how they can live outside their family of origin or marriage. Chinese culture is no place to be alone.

How does this transformation of human infants take place?

## The Life Cycle

### Genetic Predispositions

Psychologists previously regarded a child's environment as crucial in shaping his or her development. But over the last thirty years they have explored hereditary influences. By comparing identical twins with fraternal twins, it has become evident that there are genetic bases which set limits on how much a person can be shaped. Genetic influences affect intelligence, activity level, sociability, emotionality, and even aspects of morality.

Racial differences of a genetic nature may be based on heredity, especially where members of racial groups have tended to marry within their own group. Philippe Rushton has made some very arresting claims that Negroids, Caucasians, and Mongoloids (which include the Chinese) are arranged in this same order with respect to many characteristics ranging from level of intelligence to speed of development, from anxiety proneness to marital stability. Controversy surrounds some of these claims about differences and many of the genetic arguments. There is strong evidence, however, about temperamental differences in Chinese babies.

David Freedman compared Caucasian American newborns with Chinese American newborns, and found temperamental differences between them. The Caucasian babies were more irritable, more changeable in their level of contentment, more easily upset, and less consolable than the Chinese babies. These differences, with the addition of a higher level of activity among the Caucasian babies, continued during the children's first five months. Given the presence of these differences from birth, Freedman favoured a genetic explanation for them. As we shall discover, Chinese passivity and calmness dovetail smoothly into family demands for restraint and emotional control.

### Universal Variations in Parental Behaviour

Warmth and control are two fundamental characteristics of parental behaviour towards children that can vary considerably. From work in a number of cultures Earl Schaeffer has developed a two-factor map which can be used to describe the differences in how parents (or caretakers in general) raise their charges.

Ron Rohner has extensively examined the warmth dimension in a number of countries. He, like many others, is concerned with the contrast between acceptance, care, and concern for the child and its polar opposites of neglect, abuse, indifference, harshness, and rejection. These fundamental attitudes are communicated in a host of daily exchanges with the child. Their effects on the child's personality are profound and wide ranging. Children who are cherished by their caretakers develop an optimistic, generous, and responsive approach to life and to other people; those who are rejected became depressed, suspicious, withdrawn, and emotionally volatile. To borrow from Erik Erikson, parental acceptance or rejection, especially in the early stages of infancy, shapes the child's basic orientation of trust versus mistrust towards the world. This orientation will direct and colour the child's whole life.

The second dimension of parenting concerns control, as opposed to autonomy. At the restrictive end of the continuum are parents who supervise their children closely, limiting their activities, speech, and friendships to what is acceptable to the parents. At the other extreme are parents who allow their children to associate, explore, and come and go mostly as they please. This contrast is found both within and between different cultural groups. Indeed, as Lucian Pye has persuasively argued, these differing styles of parenting may be mirrored in the country's political organizations.

Using these two key aspects of parenting, one can construct a two-dimensional grid on which it is possible to locate the typical pattern of parental behaviour in any given culture (see Figure 2). Compared with other cultures, the Chinese appear to be moderately warm and very restrictive in their parenting. How caretakers show acceptance and control will of course vary during the life cycle, and it is to the stages of childhood that we now turn.

## Infancy and Early Childhood

There is surprisingly little comparative information on early patterns of caretaking. This is a lamentable state of affairs when one considers that we are talking about the formative age of almost 30 per cent of the world's population. The existing information, combined with lore, observation, and speculation, however, yields a fascinating account.

Figure 2    Universal Dimensions of Parenting Behaviour

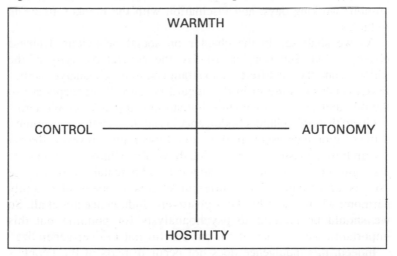

## Early Care

David Ho's work on traditional patterns of childrearing indicates that, before the age of reason (about 5 years), the infant is not regarded as a separate individual requiring adult input beyond the necessities of food, clothing, and shelter. The infant is a great source of delight and joy for all in the family, however, and is almost always surrounded by familiar people. So the infant will often sleep with his or her parents, travel strapped to mother's (or grandmother's) back, and be a part of family gatherings at all times of the day or night. The pattern of close, intense relationships with a narrow circle of other people thus begins early. It is this early indulgence, especially with food, that so interests psychoanalysts. As Warner Meunsterberger, for example, asserts:

Few children are fed and treated with so much permissiveness. As far as we can ascertain, oral deprivation does not occur during this early period. Experience with hunger is avoided by feeding the child upon hearing him cry.

This pampering at the oral stage of a child's development establishes a lifelong preoccupation which lays the foundation for what psychoanalysts have labelled 'oral-receptive mastery'. They use this basic orientation to explain a host of other behaviour, including the Chinese obsession with food, the institutionalization of a rest period, gambling, the use of go-betweens to mediate in conflicts, 16-hour working days, and fascination with the monkey figure in folktales.

As we shall see in the chapter on social behaviour, Chinese observers like Sun Long-ji criticize the general passivity of the Chinese, and their indifference to strangers, in psychoanalytic terms. Psychoanalysis is useful in this regard because its concepts are so flexible and its view of mature human development so Western.

Given that one culture's 'indulgence' is another culture's 'warmth', some caution must be exercised around this topic, however. Recent research by Lau Sing, for example, shows that Chinese respondents distinguish between parental indulgence and parental warmth. These aspects of parenting have different effects in areas like family harmony where warmth relates positively, indulgence not at all. So we should be grateful to psychoanalysts for pointing out this important aspect of parenting, but careful not to over-generalize.

Indeed, this indulgence does not occur in parts of the People's Republic of China, especially the cities, where babies are often placed in nurseries from as early as 2 months of age. There, according to Sander Breiner, a child psychiatrist, there is 'no evidence of cuddling, fondling, or "loving" of the children [of] two to nine months of age. The staff did not believe that an adult–child interaction is critical for babies or that any active play is of value'. Given the ratio of babies to staff, such personal care would be difficult to organize in any case. What is striking, however, is the lack of concern about the long-term effects of this mechanical, stereotyped, and impersonal way of raising children on their responsiveness, their depth of attachment to others, and their curiosity about the world around them.

Educators in Western countries would be dismayed by such caretaking arrangements. The findings of John Bowlby on the dangerous effects of separation of the child from the mother are widely known. In consequence, many parents would share grave concerns with the professionals about the damaging impact of such an impersonal environment on their children's emotional development. In the West, caretaking arrangements are made later in the child's life, and are marked by much greater warmth.

*Early Restrictiveness*

Control over the child's movement also begins in infancy. Babies are often swaddled in restrictive clothing and held or physically immobilized in a chair, back-harness, or cot. Parents consider the floor or ground to be 'dirty', and discourage, indeed prevent, babies from exploring and manipulating much of their accessible environment. Given the small size of most Chinese homes, there is not a great deal of space to cover anyway!

Control is exercised physically rather than verbally, especially in the early years. This pattern is similar to that of the Japanese, but the opposite of the American pattern. Many commentators have noted that the Chinese tend not to speak to their young children as much as Americans do, and treat them not as separate thinking beings but rather as physical extensions of themselves. This non-verbal pattern of relating may set the stage for the subsequent verbal inhibition of the Chinese outside their family circle and may indeed account for their relatively lower performance in verbal tests of intelligence, as we shall discuss later.

The net result of these various strands of childrearing practices can be detected in a research programme directed by Jerome Kagan at Harvard University. He and his collaborators studied matched groups of Chinese and Caucasian American infants for two years in a wide range of controlled but natural situations. To quote from David Ho's conclusions about this rigorous study:

The Chinese infants . . . were less vocal, less active, less likely to smile to many (but not all) of the laboratory episodes, and more apprehensive in social and separation situations; they were quieter, stayed closer to the mother, played less when they were with unfamiliar children or adults, and cried more often following maternal departure.

Many of these differences reflect the genetic differences in temperament that Freedman identified. In addition, however, one can see the general social inhibition that characterizes children whose contact is confined to a close-knit group like the family. The effects of parental restrictiveness may be seen even at this early stage of development. They will be amplified when socialization continues at school.

*Early Schooling*

Schooling begins very early by Western standards. In the People's Republic of China, for example, kindergarten starts as early as 18 months, with infants spending eight to ten hours a day, six days a week, in the institution. By Western standards, a typical Chinese kindergarten seems more like a primary school. Children sit quietly, neatly arrayed in rows, following rote methods of learning, receiving explicit instruction in numbers, letters, and characters. Disruptive behaviour is not tolerated. Reprimands, isolation, or striking are used to enforce discipline. Fractious children are sent to the principal, who will often call in the parents and demand that they try harder to make their child more tractable. Given the importance of education for one's future in Chinese societies, the competition for available places, and the mass of educational material to be absorbed, any concerned parent quickly gets the message! It is at this point that the idyll of childhood often ends and the child begins to feel the harsh realities of a coldly competitive society.

The net result of these pressures for diligence and restraint strikes many Westerners. William Kessen, a developmental psychologist from Harvard, led a delegation of psychologists to China in 1975 and afterwards wrote:

We were impressed . . . by the apparent absence of disruptive, hyperactive, and noisy children. The same quiet orderliness, the same concentration on tasks was to be seen in all the classrooms we visited, down to children barely able to walk.

Much the same impression would result from observing classrooms in any Chinese society from Taiwan to Chinatown in San Francisco. It certainly contrasts with classroom behaviour in more permissive cultures! The question, of course, is the human cost of this outcome. Kessen wrote: 'The docility did not seem to us to be the docility of surrender and apathy; the Chinese children we saw were emotionally expressive, socially gracious, and adept.' Others disagree. Sander Breiner, for example, described the children to whom he was granted access as 'utterly lacking in spontaneity', stereotyped in their responses, and emotionally flat.

Of course these observations reflect the classic Western concern about the consequences of social control. What is instructive here is the puzzle the Chinese experience poses for Western social science. Breiner points out that many visitors from the West:

see the conforming child, the inhibited child, the performing child, not as a problem but as healthy and freely developing. If conformity and a lack of spontaneity can be seen as obvious social symptoms of serious underlying psychopathology, then there is a serious problem ahead for China. If these qualities are seen as valuable and not indicative of psychopathology, then the basic understanding of child psychology would require revision.

There is no doubt that many Western beliefs about the child are
biased and ethnocentric, and could benefit from exposure to Eastern
models and careful assessment of that experience. We do, however,
need more careful scientific measurement of Chinese processes and
outcomes in order to understand where our own models need
amending.

## Discipline

Nowhere is this need more marked than in the area of how Chinese
actually discipline (and reward) their children. There is much research
on this topic in American psychology, with great attention being
paid to the effects of physical punishment, reduction of privileges,
shaming, isolation of the child, the induction of guilt, reasoning,
scolding, material rewards, withdrawal of love, and so forth. Different
observers emphasize different elements, often to support their own
theories. Richard Wilson, for example, in his studies in Taiwan,
considered shaming and isolation from the group to be the dominant
techniques used in Taiwanese society. These disciplinary techniques
make a child dependent, so that he is more likely to adopt group
values, inhibit aggression, and comply with the example of
authorities. These consequences fit many of Wilson's observations
about schoolchildren's behaviour in Taiwan.

Unfortunately, the available research does not indicate any pre-
dominant method of discipline in Chinese societies. As David Ho
concluded in his review:

Conflicting claims have been made about the training and disciplinary
techniques characteristically used by Chinese parents. The evidence does
not allow unequivocal generalizations to be made about a single Chinese
pattern of disciplining children. Rather, it serves to guard against assertions
that any particular technique or pattern predominates or that it is peculiarly
Chinese.

What is interesting is how Chinese persons perceive various types
of parental discipline. Lau Sing and his co-workers have shown
that Chinese, like Westerners, associate a dominating style of control
with lower levels of parental warmth. They believe that family
harmony suffers if parents are strongly authoritarian and hostile in
their discipline of children. This is a universal finding, but still
leaves us asking, 'What sorts of discipline give this impression to
Chinese, and how much?' Cross-cultural comparisons would probably
show the Chinese to be more tolerant of higher levels and stronger
forms of control in their discipline of children.

This same study found that Chinese perceive mothers as the more caring, fathers as the more disciplinarian. This pattern of distance in affection between father and child conforms to traditional divisions of roles and is found also in Western countries. It poses a problem in Chinese culture, however, where so much importance is attached to the relationship between father and son. Francis Hsu has argued that this is a key relationship which links generations within the family and builds interdependence within the family unit. Without adequate affection and warmth in this relationship, David Ho argues, children will perform their roles in the family without the emotion necessary to keep the unit viable. Filial piety will decline unless it is infused with greater paternal affection.

At this point then, we have a reasonably clear picture of infancy and early childhood in Chinese society. The infant experiences considerable warmth, especially maternal, at least in the family context. But there is some question about the impact of early removal from a caring family to rather mechanical caretakers in nurseries and other day-care centres. Everyone involved in the social training of the child restricts the child and demands obedience, control, and restraint. In this they are remarkably successful. It is uncertain *how* the Chinese discipline their children, although they are undoubtedly assisted in this process by their children's more placid temperament.

## Childhood

Three main themes dominate the development of the Chinese child during the primary school period: the control of aggression, the repression of sexuality, and the inculcation of the desire to achieve.

### Aggression

There is much debate about the proper definition of aggression, but for the purpose of our discussion we may treat it simply as the use of coercive means to control the behaviour of others. Such means extend from milder verbal forms, like insulting or threatening harm, to striking or even killing others. A number of factors in Chinese culture combine to yield low levels of aggressive behaviour. Firstly, assertive, wilful actions by an individual put family or group cohesion at risk and hence are avoided. Secondly, there are many clear indicators of status, such as age, sex, and title. The prerogatives of each party in the hierarchy are widely acknowledged. Any challenge to this established order by a junior will be regarded as 'revolutionary', and is thus promptly suppressed. Thirdly, aggression can backfire, bringing harm to its instigators. The demands for filial piety require the child not to take this risk by instigating attacks on others. For 'The body with its hair and skin is received from your parents; do not cause it harm.' All these considerations militate against aggressive behaviour.

Such at least is the reasoning; what do the data indicate? Again there are few studies, but the results of those carried out are consistent and in accordance with the frequent observations that overt expressions of aggression are very rare in Chinese societies.

Training in non-aggression begins early, of course, in the home. Chinese parents are extremely intolerant of hostility directed towards themselves and discourage fights among their children by putting pressure on the older children to concede to their younger siblings, thereby demonstrating the process of conciliation (and the responsibility of seniority). When the children begin to associate with other children, the implications of having an 'aggressive' child are magnified. Neighbours and other families may become involved, creating discord in the community. One's child may develop a reputation for being rough, disobedient, and competitive, dangerous credentials in any Chinese setting. Consequently, those taking care of children punish their charges' aggression in circumstances where such discipline would appear unacceptable to Westerners. So, for example, if a neighbour makes a direct complaint, a parent will often discipline a child without ascertaining the facts. Similarly, Chinese parents will rarely encourage their children to fight back under any circumstances. Not surprisingly, Chinese parents exercise more disciplinary control over their children's aggressive behaviour than American parents do. One expects that this difference would be true of *any* comparison of Oriental and Western parents.

There are fewer data on the actual level of childhood aggression. Again, however, the conclusions are consistent. Firstly, overall levels of aggression are very low in Chinese societies, regardless of whether the measures used are self-reports or observations. The one exception is a higher level of verbal aggression in Chinese pre-school children than in American youngsters, a pattern I expect would be reversed in older, school-age children. Secondly, the factors associated with childhood aggression in the West, such as authoritarian childrearing, negative attitudes towards school, and the amount of television viewing, are also found for Chinese children. Thirdly, there are higher levels of aggression in boys than in girls. This difference is also found in Western societies, but the Chinese difference between the sexes is relatively larger. As we shall discover in later chapters, there are powerful Chinese stereotypes about the differences between men and women. These beliefs undoubtedly affect the different ways in which boys and girls are taught to express anger, dominance, and competitiveness. Much research is still to be done in this area.

Overall, then, Chinese societies are intolerant of aggressive behaviour. Low homicide rates, an aversion to violent sports, and an absence of public brawling are just some of the consequences of the vigilant response by parents, teachers, and other caretakers to any hostility or wilfulness in their charges. Such vigilance ensures that order and harmony will prevail against the divisive forces of chaos and immoderation.

Of course there are less obvious ways of being hostile towards others. Anger and opposition may be expressed in playing helpless, going slow, backbiting, not understanding, forgetting important promises, and other forms of passive-aggressive behaviour. In authoritarian contexts this is a sensible strategy to adopt, as open rebellion will unleash repressive measures. Passive resistance is rarely labelled as 'aggressive' and hence is not punished, although it may be equally effective in undermining the pressure of superiors. Where a parent, or other authority figure, has failed to back up his or her power with affection and care, passive-aggressive responses from his or her charges are likely. Cross-cultural studies involving the Chinese would do well to include measures of these 'quieter' forms of aggression. I would expect them to be more frequent in any more hierarchical social system, like the Chinese.

*Sexuality*

Any culture with collectivist social pressures and concerns for social hierarchy will tend to suppress sexual behaviour. Like aggression, sexual attraction must be carefully suppressed and channelled. For a freer sexuality may create potent jealousies within groups and lead people to defy their parents' choice of a suitable mate. In individualistic cultures, expression of sexuality is one aspect of the pursuit of happiness, and physical attractiveness a more important factor in mate selection. When Chinese decry Westernization and 'bourgeois liberalism', it is the sexual permissiveness of the West that is one of their chief targets. Partly in consequence, pornography, provocative clothing, public displays of affection, and premarital sexual experimentation are much less prevalent in Chinese society, whether in traditional China or modern Singapore.

This process of suppression begins early. According to David Ho, sex training is the most severe of the various areas of childrearing. Parents prohibit nudity in the house, are extremely anxious about sexual behaviour like masturbation, and rarely give their children any sex education. This chore is left to the schools, where reluctance to grasp this nettle is high, lest the parents be offended. Not surprisingly, sexual knowledge is low and heterosexual segregation is high in all Chinese societies.

One would like to know more about how these outcomes are achieved, of course. The problem is that Chinese social scientists are themselves reluctant to address the topic. Sexual behaviour is of minor importance in comparison with more pressing social concerns, it is argued, and furthermore, Freud's legacy of preoccupation with childhood sexuality is a Western aberration. No visiting social scientist would be inclined to offend his or her Chinese hosts or to embarrass research subjects, and so the field of sexuality generally lies fallow.

## Achievement Motivation

Such is not the case with the area of achievement motivation, where there is a plethora of studies. This is hardly surprising, given the Chinese concerns with modernization and training for the skills necessary to advance society.

The early studies in this area were based on David McClelland's theory and measurement techniques. McClelland argued that emphases on socialization could be seen in the themes that dominated the content of educational materials. He examined such materials in a number of cultures, including the Chinese, and detected a changing pattern of needs in China from the early to the mid-twentieth century. Achievement motivation rose during this period so that by the middle of the century China was above the world average (which was calculated from over forty countries).

Further studies by Yang Kuo-shu have highlighted a number of interesting aspects of Chinese achievement motivation. First of all, achievement goals are often presented as being for the benefit of a group, be it the family or the state, rather than the individual. Secondly, other people, rather than the individual, often define the standards against which achievement is to be measured. Thirdly, tests which measure unconscious processes, like the Thematic

Apperception Test, often produce results dramatically different from those relying on self-reports, which tap conscious, more controllable processes. The former often reveal individualistic themes, the latter collectivistic themes. Fourthly, achievement motivation in boys is generally related to high parental care; in girls, to parental hostility. This difference between the sexes is also found in Western research.

The important factor is, of course, actual achievement, not motivation. In Chinese culture, childhood achievement is almost exclusively defined in academic terms. Social skills, athletic ability, or personal fulfilment are secondary to doing well in school. As many commentators have noted, traditional China was an open society in that anyone could elevate himself (rarely, however, herself!) to the mandarinate by excelling in the civil service examinations. In fact this was the *only* means of advancing beyond one's allotted station in life. The obsession with academic achievement remains today, since academic achievement is still a major escalator to higher position.

In consequence parents exert massive pressure on their children to do well in school. Homework is supervised and extends for long periods, extracurricular activities are kept to a minimum, effort is rewarded, tutors are hired, and socializing is largely confined to family outings. The result in any interethnic setting is dramatic. Chinese students, even recent immigrants, often earn the ire of local parents by outperforming their own children. They continue in education longer than children from other groups and are vastly over-represented in graduate schools and the professions in later life, relative to other ethnic groups.

What socialization practices predict academic success among the Chinese? Research by Stanford Dornbush in Californian high schools has produced an ironic finding: Chinese students who are more successful come from families reporting *less* authoritarian patterns of rearing their children. This negative relationship between grades and authoritarianism is also found within the other ethnic groups sampled. The irony lies in the fact that as a group the Chinese Americans do better at school than White Americans but are *more* authoritarian in their childrearing practices than are White American parents. Clearly the puzzle of Chinese academic success is only just beginning to be cracked. Dornbush himself concludes that his group has 'more questions than answers in examining Asian parenting practices and school performance'.

It is important for those studying Chinese achievement to realize that the Chinese have often felt beleaguered and vulnerable to the vicissitudes of famine and political change, and to the whims of authority. Wealth is often their only buffer and educational attainment its best guarantor. As the Chinese proverb puts it, 'While great wealth comes from providence, moderate wealth comes from diligence.' This diligence is inculcated early and reinforced throughout one's life. For there is no social security beyond one's achievements.

## Summary

We have been examining a number of themes in the early development of Chinese people. I began by emphasizing the importance of the family unit to all Chinese. We then considered the two key elements of warmth and restrictiveness in parenting, as they affect the Chinese infant. As the child grows, concerns about aggression, sexuality, and achievement come to the fore and are channelled with the same concerned strictness that marked the earlier years of the child.

I fear that, in my Western way, I may not have conveyed adequately the sense of mutuality, of being connected through affection, obligation, and responsibility to specific other people — the background theme which is absolutely critical to an understanding of Chinese social life. As Sun Long-ji puts it in *The Deep Structure of Chinese Culture*, 'from the very beginning a Chinese is defined by a bilateral relationship with another person'. Children develop this sense of being connected through a myriad of daily exchanges with their parents. Circular tables, shared bedrooms, late-night outings with their parents, supervision of homework by elder brothers, daily phone calls to mother after marriage — all of these weave the warp and woof of this Chinese interdependence. It is what makes life within one's family so supportive and sustaining; outside it, so rough and uncaring.

# 3

# How Chinese Think

To excel others,
master the classics!
Chinese adage

IN THIS chapter we will consider our accumulated knowledge about the way the Chinese people perceive the outside world and deal with this information so that they can respond most effectively to environmental demands. At first sight this may seem an unwarranted undertaking. Surely, all humans are born with an identical sensory apparatus and brain. Different groups will of course live in different geographical locations, so that the *content* of what they perceive and think about will differ. But the *way* in which people think will be the same. Surely!

The available evidence suggests otherwise. There are some distinctive features of the way Chinese think and these cultural characteristics appear to arise from the style of social training and the educational requirements that distinguish the Chinese from other groups.

The data base here is meagre in comparison to that available in other areas of psychology. Perceptual and cognitive psychologists generally assume that all people function in the same way. They are not too concerned with the practical applications of their work. In consequence, they tend not to focus on differences in the content of what various groups think. Nevertheless, the remarkable academic achievements of Orientals have spurred researchers with applied interests, especially educational psychologists, to examine cultural differences more closely. Early work began in the area of intelligence.

## Chinese Intelligence

### The Components of Intelligence

We normally think of intelligence as a single ability, a lighthouse beacon which varies in intensity from person to person. However, most tests of intellectual functioning consist of a number of subtests, which assess a wide range of intellectual competence. So, for example, the Weschler Adult Intelligence Scale (WAIS) consists of two broad domains, verbal and performance. The verbal tests include vocabulary items, questions of general knowledge, and serial memory for strings of digits read backwards and forwards; the performance tests include picture completion, the pairing of digits with symbols, and the reproduction of visual designs using blocks. There are many similar tests of intelligence, all consisting of different batteries of subtests measuring different aspects of cognitive functioning.

Some of these subtests are more closely related to each other than to others. So, within any test battery there are groupings or clusters of subtests, with each of the subtests within a grouping measuring the same underlying factor of intelligence. These factors vary from test to test, depending on the type of subtests included. Many scientists believe that the greater the variety of factors measured, the better the measure of intelligence.

## Comparisons of Chinese Persons' Intelligence

Early cross-cultural comparisons were laughable. A readily available group of Chinese in the West was tested against a group of middle-class Caucasians. The Chinese were often children of struggling immigrants with a poor command of English. The test items themselves were often culturally biased, based on familiarity with Western traditions, and sampled a narrow range of abilities. The lower Chinese scores which resulted were of course quite predictable.

In time the approach to such testing became more sensible. Broader, more equivalent samples were compared; more comprehensive and equally familiar test items were used; subjects were tested in their first language, and so forth. Having said all that, it should be noted that no cross-cultural testing of intelligence has been conducted by Chinese investigators using Chinese-produced tests of intelligence. This is an important caveat. As we shall see, Chinese education requires considerable time and effort to be devoted to memorization. One would therefore expect a Chinese test of intelligence to include more memory subtests. As we will see below, Chinese score higher than many other groups on such subtests, and hence would do better than Caucasians on a Chinese test of intelligence.

For the present, however, we must make do with Western tests.

It should be noted that many psychologists studying intelligence have criticized these for being too narrow in scope. Howard Gardner, for example, has pointed out that contemporary tests of intelligence fail to tap musical, bodily kinaesthetic, and personal intelligence, the last having both interpersonal and personal components. Thus, we may still not be examining a complete range of intellectual abilities in our testing.

## Overall Intelligence

James Flynn of the University of Otago has consolidated the 16 relevant studies on the intelligence of Oriental Americans. On the basis of this research he assigns Chinese (and Japanese) Americans an intelligence quotient of 98, two points *below* the Caucasian American average. This difference is small and could easily be eliminated by including more subtests of areas in which the Chinese tend to excel, like number memory, for example.

The only cross-cultural study involving a native Chinese population was a careful comparison of Taiwan Chinese and Japanese Americans, led by Harold Stevenson from the University of Michigan. The investigators selected ten subtests of cognitive ability, such as memory of items heard, spatial relations between objects, vocabulary, and general information. As they concluded:

This study offers no support for the argument that there are differences in the general cognitive functioning of Chinese, Japanese, and American children . . . by the time they are enrolled in the fifth grade of elementary school, the most notable feature of their performance is the similarity in level, variability, and structure of their scores on the cognitive tasks.

Again, this conclusion may depend on the composition of the subtests, but it seems to me a probable outcome to any broadly based sampling of cognitive abilities. Perhaps of greater interest than general levels of intelligence, then, is the *pattern* of abilities which characterizes the Chinese relative to other groups.

## The Pattern of Cognitive Abilities

Cultural groups may be similar in average ability, but show a different profile of strengths on the component abilities constituting that overall average. Obviously, results will depend on which groups are compared across which factors of cognitive ability. A general conclusion has emerged from a host of studies. In the words of Philip Vernon, a leading figure in the study of intelligence, there is a 'unanimous finding that Orientals of all ages in any cultural setting score higher relative to Caucasians on spatial, numerical, or non-verbal intelligence tests, and less well on verbal abilities and achievements'. So Chinese excel on tests like the Raven's Progressive Matrices, which assess non-verbally the respondent's ability to complete a complex visual pattern by selecting from among a variety of possible pieces. Their scores on the quantitative portion of the Graduate Record Exam for American universities are among the highest of all ethnic groups. Tests of vocabulary, verbal comprehension, and analogical thinking, however, yield relatively lower scores. The professional implications of this profile are obvious, with accountancy and computer applications being much more suitable for Chinese than law or politics, for example.

Although considerable research has been done in the area of intelligence, there is much more to thinking than simply one's cognitive output. I now turn to some of these aspects of Chinese thought processes.

## Chinese Cognitive Style

Tests of ability or intelligence present respondents with clearly defined tasks, so that they may demonstrate their speed or depth of functioning in response to these prescribed challenges. Daily reality, however, is often unstructured, and permits us to organize it in accordance with our habitual modes. Here we encounter more striking cultural differences.

### Holistic Perception

Many years ago Francis Hsu was involved in a study which asked subjects to respond freely to unstructured Rorschach ink-blots. The relative proportions of whole-card and specific-detail responses are of interest. Chinese from China gave relatively more whole-card responses than did Chinese Americans, who in turn gave more than Caucasian Americans. Apparently the stimulus as a whole has more salience for Chinese; the parts of the whole for Americans. Similar results have been found with other tests which use unstructured formats, like the sentence completion test or the Thematic Apperception Test.

In a similar vein Chiu Lian-hwang tested matched samples of Taiwanese and American children on their approaches to grouping objects. The children were presented with arrays of three familiar objects taken from a variety of categories, such as people, foods, tools, and so forth. Each child was asked to select two of the three objects which were alike or went together and to state the reason for their grouping.

Chinese children more often grouped objects on the basis of an assumed relationship or interdependence between the two items, for example, 'because the man is married to the woman' or 'because the mother takes care of the baby'. The Chinese were also slightly more likely to pair objects on the basis of similarities in the total appearance of the objects, such as 'because both people are fat'. The American children, by contrast, preferred the analytic style of grouping, that is, they identified some attribute, be it descriptive, like 'because both animals have fur' or inferential, like 'because both animals are mammals'. In short, the Chinese tend to perceive on the basis of the overall pattern uniting the objects, Americans on the basis of a characteristic shared by the objects. American children join the objects after decomposing them into parts; Chinese children join the objects after considering them as wholes.

## Creativity

The ability (and the courage) to produce a new but appropriate response to a problem is a much prized characteristic in the West. Creativity is valued for its contribution to progress and as proof of the creator's individuality. But it requires a supportive social framework, which provides time and encouragement for the trial-and-error approach that necessarily accompanies creative exploration. Furthermore, teachers must encourage children to look beneath the surface of things to detect non-obvious bases of relationship among the elements in a problem. On both of these counts, there are problems in Chinese culture.

### Sense Dependence

The Japanese philosopher, Hajime Nakamura, wrote of the Chinese:

One of the most important characteristics of Chinese psychology is its reliance on sense-perception. They reluctantly dwell on that which is beyond the immediately perceived . . . For the purposes of instruction and persuasion, they resort to images that have the appeal of direct perceptions.

In support of this assertion, comparative research indicates that

Chinese are more concrete and practical than Americans in the objects that they choose to draw, and more pragmatic in their tendency to evaluate ideas in terms of their immediate application. Both characteristics lessen creativity, which requires that people explore situations in all their possibilities without prejudging their usefulness.

## Experimentation

A number of observers have noted the inhibition of the Chinese when presented with new situations for which they have no prescribed mode of solution. In such situations an adventurous curiosity will promote the discovery of a solution by leading people to experiment with the components of the problem. This is precisely where the Chinese fall short.

To digress for a moment, the Swiss psychologist, Jean Piaget, described a number of stages through which a child passes to achieve a mature level of thinking. He labelled the final stage 'formal operations'. This term describes the ability to detect general patterns which underlie the specific elements of a relationship, such as that among a light source, the distance of an object, and the size of its shadow. Although Chinese teenagers can attain this level of thought, they do so more slowly than American children. The authors of a study on this ability explain the difference by noting that:

An aptitude for the hypothesis testing and experimentation of formal thought requires an active, searching mode of behaviour, characteristics which the Hong Kong culture may not encourage.

Such discouragement is characteristic of all Chinese cultures, as I have said in the chapter on socialization. Again, this apparent inhibition of exploratory playfulness will prevent the discovery of hidden relationships and thereby depress creative output.

## Performance on Creativity Tests

In time habits become fixed. Even when creative responses are called for, as in a test of creativity, the required skills are not readily available. Various tests of creativity involving Taiwanese, Singaporean, and mainland Chinese students unanimously confirm the expectation that Chinese are less creative than Americans. This is not to deny some extraordinary feats of creative genius by Chinese, of course. They are well represented in the ranks of Nobel laureates, for example. Nevertheless, their overall level of creative output is lower than that of Westerners.

Creativity is a two-edged sword. Its benefits are obvious, but its process disturbing. The creative act requires time, resources for experimentation, a valuing of individual expression, and a freeing of people from prescribed modes of thinking. Its favours are not bestowed exclusively on those already designated as leaders, scholars, and established artists. In consequence, creativity disturbs conservatives with its unsettling, revolutionary capacity. For the Chinese it raises the dreaded spectre of *luan*, or chaos, and hence is not encouraged.

Thus Chinese students are ideally suited for what the educational psychologist Donald Norman labelled 'additive and fine-tuning' approaches to learning. Neither adding to a core of existing knowledge nor honing one's established skills challenges what one has already mastered. Instead, it 'polishes the jade'. Additive and fine-tuning strategies are tailor-made for subjects like physics, chemistry, computer science, and engineering which Chinese graduate students have come increasingly to dominate in many Western universities.

Here, then, we see the effects of broader social considerations on the acquisition of a cognitive skill like creativity. Chinese cultural considerations influence other aspects of the cognitive process. We will now turn to these constraints and describe their implications for the ways in which Chinese people think.

## Important Cultural Considerations

### Mastering the Chinese Script

To be literate in Chinese culture one must master its written language. To quote Philip Vernon at length in this regard:

Chinese, however, represents every different word by an ideograph, or pictorial character [in fact, sometimes two or more], and there are some 3,500 of these characters to be learned in order to read an ordinary book or newspaper, and far more for uncommon words. Each character contains two parts: one is the stem, which gives the phonetic element, or sound; the other is the radical, which gives the semantic element, or meaning. Though there are many thousands of phonetics, a much smaller number is required for most reading and writing. A knowledge of these, therefore, makes it possible to pronounce a great many new words. Likewise, some 80 per cent of characters contain one of 214 radicals. Words that are related in meaning usually contain the same radical. Thus, there are many regularities or general rules that help in reading Chinese.

[material in brackets added]

Although there are rules which help, achievement of literacy in Chinese culture is a Herculean chore. First of all is the sheer amount of time required to recognize and write the 214 radicals alone. English readers, for example, will remember how long they needed to master a mere 26 letters! Chinese pupils must therefore learn early about the rigours of repeated practice and lengthy sessions of homework.

The next aspect of written Chinese is that each ideograph is formed by combining radicals in prescribed patterns to form an integrated whole. Neatness, a sense of balance among the components, and attention to fine detail are all required in order to depict the characters legibly. This early and repeated practice in perceptual detail and the relating of visual parts to wholes is, I believe, one explanation for the better performance of Chinese on pattern discrimination and visual/spatial tests of intelligence.

Continuing with the script, words are made up of single or, more commonly, double or triple characters. These word-characters must then be combined in various patterns to depict new concepts. A 'fax', for example, is represented by the four ideographs for 'picture, words, passing, [and] faithfully'. As one can readily appreciate, the demands on one's memory capacity for receiving and producing the written Chinese script are enormous.

Given these heavy demands on rote memory functions from early in life, one would expect educated Chinese to excel in any new activities which make such demands. Indeed they do, as we have seen in the section above on intellectual abilities. Chinese do well in subjects like mathematics which require early mastery of memorized materials like tables.

With respect to mathematics, the Chinese language helps in another regard. As Rumjahn Hoosain in Hong Kong has pointed out, a distinctive feature of Chinese is the shortness of the names of numbers. This phonological fact means that numerical information can be stored more efficiently in short-term memory. Hoosain believes that the processing of information can thereby proceed more efficiently because less attention is devoted to memory retention. Performance in mathematics is thus enhanced.

The types of reading disabilities found in Chinese culture also appear to be related to the use of an ideographic script. Although the overall levels of reading problems are similar in Japan, Taiwan, and America, the particular Chinese vulnerability relates to discovery of meaning rather than to pronunciation of presented words. This 'Achilles heel' derives from the importance of visual form in determining the meaning of ideographs. The importance of the visual element to Chinese readers subjects them to reading problems that Americans, who use a phonological script, do not encounter.

Conversely, Chinese will typically excel at tests of visual performance, like the Raven's Progressive Matrices, for example. As Ovid Tzeng has pointed out, 'processing logographic script involves more visual/spatial memory than does [processing] an alphabetic script' [material in brackets added]. Practice makes (more) perfect, at least in certain types of memory function.

## The Educational Context
### The Competition for Places

Many are called, but few are chosen in Chinese culture. Readers may recall that passing the civil service examinations was one of the few institutionalized ways in ancient China of rising above one's given station in life. The rewards for success were considerable, but limited to an élite few.

This consideration is still a fact of life in all Chinese societies. In Hong Kong, for example, there are two universities serving the clamorous demands of almost six million people. In New Zealand, there are seven serving roughly three million. With such odds, the struggle in Chinese societies for school success is intense. The pressure to succeed is relentless and exacts a considerable toll in student anxiety and depression, not to mention family power struggles around the doing of homework.

Class sizes are large because resources are often scarce, but more importantly because the Chinese believe that 'On one mountain, there cannot be two tigers'. A wide competition will better enable the best student to claw his or her way to the top, thereby proving that the best choice has been made. 'With fire we test our gold' seems to be the logic driving the system.

There is less opportunity for individual instruction in class. Examinations are frequent and grading is based almost exclusively on their outcome. Fairness is ensured by basing grades on objective scoring of quantifiable elements — names, dates, facts, numbers.

## The Role of a Teacher

Teaching is an exalted profession in Chinese culture, commanding the same respect as is due to one's father. So teachers are generally well provided for, except when their moral authority makes their potential opposition to a political regime dangerous. Students respond to teachers as to a stern parent — with attention, silence, and fear. They do not question teachers, or challenge their judgements, provided the teacher behaves with moral integrity. Not surprisingly, discipline problems are rare at school. Vandalism is almost non-existent.

## The Classroom

As part of its cross-cultural studies of educational practices, the Stevenson group has looked carefully at classroom practices. I quote one of their conclusions at length because it is the natural consequence of our preceding analysis:

Asian [Taiwanese and Japanese] classrooms are more efficiently managed than the American classrooms; greater amounts of time are devoted to academic activities and to imparting information in Asian classrooms. Attentiveness on the part of children is high, transitions from one activity to another occupy little time, and children in Asian classrooms seldom engage in irrelevant activities during class periods. Much less time is devoted to small-group or individual activities in Asian classrooms; most of the class time is devoted to activities where the teacher is in charge. This is in contrast with the organization of American schools, where children are more frequently divided into small groups or left to work on their own.

Western teachers who observe such a learning environment are typically bowled over by its orderliness, as the earlier quote by Kessen suggests. It is very teacher centred, indeed!

## An Educated Person

In ancient times an educated peason was a man who had memorized the classics. The discipline required to memorize produced a civilized man. Even today there is an almost magical belief in the value of memory work.

The young mandarin would then use the moral precepts found in the classics in judging individual cases brought before him. The classics contained many moral injunctions which were believed to reflect the 'Mandate of Heaven'.

Even today, moral instruction is taught in Chinese schools. Not only is this a valued legacy of the past, but such instruction also serves to bind together a larger political unit. Otherwise, the strength of the family unit would lead to an indifference for others who were not tied in some way to one's family. Public morality and concern for strangers, never Chinese strengths, would be even more difficult to ensure if moral education were not included in the school syllabus.

### How to Show Respect, Chinese Style

Liu In-mao places great emphasis on what he calls the 'respect superiors rule': 'If your superiors are present, or directly involved, in any situation, then you are to respect and obey them.' The teacher is a surrogate father or emperor and so commands the same responses. Indeed, the educational system is very like an ancient court. The consequences of this scenario are critical for cognitive development.

One of the Chinese words for disobedience is composed of two characters roughly translated as 'mouth back'. Not surprisingly, students in class show their respect by keeping quiet. Verbal fluency thereby suffers because students are not trained to develop their debating skills with a superior. And we know that Chinese performance on verbal tests of achievement is lower than that of most Westerners. They are especially weak in the development of persuasive argument in new situations.

Part of this ineffectiveness in the face of novelty derives from extensive training in memorization instead of argumentation. The emphasis on acquisition of (measurable) knowledge requires considerable memory work, a skill at which Chinese generally excel. Memorizing of course requires dedication and effort. It is these aspects of Chinese school performance which Harold Stevenson believes can be used to explain their early attainment in reading and mathematics compared to Americans and Japanese. Chinese simply do more homework than Americans — who have an almost magical belief in natural ability. It is not that Chinese have a unique collection of abilities, larger parts of certain brain areas, or what have you. Instead, certain abilities, important at early stages of academic development, are enhanced through practice and memory. Both require time, which Chinese give to the task in abundance.

But at higher levels of education, and in some disciplines especially, what becomes important is the illumination of inner, hidden patterns and meaning. Instead of description, one needs induction. One must go beyond 'surface' levels in approaching learning, to 'deep' levels. So-called 'surface approaches to learning' emphasize mastery of facts through rote learning; 'deep approaches to learning', a penetration beneath the surface to discover broad themes, underlying assumptions, directions of the argument, and so forth. Not surprisingly, Western teachers of Chinese students at university find their charges weak at general essay questions. Such questions require students to identify a pattern, select facts to support that pattern, and to organize facts and themes in a persuasive way. Instead, they often produce a paper with an avalanche of facts which fit the general topic, but lacking any sense of development and conclusion. The exasperated teachers either switch to multiple-choice questions or begin training their students in (Western-style) argumentation!

Mastery of the deeper approach requires a more playful, speculative, 'as if' attitude towards the topic in hand. It does not thrive in competitive, examination-oriented classrooms where performance is measured by the concrete enumeration of memorized facts. At higher levels of professional attainment, therefore, Chinese will be stronger, for example, in accountancy, which allows one to work within a set of given, logical rules; weaker in psychology, which requires speculation about internal, hidden processes and consideration of their possible effects on observable behaviour. Readers can make similar predictions about probable Chinese attainments in other professions (if they are natural psychologists, of course)!

## Conclusion

As one management trainer said, 'You've got to inspect what you expect'. What a responsible teacher inspects, of course, are those skills that are necessary for the society into which a student must fit. Chinese societies, like all others, require literacy and numeracy. The attainment of literacy in Chinese requires the skills and discipline needed to master an ideographic script. This fundamental requirement fosters visual/spatial abilities, attention to detail, and sensitivity to surface patterns. Memory ability is needed, along with the time and persistence to learn masses of logographs.

The acquisition of these and other skills likewise constrains development. Respecting superiors *Chinese style* entails silence and the reproduction of what the teacher regards as important. One goes beyond the given barriers with trepidation, as the consequences for exam results, one's place in school, and one's future in society are decisive. Creativity, verbal fluency, persuasive arguing, working out deeper patterns are therefore relatively less developed in otherwise smart students than they are in other cultures.

After all, you must expect what you inspect, and conversely, not expect what you don't inspect . . .

# 4

# The Social Actor in Chinese Society

We cannot enter into alliances
until we are acquainted with
the designs of our neighbours.
Sun Tzu, *The Art of War*

THIS CHAPTER prepares us to consider Chinese social behaviour by introducing us to the social actor in the drama. I say 'social' because I shall examine the internal characteristics of Chinese people that are most closely connected with their interpersonal exchanges.

So we will temporarily extract the Chinese person from his or her social context and isolate some of the ingredients that social scientists believe to be key determinants of social behaviour. We will start with the sense of self, move on to social attitudes and values, then finish with aspects of perceiving others. In subsequent chapters we will see how these elements fit in to social and organizational life.

## The Sense of Self

Philosophers, journalists, social scientists, and others often use the term 'self' as an explanatory 'ghost' to account for any noteworthy feature of Chinese behaviour. So, for example, the Chinese self is described as 'permeable' (or meek) because the Chinese often appear to defer to the wishes of other people. In effect the term 'self' becomes a substitute for the concept of personality itself. Used in that sense this whole book is about the Chinese 'self'.

The sense of self is a more limited topic. Here the question is simply, 'How do Chinese persons describe themselves, in comparison to how other groups of people describe themselves?' We are, of course, tapping conscious awareness rather than unconscious processes in asking this question. Provided we collect data that may be used in cross-cultural comparisons, we should be able to test many ideas about the Chinese sense of self.

Unfortunately, most of the research in this area has been done 'safari-style' by Westerners on sabbatical leave. The content of their questionnaires and their interpretation of the results do not adequately represent the Chinese perspective. From the research that passes muster, however, the following conclusions can be drawn:

1. Chinese people consistently describe themselves in less positive terms than do Americans (but more positively than do the Japanese).
2. Chinese think of themselves using more group-related concepts (such as, attentive to others) than Americans do; and they see their ideal 'self' as being closer to their social (or interpersonal) self than Westerners do. In describing themselves Chinese employ more terms that relate to family roles (grandson, daughter, elder brother, and so on).
3. Chinese describe themselves using the same features of personality that they use to describe other people. These features assess at least whether a person is: socially oriented or self-centred; competent or ineffective; expressive or conservative; self-controlled or impulsive; optimistic or pessimistic. Where a Chinese will place himself or herself on each of these five dimensions will vary from person to person. Only the first and the last dimensions are similarly composed to those that Americans use, and overlap with what Americans label as 'agreeable versus uncooperative' and 'stable versus neurotic', respectively. As is true with Americans, Chinese females rate themselves as being higher in social orientation and lower in optimism than do Chinese males.
4. The concept of self-esteem is broad and can be broken down into constituents such as academic, social, familial, physical, athletic, and so on. These components are better predictors of specific areas of behaviour, such as delinquency and school grades, than is the broad measure of self-esteem.

These results fit in with the Chinese emphasis on moderation and social orientation. The moderation of the Chinese is shown in the fact that they present their selves as possessing both positive and negative features. This conception of the self probably reflects their society's need for modesty and balance.

The social orientation of the Chinese is reflected in the higher endorsement they give to group-related traits and roles, as well as the fact that their ideal self is closely involved in social relationships. The dimensions they use to perceive themselves and others are likewise focused on interpersonal concerns, not on mastery of the external world or absorption with narrowly personal processes.

## Attitudes towards the Social World

In this section I shall examine how the Chinese orient themselves towards social events, other people, and values. Our data consist of responses to attitude surveys or self-rating questionnaires, so we will later want to see how these fit in with actual behaviour.

### The Cause of Social Events

One of the most widely studied attitudes is that of the individual's perception of his own influence over events. Tests of this concept ask respondents whether they believe that the events in their lives have been caused by them or by some external factor, like political forces, chance, other people, and so forth.

Not surprisingly, responses are related to one's educational level, social class, sex, age, and so forth, with people in positions of lesser influence, such as women in Chinese society, reporting that external forces are more influential in determining the outcomes of events affecting them.

It should come as no surprise that Chinese respondents regard external forces as more influential. Chinese are more 'cabined, cribbed, confined' than Westerners by family responsibilities, political authority, and classroom control. They accurately reflect this social reality in their responses, just as do persons from other cultures in which the mass of the population have little power, such as India, the Philippines, Venezuela, and so forth.

In such cultural systems, it would be unrealistic to assert that one exerted much personal control over one's destiny unless one in fact occupied a social position of considerable power. And it would be dangerous and self-destructive to struggle openly against persons whose authority over one is broadly approved. So, in place of open debate and courts of law, Chinese are much more likely to use indirect strategies of control, such as appeals to the heart (*ren qing*), intervention by more powerful third parties, gossip, and other methods which will be described in subsequent chapters.

### Basic Orientations towards Others

The two most fundamental aspects of social behaviour are control and association. How do Chinese understand the need for these basic features of our daily activities?

## Authoritarianism

This attitude involves a general tendency to defer to any person in a position of power, status, or control and can take the form of dogmatic or rigid behaviour, respect for tradition, obedience to political dictates rather than personal principles, and literal interpretation of rules. Chinese consistently score higher than Western groups on various measures of authoritarianism. Given the hierarchy implicit in the five cardinal relations described by Confucius (the *Wu Lun*) and the emphasis on filial piety, such results should come as no surprise. 'Juniors and seniors have their ranking', as one Chinese proverb puts it, and Chinese are oriented towards finding their place in this hierarchy and working within its dictates.

These results also fit in with those for control of events, where the Chinese have been shown to emphasize external factors as determining their behaviour. Again, it is 'fitting' for people to hold such values in societies where inequalities are a social fact of life and reflect the 'Mandate of Heaven'. Deference to authority in such cultures would be perceived as upright, prudent, and to the benefit of society, not as cowardly, unprincipled, and weak, the gloss that more democratically oriented persons would give it.

## Association

The anthropologist George Foster discussed the concept of 'the limited good', a basic belief system of peasant communities that the goods and resources of this world are fixed in supply. Consequently, everyone is in competition with everyone else for the most they can get. This view of the world promotes a suspicious attitude towards others, discouraging association with anyone whose fate is not linked to one's own.

This argument is compatible with the orientation of the Chinese towards collective activities and certainly fits their agricultural heritage. Data from many personality tests show that Chinese are generally less sociable and extroverted, and more 'shy' and socially anxious than Americans in particular and Westerners in general.

I suggest that these differences arise mainly from an indifference to strangers and those who are not connected by blood or long association. Indeed, Chinese show an intense attachment to these primary groups, rather than a broad spread of looser attachments. A Chinese person takes personal pride in the success of persons from his or her inner circle; shame in their failures. Personality measurements developed in the West often fail to identify the main characters in Chinese people's primary groups. Precise rather than general questions would pick up the *pattern* of Chinese associations. I believe they would confirm the hypothesis that the Chinese avoid those who are unfamiliar but are intensely involved with family and old friends.

## Trust

This point about closeness with one's inner circle is supported by recent cross-cultural research on trust. The concept of trust is typically used rather loosely. In essence it involves committing something of oneself, such as material resources or information, to the care of another, where one has no effective control over how that other person may use this trust.

In fact very few actions require such trust. Of course we frequently make ourselves vulnerable to others, but we have many ways in which we can exercise control over how they treat us. Most acts of trust involve acquaintances whom we see regularly. Should they abuse our trust we can punish them through direct criticism, backbiting, withdrawing our affection, removing their privileges, and even legal action.

Having said that, there is an element of risk involved in any act of trust, as the negative consequences could often be disastrous should betrayal occur. Zhang Zhi-tong developed a 'Chinese' trust scale which specified the identity of the person whom the subject was trusting and found that closeness to the subject was very important indeed. So, for example, Chinese trusted their inner circle much more than their acquaintances. This outcome is hardly surprising. What was noteworthy, however, was the finding that Chinese in the People's Republic of China and Hong Kong were more trusting towards this inner circle than were comparable Americans. But there was no cultural difference in the willingness to trust strangers.

This research indicates the importance of specifying the target of the behaviour being investigated when one compares cultural groups. All men are *not* believed to be created equal in collectivist societies; relationships are critical, especially those involving family. It is not by accident that Taiwanese divorcees, for example, are more willing to confide in their mothers than are American divorcees, who choose their friends as confidantes! In Chinese culture one's inner circle provides care and protection, over time, so that one can afford to expend less energy building a 'safety net' elsewhere.

## Values

Values are very abstract concepts, and very general. They refer to goals, like family security and inner harmony, or to means of achieving those goals, like modesty and intelligence. Values are thought to exert a broad influence over any related activity.

Social scientists use values to explain differences in behaviour among various groups in the same society or among various societies. So, for example, Lucian Pye explains authoritarian, one-man rule in Chinese culture as deriving in part from the high value Chinese place on hierarchy, social order, and group cohesion. Used in this way, values are generally inferred from other observations, not measured directly. Consequently, the value concept often becomes a 'ghost in the machine', trotted out by the social scientist to jump the hurdles of the behaviour differences he or she is trying to explain. There is a considerable need to know what studies of value have shown about the Chinese in order to put such theorizing to the test.

Yang Kuo-shu summarized the recent work on values for his chapter in *The Psychology of the Chinese People*. He concluded that contemporary Chinese students in Taiwan tend to value inner development, individualism, a future perspective, and mastery over nature rather than the traditional Chinese values of inner development, collectivism, focus on the past, and submission to nature. These young Chinese prefer a moderate and balanced life combining action, contemplation, and enjoyment. They accept social restraints, are concerned for others, and wish to preserve good traditions. They consider that sensuous enjoyment, sheer meditation, and silent submission to external forces should be avoided. Their interests are theoretical and aesthetic rather than economic and religious. They value conformity and benevolence more highly and interpersonal support and social recognition less than American students. They see collective welfare and social concern as more important than personal enjoyment and feeling. They value social and moral goals more than personal goals and competence, although there is a gradual change towards individualism and self-orientation.

The reader will note a few surprises in this summary. Firstly, values related to achievement and worldly success receive high endorsement, a fact also noted by Lau Sing and Norm Feather in their work with Hong Kong and mainland Chinese. Secondly, there is an inexorable movement away from the older stereotype of the Chinese as contemplative and passive. The traditional endorsement of social order and responsibility to the collective that many associate with the Chinese does, however, remain.

Nevertheless, there are problems associated with this work. Firstly, the tests of values are imported from the United States and may be culturally biased. Secondly, most studies involve comparisons between Taiwanese and American students, a contrast almost guaranteed to produce differences! What we cannot know from these studies is how Chinese societies compare among themselves and with other non-Western countries.

My own multicultural survey of specifically *Chinese* values (including moderation, self-restraint, protecting one's face, and so on) among people from 19 countries produced some fascinating results:

1. People from many non-Chinese cultures endorse certain 'Chinese' values more strongly than do the Chinese! So, for example, Indians, Pakistanis, and Bangladeshis endorsed the 'Chinese' values of filial piety, respect for tradition, and chastity in women more highly than did the Chinese in Singapore, Hong Kong, the People's Republic of China, or Taiwan.

2. Chinese cultures do not endorse the same values. On a dimension of collectivism, Singapore, Hong Kong, the People's Republic of China, and Taiwan occupied positions 10, 7, 4, and 1.

Some stereotypes about 'the Chinese' may disintegrate once broad, multicultural studies are undertaken using a comprehensive, 'culture-fair' measure of values. Shalom Schwartz is currently leading such a study, the early returns of which are fascinating. For example, one item contrasts selfless values like a world at peace and helpfulness with self-enhancing values like achievement and social power. Three groups from China score in the lowest 20 per cent of all groups on this item. Groups from Taiwan and Hong Kong are more moderate on this dimension, as their modernization might lead one to expect. A second contrast involves 'conservation' values like family security and obedience and 'change' values like independence and novelty. Here most of the Chinese cultures are close to the conservation end of the dimension which the exception of the sample from Guangzhou, China, which falls in the 'change half' of the spectrum.

Such research indicates the potential problem of using values alone as a way of explaining Chinese patterns of behaviour. The Chinese do not agree very strongly among themselves, and other cultural groups may be 'more Chinese than the Chinese', at least with respect to values. We must look to other concepts, like social rules or the probable outcomes for actions, to help us explain behaviour *along with values*. And, of course, we desperately need more usable data on values from the Chinese in the People's Republic of China. Such knowledge would be especially important in enabling social scientists to assess the best strategies for implementing China's modernization policy.

## Perceiving Others

Here we ask how the Chinese make judgements about another person's emotional state and personal character — what information they use, what categories are important, how they are combined to yield an impression, and what their implications are for behaviour towards the perceived person. As is so often the case, most of the research in this area is piecemeal and based on Western models. Some of the work, however, is most instructive.

### Emotional Behaviour

One of the reasons members of different cultural groups find one another 'inscrutable' is that they do not know how to interpret aspects of one another's emotional behaviour when they are together. Such aspects, known to psychologists as emotional cues, can originate from any number of sources — a slowing of the speech, a raising of the eyebrows, an asymmetry of the posture, a tapping of the fingers — or their absence. It is important to master this 'code' of emotional behaviour if one is to function successfully in any cultural group. What do we know about the Chinese code?

#### The Experience of Emotion

The most comprehensive study of emotions is that organized in 27 countries by Klaus Sherer. His team looked at such issues as how frequently various emotions are felt, how intensely, and for how long; the subjective elements in the perception and expression of various emotions; respondents' views on the regulation and control of emotions; peoples' views on events that give rise to emotions and methods of coping with such events, and so forth.

The results of this study are still being analysed but some preliminary conclusions may be drawn:

1. The events that give rise to the seven key emotions (disgust, shame, fear, anger, guilt, joy, and sadness) are similar in all the cultural groups.
2. There are strong cultural differences in the frequency, duration, and intensity with which various emotions are felt.
3. Interestingly, there are relatively few differences in the *experience* of controlling and regulating emotional expression. This finding runs counter to the often expressed belief that Orientals in general are trained to mask or suppress the expression of emotion. Thus, the Chinese may appear 'inscrutable' because they react less strongly to emotionally arousing events, not because they restrain the expression of intensely felt emotions. Perhaps the experience of 'swallowing anger' frequently enough leads one to feel that anger (and by extension, other emotions) less frequently, less intensely, and for a shorter time.

### The Display of Emotions

This muted strength of emotional *feelings* may result in the apparent moderation with which Chinese express emotions compared to Westerners. Certainly there are more rules surrounding the display of emotions in Chinese (and Japanese) culture. These rules may become so ingrained during socialization that, as adults the Chinese react less strongly to provocative events. They therefore appear more placid. This placidity is perfectly understandable against a cultural background which values respect for hierarchy, harmony in the family unit, and moderation in all things. Uninhibited emotional display is a disruptive and dangerous luxury that can ill be afforded. Westerners, operating under a different social logic, will often be amazed, appalled, or impressed by apparent Chinese control in the face of events they would find arousing. Thus probably arises the designation of the Chinese as 'inscrutable'.

### The Perception of Displayed Emotions

Having travelled this long road of reacting to events emotionally, experiencing the emotions, then displaying the emotions, we are left wondering whether Chinese perceive these displayed emotions in the same way as do other cultural groups.

The face is perhaps *the* major source of information about feelings as they arise during social interaction. The research of Paul Ekman in many countries shows that Chinese judge posed expressions of emotion to communicate the same feelings, for example, joy, anger, sadness, and so on, as do members of other cultural groups. The same appears to be true for vocal expressions of emotion. Given our common physiology and biochemistry, these findings may come as no surprise. They suggest that cultural heritage has little or no effect on what emotions are perceived *provided they are first given overt expression.*

## Perceiving Another's Character

Appreciating another's emotional state gives us information about his or her moods which can be thought of as temporary responses which take place during the course of social interactions. Also important is information about the deeper structure of personality, the more abiding core that we refer to as character or traits. How do Chinese know that a person is, for example, lazy, dependable, adventurous, or neurotic? Researchers have explored three processes that can help in identifying personality traits — attributions, stereotyping, and implicit personality theories.

### *Attributions*

The work here is based upon Western assumptions that the behaviour of a person may not provide information about his or her personality but may, rather, occur as a result of some external influence, such as luck or pressure from a third party. So, before one decides that the behaviour of another does yield clues about his or her personality, one must first eliminate explanations based upon external forces.

Chinese explain behaviour in terms of many factors. These factors include 'internal' aspects such as ability and effort, as proposed by Western theorists like Fritz Heider, but also items like mood and habit. External factors include the Western concepts of luck and the difficulty of a task but extend to items like *yuan* (the sense of shared fatedness) and health. How we use such terms for analysing the causes of behaviour has important implications for ourselves and for others. As an example, depressed people explain their failures as being due to internal or personal causes and their successes as being due to external factors. Thus, they take no credit for their victories in life and accept blame for their shortcomings.

How do Chinese explanations of other people's behaviour compare with those of people from other countries? Recalling our previous discussion of control over events, readers might surmise that Chinese would be generally inclined to use more external factors in accounting for human behaviour. In fact there is evidence to suggest that Chinese students explain their achievements and relationships in a less self-serving way than Americans or South Africans, taking less personal credit for successes and denying less blame for failures. This relative self-effacement is of course consistent with the Chinese emphasis on modesty, but, as it also occurs in anonymous questionnaires, it indicates a lower perceived emphasis on the role of the individual in achieving an outcome.

Achievement in school is of particular interest in the light of recent findings by Harold Stevenson that Chinese and Japanese children outperform their American counterparts in mathematics and reading skills. One reason for this striking disparity in achievement is that the Oriental children spend much more time doing homework. It turns out that Oriental mothers explain school success as resulting more from effort than from ability, whereas American mothers believe that ability is relatively more important. Stevenson believes that Oriental mothers push their children much harder to do homework than do American mothers. So, different explanations have momentous implications for achievement-related behaviour. Further explorations of Chinese explanations will undoubtedly reveal other important differences in their understanding of other social events.

*Stereotypes*

An observer requires considerable information about a person in order to make an attribution. We make many judgements about others more rapidly, however, on the basis of inferences we draw from salient features of the other person. For example, from research done in a number of countries, we know that baby-faced persons (that is, those with big eyes and a large forehead, and so on) are believed to be more dependent, less forceful, and more naïve than are those with more normal faces for their age. It is highly probable that Chinese make the same judgements about baby-faced adults as do the Koreans and the Americans, but as yet no data are available.

These ready-made packages of beliefs about particular groups of people are called stereotypes. They are quick and easy ways to structure our social world, anticipate what others will be like, and guide us in our behaviour towards those who fall into the appropriate categories. A few such stereotypes have been documented.

The characteristic of physical attractiveness has been widely studied in America, where a 'beauty stereotype' has been thoroughly detailed. In essence, persons judged as physically attractive are also judged as more extroverted and sociable, more competent and successful, but also as more egocentric and materialistic. Exactly the same double-edged sword of beliefs has been found in studies done at the Chinese University of Hong Kong. Both males and females hold these beliefs about both sexes. What is perceived as physically beautiful is also perceived as (mostly) good. The implications are the same, whether a person is likely to be chosen for a job, as a spouse, or for praise from a teacher.

Although physical attractiveness is a powerful determiner of impressions on its own, we do not yet know about its *relative* strength. Ken and Karen Dion, for example, have argued that:

Stereotyping based on facial attractiveness may be more prevalent or more likely to occur in societies which value a more distinctive and differentiated identity for the individual . . . than in societies in which an individual's identity is defined more by one's family, social position, and group allegiances.

Chinese students report that physical attractiveness is less important in their choice of friends than do American students. We do not know whether these self-reports accurately reflect the true role of physical attractiveness in actual encounters, but they are most suggestive.

There are probably many other physical characteristics that Chinese believe indicate personality characteristics. Chubbiness may be associated with health and success, height with intellect and dominance, and so forth. Also, some of the lore associated with the ancient art of face-reading may have filtered down to the general public.

Stereotypes about physical characteristics such as beauty may be universal. But attitudes towards specific groups of people reflect historical, economic, and political relations with these groups. One important group for the Chinese is Westerners, loosely defined as any Caucasian from Europe, North America, Australia, or New Zealand.

Chinese responses towards this group were set in the early days of gunboat diplomacy when Western economic expansion into China forced the Chinese to confront these aggressive foreigners. The salience of this group continues to the present day, as all Chinese societies are intimately involved with Western countries politically, economically, socially, and culturally.

The response to Westerners is epitomized in Chang Chih-tung's phrase, 'Chinese learning for the essentials, Western learning for practical applications'. This nineteenth-century guideline has

structured Chinese responses to Westerners from that time down
to the recent campaigns against 'spiritual pollution'. Westerners are
perceived as a threat precisely because of their technical competence and economic success. Persons from less 'advanced' cultures
do not merit serious consideration. The acknowledgement of Western prowess in the material realm is counterbalanced, however, by
a constant hand-wringing about their decadence in moral or spiritual matters.

This at least is the official line. In fact the average Chinese is
positively disposed towards Westerners, rating them only slightly
below the Chinese themselves on social morality (that is, kind,
honest, co-operative, and so on). On the positively valued dimension
of extroversion (adventurous, outgoing, enterprising), the Chinese
actually rate Westerners as higher than their own group. The generally
positive stereotype of Westerners held by Chinese is one that actually
facilitates the Chinese drive towards modernization.

One of the five cardinal relationships in traditional Chinese thinking
was that of husband to wife, with the wife playing handmaid to the
dictates of her husband. 'A husband sings, the wife hums along',
as one Chinese saying puts it. In this scenario a woman did not
serve her family of origin after marriage and so was lost as an asset
to her parents. Not surprisingly, even to the present day, male
offspring are strongly preferred, to the point where China's 'one-
child policy' foundered in part on the shoals of this prejudice.

The demands of Confucian social logic, coupled with a labour-
intensive, agrarian economy, conspired to assure women a subordinate
and decidedly second-class citizenship with respect to men. Rigid
role differences meant that when women did work, they occupied
jobs of lower status than men and received unequal pay for whatever
work they did. This role discrimination persists today despite
women's access to education and skilled jobs in such societies as
Singapore and Hong Kong.

Even in contemporary China, and despite the egalitarian cant,
women are conspicuously absent from positions of political authority
and are still lumbered with the primary responsibility for childcare.
They are the first to be laid off in times of economic crisis, with
employers then being relieved of liability to pay maternity benefits.
Many employers refuse to hire women in the first place, claiming
that they are illiterate. In fact four-fifths of children not at school
are female. Parents often consider it a waste to educate girls and
want an economic return before their daughters are lost to them

through marriage. Thus the cycle of female bondage and dependence is perpetuated.

These daily realities are reflected in the stereotypes that both men and women hold about the sexes. Women are endowed with the 'communal' virtues of kindness and consideration, but also with the deficits of subjectivity, unpredictability, and weakness. Men on the other hand are graced with the 'agentic' (purposive) qualities of courage and energy, logic and independence, although they are also perceived as aggressive and thoughtless.

Similar beliefs are found in other countries, although agreement on the stereotypes of men and women varies. John Williams and Deborah Best examined sex stereotypes in 25 countries, with smaller samples from three other societies, including Taiwan. The investigators assessed respondents, using check-lists of items associated with men and with women. The items on the list for the male stereotype were endorsed by 90 per cent of the Taiwanese sample — the highest level of endorsement in any of the societies! The corresponding rate for the female stereotype was only 79 per cent, about mid-point in the ranking of the 28 groups. So, the male stereotype in Chinese culture is very strong while that of the female is less definite. This outcome suggests that considerable effort would have to be expended in order to 'feminize' the male stereotype held by the Chinese. Perhaps Chinese women will have to become more masculine, instead!

*Implicit Personality Theory*

Information about others is valuable in part because it allows us to make guesses about other, unknown aspects of their character. If we know that someone is punctual, we are more likely to infer that the person is honest, considerate, and neat than vice versa. We are not, however, able to make inferences about whether the punctual person is talkative, neurotic, or intelligent. This is because people use a fixed number of clusters or attributes in perceiving others. If a trait like neatness falls within a cluster, then we presume that the neat person possesses the other traits in the cluster. But the person's neatness provides no information about traits falling into other clusters. This collection of clusters for any particular group is called its 'implicit personality theory'. It is 'implicit' because most people are unaware of its existence; it is a 'personality theory' because it allows those who hold it to make predictions about the character of others on the basis of limited information.

How many clusters are found in the implicit personality theory of the Chinese and why are these particular clusters important? As mentioned in the section above on the 'sense of self', Chinese use the same five clusters in perceiving others as they do in perceiving themselves. These clusters vary slightly in composition depending upon who is being described (father, friend, teacher, and so on), but contain certain core elements. So, for example, a 'socially oriented' person possesses the following characteristics: honest, good and gentle, loyal, cordial, kind, not selfish, not opportunistic, and not shy. A 'competent' person possesses these characteristics: determined, resolute, and firm, capable, not dependent, and not timid.

One purpose of perceiving people is to help us decide what to do with them — to join them in a project, to lend them money, to tell them our personal secrets, to criticize their clothing, to avoid them altogether. Research with Chinese and Westerners shows the same pattern of results in this regard. If a person is perceived as 'competent', that is, extroverted, then Chinese are more likely to want to associate with that person across a whole host of activities. Or if the person is perceived as socially oriented, that is, good natured, then Chinese are more likely to trust that person in a variety of ways.

What is instructive, however, is the *relative* emphasis the Chinese place on a person's extroversion and good nature in guiding their behaviour with that other person. Compared to Westerners (Australians, actually), Chinese place greater emphasis on good nature and less emphasis on extroversion in helping them to determine whom they will associate with and trust. This is because good nature is more useful than extroversion in a collectivist culture in which the maintenance of group strength is an important consideration.

## Summary

In this chapter I have been setting the stage for the discussion of Chinese interpersonal behaviour in the following chapter. We examined some of the characteristics of Chinese people that are relevant to social behaviour. These included the sense of self, key attitudes towards the social world and other people, values, the perception of emotion, and the assessment of character. These are elements in the collective consciousness of Chinese actors and provide us with an added perspective on the unfolding drama of their day-to-day exchanges with others.

# 5

# Social Behaviour

Virtue is the establishment of perfect harmony.
from *The Complete Works of Chuang Tzu*

IN THE LAST chapter we examined the internal characteristics of Chinese persons. Western social scientists, steeped in an unconscious philosophy of individualism, believe that these characteristics provide the foundation for the individual's social interactions. Rather like a lighthouse beacon, these individual dispositions sweep the ocean of one's daily encounters, the intensity of that beacon light remaining constant regardless of what is illuminated. So, an altruistic person, for example, will be generous towards beggars, colleagues, spouses, tourists — the lot. In consequence of this belief, Western social scientists place great emphasis on measuring individual dispositions of the general sort we examined in the last chapter.

The collectivist society is dramatically different. It pays close attention to the target of a person's social behaviour and the context of the interaction, historically and socially. As an example, Hwang Kwang-kuo has developed a model for understanding one element of social interaction — how people ration their input (their resources) in a social exchange. He argues that in Chinese society, with strangers one ensures that there is a constant ratio between both parties' inputs and gains. With family members, however, one does whatever is needed. In other words, resources are allocated according to need, not fairness.

A close examination of social behaviour in collectivist societies like the Chinese may be most instructive. It may reveal patterns and considerations that do not fit into present Western theories and results. These inconsistencies may spur us on to develop new or more sophisticated approaches to understanding social behaviour, Chinese or otherwise.

## The Non-verbal Realm

It is widely believed that people from individualistic cultures emphasize the content of speech as the key element in exchanges with others. 'My word is my bond', and the vehicle which bonds us together is our words. But we can convey any verbal message with a host of inflections, movements, and expressions, at different moments in our relationship, in many social contexts, and from any distance. These stylistic elements define the non-verbal context of an exchange. Edward Hall labels those cultures which emphasize the importance of these 'background' factors 'high context'. In such cultures, he says, 'most of the information is either in the physical context or internalized in the person, while very little is in the coded, explicit, transmitted part of the message'.

Although the scientific data are sparse, most psychologists would characterize Chinese culture along with the Japanese as high context. Using this assumption, we will examine the elements of time, space, and interpersonal synchronism in the encounters between Chinese. These are themes that are woven into our exchanges with others and play an especially important role in Chinese culture.

## Time

Robert Levine examined the pace of life in six societies, using measures such as walking speed, the accuracy of bank clocks, and the promptness of financial transactions. Taiwan was one of the slowest in his sample. On a recent visit to Hong Kong, however, Levine decided that this Chinese society was probably faster paced than Japan, the most time conscious of his original six. So, pace varies in different Chinese cultures, as anyone who has visited China and Singapore can attest! Levine's measures probably tap the degree of a society's modernization and Chinese societies span the spectrum in this regard.

What is less affected by industrialization is the way time is structured. Edward Hall contrasted two modes of structuring time, which he terms monochronic and polychronic time. As he has written:

I have termed doing many things at once, Polychronic, P-time. The North European system — doing one thing at a time — is monochronic, M-time. P-time stresses involvement of people and completion of transactions rather than adherence to preset schedules. Appointments are not taken as seriously, and, as a consequence, are frequently broken. P-time is treated as less tangible than M-time.

The approach of those on M-time is to put each event into a compartment, focus all energies on the completion of that event, and to remove all distractions, especially interpersonal ones, so that they can finish one event before proceeding to the next. Imagine such a person supervising, negotiating with, working under, or making love with a person on P-time! Phones are ringing, other friends are dropping in, medical emergencies are cropping up, repairmen are arriving, meals are being served, secretaries are needing your signature, and on and on, assuming, of course, that you have met at the appointed time in the first place!

Although there are no tests for measuring P- and M-time orientations, it is my judgement that Chinese are and will remain on P-time despite the demands of twentieth-century industrialization. The Chinese are fully capable of structuring events within their P-time framework by relying on the dictates of hierarchy and relationship to direct the unfolding of their lives together. If a particular interaction is not completed, a longer time perspective and a cyclic view of time will reduce any sense of panic. Everything will happen in *its* own time!

## Space

The study of the distances we keep between us and the amount we touch one another was brought to wider attention by Edward Hall's book, *The Hidden Dimension*. He argued that people use distance to regulate their privacy and the level of intimacy in an encounter, with greater distances being observed the more formal the gathering. Cultural groups vary, however, in the distances they keep and from whom. Hall used the terms 'high contact' and 'low contact' to characterize cultures in this respect, but these terms may be too general to capture the full picture. Studies have shown, for example, that Japanese touch members of the same sex more than do North Americans but members of the opposite sex less. Age, status, length of acquaintance, and so forth produce such wide variations in spacing and contact that it becomes difficult to characterize any group generally.

To my knowledge no comparative studies have measured the Chinese use of interpersonal space. Casual observation in urban environments would suggest that they are very tolerant of physical contact indeed, at least in public situations with strangers. Living in crowded environments with inadequate public facilities necessitates such a tolerance, of course, but there are many cultural groups that would refuse to strike this bargain. I expect that the Chinese experience of family living in close quarters predisposes them to prefer physical closeness, in all encounters except those with acquaintances of the opposite sex. This tolerance of limited space contrasts with a secretiveness about discussing personal matters with strangers, as we shall discover later.

## Interpersonal Synchrony

Again we are indebted to Edward Hall, who first pointed out in *The Hidden Dimension* that people carefully monitor their conversational distances, thereby creating a rhythmic dance as their interaction progresses. Hall later extended this analysis to all aspects of behaviour, claiming that, 'It can now be said with assurance that individuals are dominated in their behavior by complex hierarchies of interlocking rhythms.' He observed that this interpersonal synchrony or meshing was stronger among those in Latin American, African, and Asian cultures than among people from North America and Northern Europe.

Hall meant that members of these high-context cultures paid more attention to the interaction process itself. 'Getting into synch' became necessary for an exchange to succeed. So, interactions would take longer, especially greetings and farewells; verbal exchanges would be less explicit and important; careful note would be made of the pauses and the stillnesses during the exchange. A competent communicator in such a culture monitors the other's non-verbal displays carefully, proceeds with circumspection to discover the balance-point with the other, and considers fostering the relationship to be more important than prosecuting the business being discussed.

People from low-context cultures approach interactions ahistorically and purposefully, placing greater emphasis on verbal exchanges and agreements in structuring their relationship. Utterances are more explicit and binding. Exchanges are shorter and less formal. A competent communicator in such a culture is fluent, persuasive, precise, organized, and extroverted.

Hall's contrast between high- and low-context cultures in the area of interpersonal synchrony is rich and consistent with a host of observations about the Chinese, especially those concerning their negotiation behaviour. Hall emphasizes the difference in the relative importance of the verbal and non-verbal components of an interaction. To date no experimental tests of this difference hypothesis have been undertaken to compare members of any high-context culture, like the Chinese, with those of any low-context culture. Perhaps it would require a person from a high-context culture to design such an experiment!

## The Verbal Forum

The issues I wish to consider in this section are: with whom, and in what way? Observers from other cultures are often puzzled by Chinese talk and I hope that my consideration of these fundamental issues will help clarify the confusion.

### With Whom? Friends First

Chinese are reluctant to talk with strangers and will rarely initiate a conversation with someone they do not know. Americans, by contrast, place a high value on conversation as a vehicle for establishing relationships and hence find the Chinese stand-offish. The Chinese, however, make a critical distinction between established acquaintances and others. They communicate mainly with people they know and, within this circle of acquaintances, with family members in particular. Given that Chinese social needs are met by these existing associations, they see no need to interact with others. They ignore other people or regard any who initiate conversation with suspicion.

Of course Chinese do make new acquaintances. Usually, however, an intermediary known to both parties makes these introductions. This trusted intermediary is part of both social circles, effectively bringing the two strangers into contact. They will channel much conversation through this intermediary, especially during the first meeting. For this reason there is little need in Chinese society to develop the social skills needed to meet and talk alone to strangers.

### In What Way? The Indirect Approach

The verbal content of talk in high-context cultures like the Chinese tends towards indirectness. As William Gudykunst has written:

The direct verbal style refers to [the use of] verbal messages that embody and invoke speakers' true intentions in terms of their wants, needs and desires in the discourse process. The indirect verbal style, in contrast, refers to [the use of] verbal messages that camouflage and conceal speakers' true intentions in terms of their wants, needs, and goals in the discourse situation.

The indirect style is marked by features like questions instead of statements, adverbial modifiers like 'fairly', 'somewhat', and 'rather', the less frequent use of the first-person forms 'I', 'mine', and 'my', flattery in place of criticism, considerable repeating of the other's stated position before presenting one's own, more frequent referral to previous discussions, or parts of the present discussion, and so on.

The aim of such a style is to protect the relationship and allow the parties to the conversation maximum freedom of manoeuvre. A tentative approach permits the relationship to evolve harmoniously. No party will be frightened away from eventually presenting his or her true position by another's assuming an uncompromising stance. So, the Chinese feeling is that the truth is discoverable if people proceed circuitously. Silences are an important element in this process, and research indicates that Chinese are more comfortable and less threatened than Americans by such silences in a conversation.

This approach also makes good sense in a culture marked by strong differences in power and status. Given that 'One mountain cannot hold two tigers', an indirect style is sensible when one is, or may be, dealing with a superior. It is the superior's prerogative to command and a junior could be seriously compromised by making too forthright or precise an utterance. It is wise to remember that 'A word once uttered cannot be drawn back, even by a team of four horses.'

## Self-effacement

Social scientists observing Chinese verbal behaviour often mention their modesty, a tendency to play down one's own skills or efforts publicly, to flatter the other effusively, and to speak about group accomplishments rather than individual contributions. Of course, it is only those from an explicit tradition who would label this mode of discourse 'self-effacement'. Within the indirect tradition it might be labelled 'relationship honouring'. For the deflection of self-enhancing remarks protects a group from fragmenting and becoming a vehicle which serves only narrow individual interests. As Francis Hsu has written: 'The Chinese lack of emphasis on self-expression not only leads the Chinese child to develop a greater consciousness of the status quo but serves to tone down any desire on his (or her) part to transcend the larger scheme of things.' Given the importance of the group in Chinese society, the *I Ching* provides wise counsel when it advises that, 'Haughtiness invites ruin; humility receives benefits.'

*Self-disclosure*

The emphasis on an indirect approach means that Chinese will also reveal less about themselves, at least in the initial stages of a relationship. This slower revelation of intimate information is necessary in order to establish trust before one makes oneself vulnerable to possible danger through public exposure. And these dangers are considerable in a society which emphasizes moral rectitude and unchanging circles of acquaintances.

Once established as a 'close' friend, however, one will be made privy to wide-ranging and deeply personal knowledge about the other. It is as if, having crossed the moat of a carefully guarded castle, one meets no further resistance. Few, however, are allowed across.

Certainly the Western approach to the development of relationships is different. One reveals information about oneself as a strategy for establishing a relationship. Reciprocal exposure reveals whether there is sufficient similarity and trust for a viable relationship to develop. An individual's degree of self-disclosure varies according to the nature of the specific relationship. Each person retains a residue of personal privacy more resolutely than in cultures more focused on relationships.

*Instrumental versus Affective Communication*

An instrumental style of communication is goal oriented, and aims to bring the individual into a verbal exchange. People use words as tools to chisel an agreement from the intersection of everyone's goals for the interaction. Those in the instrumental position, like Americans, perceive speech as a resource for control and self-extension.

An affective style is relationship oriented, and its verbal content reflects the attempt of the speaker to adjust to the feelings of the other parties to the conversation. The participants are more concerned about the attitudes of the other parties than about the outcome of the conversation. Indeed, the enhancement of the relationship itself is likely to be the important outcome, even in business encounters. Chinese fall within this affective tradition, since one component of the indirect style values group harmony over individual assertion.

The emphasis on relationship and affect during verbal exchanges also means that people avoid confrontational, argumentative talk. In Chinese culture the light of truth does not arise from the clash of opposing opinions; too much is at stake. Disputants have long memories and the tide of power ebbs and flows in unpredictable directions. Yesterday's opponent may be tomorrow's superior and is likely to construe prior disagreements as proof of disloyalty. It is best to bite a fiery tongue.

Instead, people use their superior as a filter or arbitrator. Traditional court practice was for the magistrate to hear the evidence from each party, to send out his own underlings to assess the situation, and then to render a verdict. Superiors in any organization, be it family, club, or business, are constantly assuming this magistrate's role with conflicting subordinates who will not confront one another. There is thus what appears to those from an instrumental tradition of talk an inordinate amount of backbiting, gossiping, innuendo, and rumour in Chinese groups.

The Western tradition of straight talk, open debate, friendly disagreement, and loyal opposition has no place in an interpersonal system focused on relationship rather than 'truth', given that relationships are mostly hierarchical and involve wide discrepancies in usable power. Indeed, it is precisely this hierarchy that constitutes 'truth', not some Platonic form discoverable by logical or scientific enquiry. As the *Tao Te Ching* puts it, 'A good man does not argue; he who argues is not a good man.' This is the Mandate of Heaven and sound guidance to Chinese leaders below.

## Patterns of Associating

In discussing the verbal and non-verbal realms of social life, I have touched on many basic themes which characterize Chinese interpersonal behaviour. Many of these themes will reappear as we discuss more specific features and types of Chinese association.

### Interaction Profile

Ladd Wheeler developed a technique for recording peoples' daily interaction patterns, asking his informants to indicate various features of every encounter over a period of ten minutes. He and his colleagues then compared undergraduates in Hong Kong and the United States, confirming casual observations that had been made for decades.

A person who has a collectivist orientation towards social life concentrates his or her energy on a narrow group. One with an individualistic orientation, on the other hand, favours less intense interactions with a wider range of people. These encounters usually occur in groups of two, in which the individual can exercise greater personal control over the development of the relationship.

Research findings show that Chinese undertake fewer interactions than their American counterparts. But these interactions are longer, more often in groups, and with a smaller variety of associates than those of the Americans. Brian Little's work with undergraduates in Canada and China confirms that Chinese involve themselves in group activities both inside the university and in the wider community more frequently than their Canadian counterparts. It is probable that these characteristics of interactions apply also to other categories of Chinese, as none of the outcomes is dependent on the nature of university life.

## Social Categories

Hwang Kwang-kuo has argued that Chinese distinguish three main social groupings — family, strangers, and associates — with whom different sorts of relationship take place.

### Family

'Blood is thicker than water', especially in societies characterized by relatively fixed residence and the absence of government-sponsored social welfare. One's family is the only constant in a shifting, indifferent world, so this relationship is constantly emphasized and nourished throughout the lifespan. Resources are shared on the basis of the donor's sense of responsibility and the need of the recipient. One gives what and when one can without expecting early (or any) repayment. A sense of filial piety and parental responsibility fuels this pattern of open-handed exchange.

How widely the family is deemed to extend will vary. It may even include non-family members, if they are sufficiently close friends. Such close friends will often call themselves 'older brother' and 'younger brother', indicating the way in which they will treat one another.

### Strangers

Daily life throws Chinese into contact with a host of persons with whom they have a transient association which is unlikely to be repeated — taxi drivers, fellow passengers, sales staff, fellow spectators, tourists, waiters, and so on. There is no affective response towards such people, for they are outside one,'s established groups.

The law of the jungle tends to prevail, with people seeking their own personal advantage, totally indifferent to the needs and 'rights' of others. A careless pushiness, released by the absence of authority, is the order of the day. What Westerners would call rudeness and callousness are endemic to such encounters and result in some testy exchanges across cultural lines! They were certainly the inspiration for this remark by Ralph Townsend (an American consular officer posted to Shanghai in the 1920s) in *Ways that are Dark*: 'What we see among them [the Chinese] is complete indifference to supreme distress in any one not of their immediate family or associations, even where the most trifling effort would assist the afflicted person.'

The Chinese response is always based on the nature of a pre-existing, specific relationship. Strangers have no place in this social logic and are not mentioned in any of the Five Cardinal Relations. In this vacuum there are no constraints beyond self-interest to bind people together. And it was surely to this area of public behaviour that Sun Yat-sen was referring when he described the Chinese as 'a pile of loose sand'. Similarly, Sun Long-ji has written:

We may say that from birth, a Chinese person is enclosed by a network of interpersonal relationships which defines and organizes his existence, which controls his Heart-and-Mind. When a Chinese individual is not under the control of the Heart-and-Mind of others, he will become the most selfish of men and bring chaos both to himself and to those around him.

The only principle that might guide behaviour towards strangers is the Chinese 'golden rule' of Confucius, 'Do not do unto others as you would not have them do unto you.' This counsel, however, is in the negative and prohibits harmful acts rather than promoting helpfulness. It is quite different in its consequences from doing unto others as you would have others do unto you. This Judaeo-Christian dictum is another universal principle, but one that endorses an active reaching out to strangers. It finds its expression at the broader political level in constitutional safeguards for minority rights and a social welfare system; at the interpersonal level, in a greater willingness to assist the underdog. Such a principle operates less strongly in Chinese society.

### Associates

This is a broad category of persons to whom one is connected either directly or indirectly. Direct relationships include those deriving from school, shared residence, recurring economic exchanges, occupation, recreational activities, and so forth. Indirect relationships are those with persons who are themselves associates of one's direct contacts. One makes these indirect relationships by 'pulling' on one's direct relationship with someone who knows the party one wishes to meet.

This spider's web of interconnections, called the 'sodality' by Sun Long-ji, provides protection against an unpredictable world. In Chinese society, 'You cannot clap with a single hand', as Han Fei-tzu so aptly put it. One must therefore expend considerable effort to maintain and extend one's social bank account, thereby nurturing the sodality.

This is the territory of what Lin Yu-tang termed 'the female triad', favour, face, and fate. These three ladies dance at the ends of the loose threads dangling from the tattered robe of impersonal Justice. As Lin lamented, 'The most striking characteristic in our political life as a nation is the absence of a constitution and of the idea of civil rights.' Instead of rule by law, there was a long tradition of rule by magistrate's judgement. This in turn was a legacy of the Confucian belief that rulers would be virtuous, benevolent, and wise and hence need not be constrained in their administration of justice by Common Law. The social beliefs of most Chinese, however, are much closer in spirit to Lord Acton's contention that 'Power corrupts, and absolute power corrupts absolutely'. So, there is no refuge in the law. Rather, one's hard-earned achievements and one's personal relationships constitute the only source of stability in the fickle social world. Enter the female triad.

All social encounters may be regarded as exchanges of resources. We need others to provide us with the material resources, like food and shelter, necessary to sustain life. We also need others to provide us with the knowledge and skills necessary to interact efficiently with the social and physical environment. Finally, we need others to provide us with the acknowledgement, love, and respect necessary to sustain our spirit.

Of course, others need us just as we need them. We interact with these others, exchanging our labour, our friendship, our information, our affection, our appreciation, on a *quid pro quo* basis. Naturally, some people have a relative advantage in this process by virtue of their wealth, intelligence, attractiveness, skills, or position. In consequence they can command greater resources in the process of social exchange. They are worth more and, if they play by the rules of the social game, the Chinese say that they have 'face' (*mian zi*).

In the process of acquiring such face, these powerful people will have indebted themselves to various associates who have helped them, such as teachers, former bosses, confidants and so forth. The norm of reciprocity (*bao*) requires that they honour these social debts should they ever be called on to do so. Failure in this regard results in the loss of *lian*, also translated as 'face', but referring here to one's moral integrity as a civilized person.

This process is fair, but in the Chinese culture the *quid pro quo* is extended across greater periods of time than in other cultures and can be repaid indirectly to a third party. This is where the Chinese world of associates becomes so important. If an individual (X) needs a resource from a stranger (Y), he may be able to obtain it by 'pulling on his relationship' (*la guanxi*) with an associate (Z), who is also associated with Y, so long as Z is indebted to X and Y is indebted to Z. This Z may then be able to repay the debt which he owes to X by allowing Y to repay the debt owed to Z indirectly by granting Z's request. Complicated!

Of course the intermediary must first decide if he has sufficient 'face' in his relationship with the more powerful person to ensure that the request is granted. After all, to ask and be refused would be acutely embarrassing, since one would clearly have miscalculated one's own 'face value'. And a man who does not know his place in Chinese society disrupts the fine balance of privilege and obligation.

Given the importance of having face and of being related to those who do, there is a plethora of relationship politics in Chinese culture. Name dropping, eagerness to associate with the rich and famous, the use of external status symbols, sensitivity to insult, lavish gift-giving, the use of titles, the sedulous avoidance of criticism, all abound, and require considerable readjustment for someone used to organizing social life by impersonal rules, frankness, and greater equality.

A word or two is in order at this point about the concept of lying. Research by William Carment indicates that, compared to Canadians, Chinese rate lying as less morally wrong and believe that liars show fewer behavioural changes when lying. The overriding issue with Chinese is maintaining smooth relationships, finding one's way as harmoniously as possible through a potentially contentious interpersonal world. As Carment has shown, Chinese rate the telling of 'altruistic' lies to strangers as more acceptable than do Canadians. It is embarrassing to argue with strangers, so one saves the face of all parties concerned by lying, as long as this is in the other party's 'best interests'.

Indeed, one may avoid conflict even more effectively by telling white lies, 'bending reality', and side-stepping differences. In a high-context culture such protection of relationships is often construed to be a higher good than a slavish adherence to what is, after all, only one person's limited perspective on reality. This kind of thinking can in fact dispel much of the anxiety associated with lying, so that one shows fewer behavioural changes when lying, just as the Chinese believe. In low-context cultures where the pursuit of truth supersedes the maintenance of relationships, false utterance is a serious matter indeed. These different forms of social thinking are basic sources of irritation in cross-cultural interactions. Westerners accuse Chinese of being 'evasive' or 'duplicitous'; Chinese (but only when pushed) accuse Westerners of being 'insensitive' or 'blunt'.

Lest this social logic seem too starkly oriented around power, there is the redeeming leaven of favour. If all decisions were made solely on the basis of one's already acquired face, then no one could 'pull' on connections beyond his own status. There would simply be no pay-off for the person with more face to grant the request of someone with less.

In such a case the petitioner can request that the allocator show favour (*ren qing*). Such a request implicitly acknowledges that the petitioner lacks the present face legitimately to claim a *quid pro quo* exchange. Instead of appealing to the allocator's social bank balance, the appeal is to his compassion, vanity, or sense of responsibility. In exchange for this undeserved favour, the recipient will show his gratitude in a variety of ways — dedicated service and unswerving loyalty, 'padding' the superior's face by lavishly praising his bene-factor and undermining his detractors, and so forth. If there are no opportunities to repay through such acts of respect, there is no cause for worry, because memory persists and our circles of association may intersect in the future, even if that future is a generation away.

There is, of course, a more self-serving component in the showing of favour. Position in Chinese society was never guaranteed by virtue of class, caste, or clan. Nor was political fortune ever stable, even within one person's lifetime. 'Heaven's way always goes round', and it would be wise to anticipate such personal vicissitudes as well as merely resigning oneself to accept them in the fatalistic, Chinese way. In such anticipation one would be prudent to show favour to others on the way up since one might well need it from these others on the way down! And if not oneself, perhaps one's prodigal son . . .

Indeed, the Chinese have a rather affectionate relationship with Fate, the great leveller. Westerners are very combative with Fate, regarding her (feminine, of course) as the measure of their ignorance and their inability to bend Nature to their wills. They struggle mightily against her dictates and often respond to failure in life's struggles with depression. As we have seen in the previous chapter, however, the Chinese believe that there is a much larger element of the unpredictable, the uncontrollable, and the predestined in our lives. In the interpersonal sphere this aspect of Fate is termed *yuan*. As Yang Kuo-shu has argued, an acceptance of *yuan* provides a ready external explanation for both propitious and calamitous outcomes in social life, thereby buffering people from intense feelings of elation or regret. Given the instability of the Chinese form of government and the arbitrariness of those in powerful positions, a cheerful submission to the vagaries of Fate is a functional response, indeed. It is a major component of that marvellous equanimity one so often admires in the Chinese.

### Basic Social Behaviour

The features of Chinese social behaviour discussed above weave their influence throughout the two major dimensions of interpersonal behaviour, affiliating as opposed to fighting, and leading, as against following. In this section I shall consider various aspects of association and hostility and shall leave the question of leading versus following until the next chapter, which deals with behaviour in organizations.

### Affiliating or Fighting

This contrast is concerned with whether two or more people support, ignore, or oppose one another; form a union, leave one another alone, or draw battle lines. These basic orientations take many forms, of course, and I shall explore only those for which social scientists have collected evidence.

#### Affiliating

Chinese spend a great deal of their time associating with their family. Indeed, many parents put pressure on their children, even when grown, to do so, regarding it as an aspect of filial piety. The parents also influence their children's associates to a degree that Western offspring would regard as oppressive, intrusive, and restrictive. The epitome of this control is found, of course, in the parents' selection, or capacity to veto the selection, of their child's spouse. The unity of many Chinese families has been cemented or irrevocably destroyed by this issue.

Outside the ambit of the family, however, there is some freedom in choosing friends. At school, for example, one has a range of possible companions and those chosen as friends will often remain close companions throughout life. Who is chosen? When American high school students are asked, they indicate that they select as friends class-mates who are cheerful, enthusiastic, good-looking, friendly, and sociable. Chinese high school students, however, report that they make friends with those who are humble, altruistic, honest, hard-working, tidy, good at schoolwork, and amiable.

The contrast is striking. The Americans emphasize sociability and prize those attributes that make for easy, cheerful association. The Chinese emphasize deeper attributes, focusing on moral virtues and achievement. These characteristics are essential components to long-term relationships requiring loyalty and sacrifice. They are especially important in a collectivist society, and Chinese will place more emphasis on these qualities in their choice of friends at any time of their life and in any social context than will people from less collectivist cultures.

*Heterosexual Behaviour*

In Brian Little's research on the activities of undergraduates, he found that Canadians spent proportionally more of their time engaged in 'intimate' projects than did the Chinese. These intimate projects involved various activities with a single other person of the opposite sex. This finding, corroborated by Ladd Wheeler's research, supports Francis Hsu's contention that Western society is dominated by the husband-and-wife pairing. One's destiny in this system is to break free of one's family of origin and establish a lifelong relationship with a mate who will facilitate one's own growth through love.

In consequence of this thinking, Western parents give their children training, opportunity, and encouragement in the development of skills for dealing one-to-one with members of the opposite sex. The media in particular pander to the concerns of young people to be physically attractive, socially engaging, and interpersonally adroit. Not surprisingly, then, young adults in Western societies spend relatively more time in heterosexual interactions and are more comfortable in such exchanges than are Chinese.

It is very difficult to obtain comparative data on sexual behaviour because the subject carries such a taboo in Chinese society. The extent of its suppression may be judged from the results of a survey of basic knowledge conducted in China by Pan Sui-ming. He discovered that only 50 per cent of urban men and 30 per cent of urban women could give four 'yes's' to these questions *on the eve of their wedding*: Do you know (1) what the genitalia of the opposite sex look like? (2) that there is a female orgasm? (3) at least one basic position for intercourse? (4) that ejaculation is not harmful for a man? Books about sex, instruction in school, discussion in the media — all are markedly absent in Chinese culture and result in a sexually naïve populace.

The topic is so fraught with embarrassment that it is difficult to find respondents who will tell you what they know or what types of sexual behaviour they have undertaken. In a recent report from the Family Planning Association of Hong Kong, 16 per cent of the males with brothers reported that their brothers had had premarital 'sex'; 14 per cent of the females with sisters said the same about their sisters. The response rate, however, was only 42 per cent, so one is left wondering how many of the remaining 58 per cent of the interviews were prematurely terminated by upset respondents and by how much the figures obtained were therefore inflated. But no amount of hand wringing about difficulties in data collection can mask the striking differences. Vernon Raschke found that seven times as many American undergraduates reported experiencing coitus in the preceding year as did Hong Kong undergraduates. Other forms of sexual activity were similarly low.

These findings can all be related to the importance of the father-son bond in Chinese society. As Francis Hsu and others have pointed out, the dictates of filial piety bind the son to the authority of the father, demanding loyalty and obedience in repayment for care and protection. The sex drive pulls sons away from the exclusive bonding to their parents. It also interferes with the father's involvement in the activities of the son, by focusing the son on the attraction he feels for his wife. And finally, an acknowledgement of sexuality undermines the power structure of the family by humanizing the parents with desires shared by their adolescent children. The net result, as Sun Long-ji concludes, is that: 'To maintain social harmony they must desexualize the individual, that is, make him unaware of his own sexuality.' The consequences of this silent conspiracy are an avoidance of contact(s) with the opposite sex before marriage, ignorance about the biology of sex, low levels of sexual activity, and a widespread moralism about sexual propriety.

## Pragmatic Love

Godwin Chu is a sociologist who has studied courtship in contemporary China. He reports that the listing of desired traits in a spouse there emphasizes very practical considerations, such as the prospective spouse's income, ability to provide housing, unwillingness to have parents living with them after marriage, and so forth. Romantic considerations like intense feelings, physical attractiveness, a sense of spiritual partnership were relatively less important. Similarly, research on types of loving carried out by Clyde and Susan Hendrick showed that students of Oriental origin in the United States endorsed pragmatic and friendship-based styles of affection much more than affection based on passion and emotion, while Americans did the reverse. The Hendricks concluded that, 'Oriental students seemed relatively low in affect.' Given American divorce rates, many Orientals would heave a sigh of relief, of course!

In this regard it is worth noting the low rate of outmarriage among Chinese. A Canadian study reported that only 0.4 per cent of Chinese marriages of Chinese people in Canada involved a non-Chinese partner. This figure was comparable to the rates for Portuguese and West Indians but greater than those for Jews, Italians, and Ukrainians, and strikingly lower than those for Germans, English, and native-born Canadians. This indication of pressures for marriage within the group is related to a number of possible themes in Chinese social life, not the least of which is the favouring of practical over romantic considerations in the choice of marriage partners.

Relationships in general, and marriage in particular, are very much family affairs in Chinese and other collectivist cultures. The interests of the two key partners are relatively subordinated to those of the families involved. Passion is a volatile and disruptive element in this arrangement and must therefore not be allowed free rein. The demand for social order thus extends its reach into public conceptions of romance, just as it does into the privacy of one's sexual behaviour.

## Violence

The polar opposite of warm association is destructive fighting. The basic Chinese orientation towards any form of assault is encapsulated in the stark aphorism: 'It is better to be a dog in times of peace than a man in times of war.' Since fighting usually breaks out over a dispute about some resource, an attack signals a breakdown in the social pattern by which privileges and responsibilities are assigned. Given that the Chinese order relationships by hierarchy, the ensuing struggle is often therefore a fight to the finish followed by vindictive retaliation to re-establish undisputed ranking. With this social logic and their history, it is not surprising that Chinese avoid open hostility like the plague. It portends the dreaded spectre of *luan* (chaos).

Rates for violent crime in Chinese societies are therefore low compared with those in other cultures. Of 51 political entities reporting homicide to the United Nations in 1986, Singapore and Hong Kong were twenty-first and thirty-first respectively. By contrast, the United States was eighth, with 8.5 persons killed per 100,000 population. Had China reported its rate of 1.0 per 100,000 (for 1985), it would have assumed forty-first position, just ahead of the Netherlands and Greece. Rape is ten times as frequent in Guam as in Singapore; physical assault figures are about 50 per cent higher in England than in Taiwan. These relatively lower rates of violence are of course reinforced by harsher punishments for such crimes. Retribution in a basic concept in Chinese social life and probably supports beliefs about the deterrent effects of sentencing and punishment.

## Conflict Management

Chinese believe that the initiation of any kind of dispute is an invitation to chaos. In consequence they will avoid direct confrontation if possible, and arrange it indirectly if necessary. This tradition of aversion to disputes leads to many surprises for social psychologists conducting experiments on aggression that were originally devised in the West. Michael Madsen designed a board-game for assessing competitive and co-operative responses in children. When he changed the reward structure with children in the United States, he found that they would quickly shift from co-operation to competition. He could not, however, effect such a switch with Taiwanese or Hong Kong children by changing the reward structure. They continued to co-operate even when it was in their own interest not to do so. The demands for interpersonal harmony are too strong to be overcome by temporary economic advantage.

Of course situations inevitably arise in any cultural system where one person's interests clash in important ways with those of another. The research of Kwok Leung has shown that whenever such incendiary conditions arise, Chinese respondents will opt for non-confrontional approaches to their resolution to a greater extent than, say, Canadians or Dutch. These strategies include 'indirect' confrontation through mediators or arbitrators, or avoiding reactions, like falsely promising or withdrawing and waiting. They perceive these styles of responding as more likely than, say, face-to-face negotiation to enable them to avoid hostility while still securing control over the outcome of the dispute for themselves. Westerners place an equally high premium on avoiding hostility and controlling the outcome of disputes, but believe that direct consultation between the two key parties is more likely to achieve these goals. The cultural differences here revolve around contrasting expectations about the consequences of direct versus indirect approaches to potentially volatile situations. The Chinese shun the adversarial logic of the West, as they believe it will leave lingering animosity.

### Verbal Abuse in Public

Encounters between contending parties do, of course, occasionally degenerate into open abuse and name-calling. Although these verbal slinging matches (*ma zhan*) are infrequent, they typically arise in public situations involving strangers, such as hawkers and their customers, motorists and pedestrians, fellow travellers on a bus, and so forth. Both sides unleash a torrent of shouting and criticism, drawing a great crowd of bemused onlookers. Despite the provocations these vocal duels rarely lead to physical assault. Usually, of course, friends are present to restrain the two parties, but in any case the pay-off appears to reside in verbally bettering one's opponent, not in humbling him or her physically. Again, the powerful restraints against doing bodily harm dictate the manner of the attack on the other. 'A civilized person uses his mouth, not his fists!'

### Summary

Yang Kuo-shu has written extensively about the 'social orientation' of the Chinese. By using this term, he wishes to emphasize the importance that Chinese people attach to harmonizing the various interpersonal forces and social interests which are at work in any social situation. Training in this awareness begins early, under the tutelege of those holding unquestioned authority — parents, elder siblings, older relatives, senior school-mates, and teachers. The 'forces at work' in social situations thus tend to be those one knows closely who occupy positions of power. This basic consideration imparts a collectivistic, authoritarian character to Chinese social life. Like its opposite, democratic individualism, this approach to the complexities of living is Janus-faced, yielding both attractive and destructive consequences. This chapter has explored these consequences in the verbal and non-verbal realms, in patterns of association, and across the primary dimension of social behaviour — co-operation and joining, as opposed to fighting.

# 6

# Chinese Organizational Life

Do not repeat the tactics which have gained you one victory,
but let your methods be regulated
by the infinite variety of circumstances.

Sun Tzu, *The Art of War*

THE ECONOMIC success of the overseas Chinese is legendary. The 1987 figures for GNP per capita for Hong Kong and Singapore (expressed in US dollars) were $8,070 and $7,940 respectively, extraordinary indeed given their humble position in the early 1960s; during the past twenty-five years Taiwan, China, Singapore, and Hong Kong have recorded economic growth rates of 7.0, 5.2, 7.2, and 6.2 per cent respectively, while the United States could only manage increases averaging 1.5 per cent. In the Philippines, Indonesia, Malaysia, and Thailand, the overseas Chinese account for a minority of the populations but control about 75 per cent of each country's private-sector capital.

These stunning levels of performance have drawn considerable commentary by pundits eager to solve the Chinese puzzle-box and isolate the magic formula for success. There are, of course, important economic factors sustaining the 'East Asian economic miracle', such as an absence of powerful labour unions, stable political climates, governments supportive of business, and a world economy hungry for the light manufactured goods produced by the 'dragons' of Asia. Many also believe that there are important psychological components to this successful alchemy, such as an abundance of entrepreneurial vigour; the Confucian values of obedience, thrift, self-restraint, and the importance of the family; and the genius of Chinese organization.

In this last regard there is some dissent. Writing about Chinese organizational behaviour in *Ways that Are Dark*, Ralph Townsend asserted that:

They have most of what it takes, in the modern world, to make things work. They have a talent for obedience, when well supervised. They have industriousness and intelligence. But two other essentials, honesty and willingness to coöperate, they emphatically lack, and some deeply inner ingredient of character seems to militate against remedying this lack. They simply cannot work among themselves in large undertakings. And they do not have a satisfactory mental connection between academic ability and practical application. But the worst of their deficiencies is their treacherous disloyalty. They seem ever prone to work against one another rather than coöperatively, though they are very fond of membership associations expressing a theory of coöperation, but never achieving it. (p. 13)

This vitriolic portrait gives one pause when one is considering what contributions Chinese organizations and Chinese behaviour in organizations could possibly be making to economic success. Of course, Townsend was an American diplomat describing China in the 1920s. Perhaps he was exposed only to that limited sector of China seen by foreigners. Perhaps the psychological realities of early twentieth-century Shanghai are irrelevant to contemporary Chinese cultures. Or perhaps more simply Townsend was perversely biased in all his interpretations regardless of what he experienced.

Clearly, the role of culture in business practices is both provocative and contentious. I propose to begin exploring this interface by relating Confucian philosophy to management and economic growth. Then I will consider some important features of Chinese organizations. Most of these data are drawn from research on businesses in Hong Kong, Taiwan, and Singapore, but their connection to recent experiments with bureaucracy in China is instructive. Then we will move to the interpersonal level and summarize research on leadership, following, and human relations in the workplace. This chapter will attempt to apply the ideas and findings about the psychology of the Chinese people already presented in earlier chapters.

## The Confucius Connection

Much has been laid at the door of the Confucian legacy — Max Weber used it to account for China's economic backwardness, just as Herman Kahn invoked it fifty years later to account for the economic brilliance of the overseas Chinese. Obviously, Confucianism is a mansion with many rooms! In the hands of a creative writer it can be used to decorate a number of designs.

It fits the purposes of social scientists especially, because its teachings are so thoroughly this-worldly and interpersonal. However, it must be remembered that as few Chinese have read Confucius as Westerners have read Aristotle or John Locke. The question is not what Confucius and his disciples said, but what contemporary Chinese believe. Even those beliefs are only of value to social scientists if they relate to how people behave. How Confucian are Chinese people and what difference does it make?

## Confucian Values and Economic Growth

George Hicks and Gordon Redding have applied their considerable skills to reviewing the various explanations offered for the 'hyper-growth' of the East Asian dragons. After reviewing the economic explanations for the unpredicted and unprecedented levels of growth in these countries, they conclude that:

the determinants of the post-Confucian 'economic miracle' are immensely complex . . . It is possible to see any full explanations as including elements from three categories of 'fact', all three layers being interconnected within themselves:
1. Economic policies adopted in a country.
2. Structural and institutional elements within a country, such as the forms of government, of industrial organization, and the legal and other infra-structures.
3. Cultural elements drawing from the country's history, carried partly by its religions, and evident in social values and ideals.

Herman Kahn earlier surmised that these key values and ideals include:
1. Family socialization to promote sobriety, education, skills, and diligence.
2. Devotion to group over individual interests.
3. A respect for hierarchy and an acceptance of the complementarity of relations.

Subsequent research by a group of psychologists called the Chinese Culture Connection identified a cluster of Chinese values which have been associated with high levels of economic growth between the 1960s and the mid-1980s. They labelled the cluster 'Confucian dynamism'. It involved the following items:

| *Relatively important* | *Relatively unimportant* |
|---|---|
| Persistence and perseverance | Personal steadiness and |
| Ordering relationships by status | stability |
| and observing this order | Protecting one's face |
| Thrift | Respect for tradition |
| Having a sense of shame | Reciprocating greetings, |
| | gifts, and favours |

The three political units with the highest scores on this bipolar dimension are Hong Kong, Taiwan, and Japan, with average annual growth rates of 5.9 per cent; the three with the lowest scores were Pakistan, the Philippines, and Nigeria, with a corresponding rate of 2.6 per cent.

Clearly the average endorsement of certain Confucian values, like hierarchy, is connected to economic buoyancy; that of other Confucian values, like reciprocation and face, to relative stagnation. The Confucian legacy is multifaceted and only some aspects of it are related to contemporary economic vibrancy. Some of the Confucian heritage appears to be progressive; some, retrogressive. Ironically, many non-Chinese societies endorse some of these Confucian values more strongly than do many Chinese societies. We should therefore regard glib generalizations and *ex cathedra* pronouncements by pundits with scepticism and subject them to empirical scrutiny.

### Confucian Themes in Modern Management Theory

The universal practicality of certain Confucian principles is reinforced when we relate his philosophical themes to current Western speculations about management. Oded Shenkar has identified a number of similarities between the Confucius of the *Analects* and the Human Relations School of management theory, as represented in the writings of Douglas McGregor, Warren Bennis, and Rensis Likert:

— formalized, detailed rules are destructive to human relationships;
— flexibility and versatility are essential qualities for a leader;
— leaders must delegate their authority and develop responsible subordinates;
— the leader must set a personal example of the commitment and morality he (or she) enjoins on subordinates; such modelling will influence those led to internalize such standards themselves;
— economic incentives are incomplete as a means of motivating subordinates;
— a leader must be courteous, friendly, helpful, and sincere in dealing with subordinates.

It is fascinating how basic ideals continue to resurface. As we will see, however, some ideals are easier to realize in certain cultural settings than are others!

## Characteristics of Chinese Organizations

An organization is a social setting within which human actors play out their interpersonal roles and psychological dramas. It is a context within which behaviour occurs, so that if we understand organizational features we will learn about the external constraints under which the Chinese operate. Most research in this area has been driven by our fascination with Chinese businesses. There are, of course, other organizations in which Chinese spend much of their time — academic, social, governmental, and so forth. We must take care in applying the findings in business to these areas.

### Structuring

One can ask many questions of an organization: who does what and how clearly is that 'what' specified? How many people report to which persons and across what range of responsibilities are they held accountable? Answers to these and other structural questions are in part determined by the size, products, and technology of the organization. There will, for example, be greater specialization of job function in larger organizations and less formalization of role requirements in a research team than on an assembly line.

If, therefore, we are to examine Chinese patterns of organizational structure, we must equate these background factors of size and type of output across the cultural groups being compared. We know from Gordon Redding and Gilbert Wong that, 'there is a tendency for [Chinese] companies to act as manufacturers or providers of a specific service within a larger chain of operations, but not to manage a whole chain by vertical integration.' So, Chinese companies will tend to be small providers of goods or services. Bearing in mind such background factors, what conclusions can we currently draw about Chinese organizational structure? Redding and Wong include the following:

(a) Centralization of the power of decision making, usually to a single dominant owner, manager, entrepreneur, founder, or father figure.
(b) A low level of specialization, with fewer and/or less breaking up of the organization into specialized departments, and with more people responsible for a spread of activities across a number of fields.
(c) Less standardization of activities and thus fewer routine procedures.
(d) A relative lack of ancillary departments such as research and development, labour relations, public relations, market research, and a tend-

ency instead for all employees to deal with the main product or service of the company.

The foregoing portrays a typical family business — hierarchical, informal, and intimate — with everyone undertaking a variety of activities to meet daily performance demands. In another study Gordon Redding and Richard Whiteley conclude, 'The erection of alternative co-ordination systems of a more classically bureaucratic nature, involving neutral, objective, contractual relations appears to be resisted in this culture.' What then happens in actual Chinese bureaucracies, especially government ones?

## Bureaucracy — Chinese Style

Many people regard the terms 'bureaucracy' and 'bureaucratic' as negative. They associate them with the evils of over-regulation, indifference to the man in the street, and excessive paperwork, since most people have had frustrating encounters with rigid bureaucrats, Chinese or otherwise.

The essential elements of any bureaucracy are usually derived from Max Weber's analysis and include the following, as outlined by Richard Hall:

(1) A well defined hierarchy of authority, (2) a division of labor based upon functional specialization, (3) a system of rules covering the rights and duties of positional incumbents, (4) a system of procedures for dealing with work situations, (5) impersonality of interpersonal relationships, and (6) selection for employment and promotion based upon technical competence.

Organizations having these attributes are an essential feature of twentieth-century life and people often overlook their beneficial aspects in their eagerness to find a scapegoat for their own personal frustrations. The Chinese have been confronting the frustrations of bureaucracy for over two thousand years and their experience is instructive.

Max Weber labelled the Chinese form 'patrimonial bureaucracy' and attributed China's stability and resilience to it. It is not a pure form, however. As C.K. Yang has written:

In China, the bureaucracy developed in a social system characterized by a diffuse social pattern, local self-sufficiency, local homogeneity by national heterogeneity, emphasis on the primary group with its network of intimate personal relations, and the importance of an informal moral order.

Many of the Confucian elements in the above description stand in marked contrast to the centralization, standardization, formalism, and impersonality of 'pure' bureaucracy. Not surprisingly, there were conflicts and tensions in the interplay of these two systems which paralleled the balance of power between imperial authority and local autonomy. Periodically, the bureaucracy broke down. The government of such a vast country as China, however, requires some form of bureaucracy, and the system has proved remarkably resilient throughout Chinese history. A brief look at the mainland Chinese experience with dismantling bureaucracies during the Cultural Revolution provides a sobering antidote to dissatisfaction with such organizations and speaks powerfully about the persistence of Chinese cultural themes.

### Debureaucratizing China

Oded Shenkar claims that, ironically, the Maoist opposition to bureaucracy was rooted in Confucian tradition. In the *Analects*, Confucius asserted that a gentleman becomes qualified for leadership as a result of his moral rectitude, not his technical and specialized talents. 'Once a man has contrived to put himself aright, he will find no difficulty at all in filling any governmental post.' Breadth and propriety are the key virtues. Furthermore, the ideal leader must not be trammelled by rules and regulations, nor must he impose a prison of guidelines on those he rules. An effective leader rules by force of personal example and astute assessment of each situation.

It was this Confucian resistance to technical specialization and restrictive regulations that formed the backbone of Mao's assault on government bureaucracy. For Mao, 'complete' knowledge required practical experience and political purity in addition to formal training. Detailed multiple rules strangled initiative from the lower echelons and gave higher echelons the means of 'control, restriction, and suppression' (*China News Summary*, 1975) — not to mention the means of resisting external authority outside their local domains!

The assaults on technocrats and regulations exploded during the Cultural Revolution, with attacks on 'bureaucratism', trained specialists being dismissed to the countryside for 'practical experience', and condemnation of the 'revisionist shackles' of procedural guidelines. Shenkar concluded, however, that 'the attempt to manage without a detailed division of labour and with virtually no regulations appeared to fail, producing minus consequences.'

These excesses have been reduced in recent years, with technical competence and procedural regulations assuming greater importance. The public demand for the establishment of moral (political) credentials continues, however, and is in line with the traditional Chinese practice of concentrating power into the hands of a worthy élite and ensuring that this power is legitimate. The Chinese tradition of trusting the unfettered leader means that there is a continued resistance to, or ignoring of, regulations which bind the hands of this élite from exercising unchallenged authority. As Geert Hofstede has argued, these fundamental beliefs about proper management are typical of cultural systems that are high in power distance, or hierarchical.

What is striking in this analysis of bureaucracy in China is the persistence of cultural themes over great spans of time. The alert reader will also see the connection between these themes and the research on organizational structure described earlier. Like Chinese bureaucracy, Chinese businesses outside China have low levels of formal control and specialization but high levels of centralization. Different political, social, and economic climates do not appear to change the basic cultural thinking on how to organize people. As the French are fond of saying, 'The more things change, the more they are the same!'

## Distinctive Features of Chinese Businesses

### Ownership

Chinese businesses are typically owned by a founding father. Because of the difficulty in Chinese culture of trusting outsiders with capital, a core group of family members retain proprietorial rights. The businesses generate money for development internally or from trusted associates of long standing. Ownership involves 'hands-on' management for the Chinese and it is rare to find technocrats and professionals in key positions, unless they are also insiders. Positions of financial control are especially sensitive in this regard.

### Size

Chinese business units tend to be smaller on average than their Western counterparts. For example, 92 per cent of all manufacturing companies in Hong Kong in 1981 employed fewer than 50 people. The result is that there is one business unit for every 18 people in Hong Kong; one for every 36 in the United States. This smaller figure arises from the Chinese view of the tight association between ownership and control. Given that ownership is confined to a small group of trusted family members, Chinese businesses only become large if they concentrate in one narrow sector where the owner is skilled and experienced, or when the company enjoys a politically assured monopoly, thereby permitting inefficiency.

## Impermanence

The decisive role of the owner-founder in Chinese businesses has a number of consequences. Given his distrust of outsiders, he fills key positions with close associates loyal to him. This inner circle tends to comprise direct family members or those related by marriage and may not include the most competent people available. When the owner-founder begins to step aside, the members of the inner circle often begin to struggle for control. Their loyalty is to the father-figure, not to one another or to some abstract code of professional procedure or power sharing. Tension and acrimony surface, typically among brothers and sisters. The company may be broken down into smaller units. But as the heirs who control them may not enjoy their father's skill, the company frequently disappears by the third generation. The exceptions to this rule are noteworthy by their scarcity.

## Interpersonal Relations at Work

Let us now consider interpersonal behaviour at work. We focus upon activities which occur when people interact to perform a task. Most of the available data come from observations in the workplace, but the reader will appreciate that many jobs are done outside the workplace, by teams whose members vary from strangers to family members. So these findings may apply in many situations, and overlap considerably with material presented in the previous chapter on social behaviour.

## Leading and Following

In all cultural systems some people have more experience, knowledge, training, strength, energy, skill, resources, and connections than others. These people assume or are granted positions of authority over their subordinates. Given the potential for abuse of such power, strong rules about leading and following are needed. In Chinese culture, the problem was broadly addressed by the

Doctrine of the Rectification of Names which asserted that 'The king shall be king, and the subjects shall be subjects.' Social harmony will be assured if a wise and benevolent leader makes decisions which loyal subordinates sincerely follow. This was the Confucian ideal of 'government by gentlemen', as Lin Yu-tang aptly put it. It required for its success that the leader was in fact the most capable to lead and unwilling to use his considerable power for his own narrow advantage. This of course was the ideal. What is the reality?

## Chinese Leadership

### Dimensions

Any task-oriented group has two basic concerns: to achieve the goal for which it was created as successfully as possible within the environmental and interpersonal resources at its disposal; and to maintain a level of morale among the team members so that their work sustains their spirits and members assist rather than hinder one another's performance. Research on leadership behaviour has consistently identified two groups of activities which relate to these two requirements. The first is called 'initiating structure' and involves all the actions of a leader that are directed towards planning and controlling the group's output. The second is labelled 'consideration' and refers to all the actions of a leader that are directed towards maintaining group harmony and enhancing positive sentiment among the group members.

Within this general framework a number of cultural issues may arise. The first answers the question, 'Which type of leader is most effective, the one who emphasizes initiating structure or the one who emphasizes consideration?' The consensus from research in Western cultures, such as England, the United States, and Holland, is that successful managers are high in *either* consideration *or* initiating structure. The type of leadership important for the group's performance depends on aspects of the job in hand and the external environment.

Similar research conducted in more collectivist cultural systems, such as the Chinese in Taiwan and the People's Republic, the Japanese, and the Indian, shows a marked difference. In these settings a leader has happier subordinates and higher outputs if he, or occasionally she, is high in *both* initiating structure *and* consideration.

In collectivist systems a leader has broad and unquestioned authority. He must therefore be more skilled in the performance aspects of the job, because no subordinate will compromise the leader by correcting him. He must, however, be perceived as kind and considerate to lessen the fear and avoidance his subordinates will show in the face of his unbridled power. The effective model for leadership in systems like the Chinese is thus the wise and loving father.

This combination results in a management style which Gordon Redding labels 'paternalism' in his *The Spirit of Chinese Capitalism*. The concept of paternalism includes 'the themes of hierarchy, responsibility [for the whole organization], mutual obligation, family atmosphere, personalism, and protection [of the employees]'. This style suits workers' desire for a more familial context at work and is in line with traditional deference to paternal authority. A paternalistic approach to leadership glues the organization together in a Chinese way, but does have consequences for how both managers and subordinates spend their time at work.

Although research on leadership behaviour repeatedly shows the two dimensions of consideration and initiation, recent research from China has revealed an additional striking dimension. In the mid-1980s Xu Lian-cang directed massive studies of workers in different sections of the Chinese economy. His team from the Institute of Psychology in Beijing identified a distinct third factor of leadership behaviour, labelled 'moral character'. This measure includes such characteristics as:

— a commitment to abide by the law and avoid corrupt practices;
— a (positive) attitude towards the Party and willingness to follow Party dictates even when they conflict with one's personal views;
— fairness to all employees;
— a (positive) attitude towards political workshops held during working hours;
— receptiveness to suggestions from workers.

Research with Chinese subjects outside China has not found this third dimension and its presence reflects the intense politicization of the workplace in post-revolutionary China. The concept of work and hence leadership is thereby broadened.

### Demonstrating Wisdom and Concern

As we have seen, a combination of high consideration and high initiating structure (and high moral character in China) is related to high performance in Chinese cultures. The obvious question which follows is *how* a leader shows initiating structure and consideration, the answer to which again shows cultural differences. In Hong Kong, for example, a leader behaves considerately by discussing a subordinate's personal difficulties with others in the subordinate's absence, spending time with subordinates both at work and after hours, and talking about work problems. Subordinates rate British managers as high on consideration if they demonstrate the use of equipment, give instruction on how to increase job skills, seek suggestions on improvements to working methods or conditions, and respond positively when they receive such suggestions. The contrast in how to demonstrate consideration is striking, with the Chinese manager more interpersonally oriented and the British manager more task focused.

Hong Kong managers show initiating structure by responding to suggestions for improvements, meeting frequently with subordinates, encouraging co-workers to help one another, and discussing the subordinate's career and plans. American managers demonstrate this emphasis on performance by dressing like their subordinates, showing disapproval of latecomers, and talking about the progress of work. Again, the contrast is striking and consistent with the Chinese emphasis on the general relationship rather than specific tasks. As with consideration, the potential for cross-cultural misunderstanding is enormous when managers from one group supervise those from another. Although they have the best of intentions, they may behave in ways that fail to have the impact they expect, or in some cases have a different impact altogether!

*How Leaders Spend their Time*

There is surprisingly little information on how leaders in different cultures spend their time, but general observation and the available research data suggest that Chinese leaders are 'bossier' or more authoritarian than their Western counterparts. Given the concentration of power in any position of leadership, they spend *less* time consulting in large meetings, reasoning with peers, persuading subordinates, making concessions within the workplace, writing memos, defining job specifications, developing subordinates, and instituting formal systems of control. Conversely, Chinese managers spend *more* time making decisions alone, giving orders, supervising the execution of these directives personally, participating in social and family gatherings with workers, dealing with employees' welfare concerns, managing the financial aspects of the operation, listening to complaints of subordinates about other employees, placating those whose 'face' has been insulted, having 'a quiet word' with a fractious team member, and using moral suasion to bring disaffected disputants into a grudging truce (privately, of course). Such are the consequences of paternalism, a management style that is centralized, personalized, and resists explicit formal guidelines and contractual obligations.

## Who Leads?

Those who lead in Chinese society are, simply, older men. Two of the Five Cardinal Relations involved the subordination of the younger brother to the elder and of the wife to the husband. Those basic rules permeate Chinese social life even in modernized societies like Singapore and Hong Kong. For example, a recent report by the Population Crisis Committee rated 99 political entities on the relative status of women and men. One of the key subscales in the area of employment concerned the proportion of females in the élite professional class, from which leaders are typically drawn. The Chinese societies of Hong Kong, Singapore, Taiwan, and China all scored in the bottom half of the societies studied. Similar conclusions may be drawn from the political realm, with the qualifier that age is an added advantage. To some degree these patterns will moderate with increasing wealth and modernization, but the cultural legacy of Confucianism will continue, giving men power with respect to women and the older with respect to the younger. Traditional stereotypes are very resilient.

## Chinese Entrepreneurs

A number of organizational and societal considerations produce a high level of entrepreneurial vigour in Chinese communities outside China. Firstly, the close relationship between ownership and control in Chinese businesses means that talented, enthusiastic outsiders are rarely promoted to responsible positions in somebody else's company. Secondly, Chinese outside China are often refugees or resented minorities. They therefore feel vulnerable, and this, combined with the Chinese drive to acquire social power, leads to a preoccupation with accumulating wealth. The result is the proliferation of small business units formed by entrepreneurs eager to exercise their own control and generate wealth for their own family.

Entrepreneurs are vital catalysts in any economy. They introduce new products, develop innovative production methods, open untapped markets, obtain access to fresh sources of supply, reorganize industries, connect suppliers to purchasers, orchestrate financial resources, and so forth. In short, they breathe economic life into a community.

Despite legendary stories of Chinese entrepreneurs, it should be noted that their failure rate is very high. In Hong Kong, 52,000 firms are incorporated every year, but another 35,000 disappear. Also, the entrepreneur is not responsible for the economic success of the overseas Chinese on his own. He needs a loyal cadre of diligent, flexible, and efficient workers to provide a commercial edge in a competitive vortex. The co-ordinating functions which this oft-neglected group perform are essential supports to entrepreneurial initiative.

These considerations aside, it must be acknowledged that there is a widespread hunger in Chinese culture to begin one's own business. One consequence of this eagerness is the high turnover of middle-level management in Chinese organizations. This attrition of ambitious and often talented persons limits the potential of these companies for organizational growth. It does, however, fuel a vigorous enterprising economy of small resourceful businesses. Given recent demands world-wide for export-oriented labour-intensive manufacturing, it is understandable that the overseas Chinese have prospered. Whether future conditions will favour Chinese entrepreneurship is, however, another question.

## Managerial Values

A word or two of caution is in order about the recent proliferation of 'research' on managerial values, especially that involving respondents from China. The typical scenario is that a teacher from a Western business school is invited to lecture on management at a sister university in China. Deciding to 'shoot two birds with one arrow', the enterprising Westerner takes along his or her favourite value survey and administers it to his or her class as part of the training. Upon returning home, the teacher finds a 'comparison' group of trainees, analyses the responses of the two samples, and draws a number of conclusions in an article on international management.

Such 'parachute' research is fraught with danger. Firstly, the teacher usually has no idea about how and why the Chinese respondents came to attend the course. Finding a genuinely comparable group at home thus becomes impossible. Secondly, although the measurement of values is cheap, easy, and quantifiable, it is a 'sensitive' topic and few respondents would expect or believe that their responses would be kept confidential. Therefore they will often modify their responses in order to look politically correct. Finally, research from a variety of cultures is questioning how close is the connection between one's stated values and one's actual behaviour anyway. So, if the reader is interested in values as a short cut to understanding how and why a person behaves, his or her strategy needs reassessment. Other issues, including translation (if it occurs at all), methods of data analysis, and selection of the values to be measured, add to the confusion. In short, *caveat lector*! For these reasons I will not review such research here, but add my voice of hope that future work in this area will be more carefully thought out.

## Chinese Followership

Leaders and those they lead live in the same society, so much of what will be said about following can be predicted from the preceding discussion on leading. Indeed, some topics, like staff turnover and deference, have already been considered. As always, conclusions are subject to political and economic considerations. Turnover, for example, is not a problem in China where one's work group provides housing, community life, political education, and permission to transfer elsewhere.

### Conformity

In a cultural system that gives wide-ranging power to those in authority, there must be a reciprocal emphasis on compliance and loyalty in those subject to that authority. As we have already seen, this socialization begins early in family life, with the prizing of quiet and tractable children. 'Instant, exact, and complete obedience' is the ideal.

In general, the available comparative data suggest that the Chinese conform readily. Most of these findings, however, relate to strangers thrown together into unusual research settings for the purpose of assessing their compliance to some distant authority's request or opinion. In such settings most subjects are probably more concerned about avoiding unnecessary conflict with these strangers through compromise than with assessing the issues.

What is obviously needed for a full understanding of this issue is observation of subordinates in actual interaction with their real-life superiors — parents, teachers, bosses, school seniors, and so forth. In this regard observation and research confirm the effects of the Confucian hierarchy. Subordinates are less likely to volunteer opinions, take individual initiative, or depart from standard operating procedures without a superior's approval. For the consequences of making a mistake will devolve upon the subordinate and there will be little institutional protection against the superior's wrath. Risk taking does not benefit subordinates, and so they conform.

*Disagreeing*

In every culture superiors take positions and subordinates sometimes disagree with their judgements. Society must cope with this fact of life in order to guarantee some degree of efficiency and co-operation. How is the revolutionary act of verbal opposition achieved in Chinese culture?

The basic rule is: 'Honour the hierarchy first, your vision of truth second'. The superior must always be accorded face, so one first agrees with whatever he or (occasionally) she has said. Only then is difference voiced, if possible through a third party, *and* in private. If a face-to-face confrontation is unavoidable, the subordinate will use mild ambiguous language in the hope that the superior gets the message without getting offended. Should these appeals prove ineffective, continued resistance may take the form of a 'go-slow' approach to the task, buttressed by energetic excuse making when called to account by the superior. At this point both parties will be aware that they are engaged in a power struggle and neither is likely to back down. They must then involve a superior third party to use his or her authority to forge a truce. As the face of both parties has now been compromised, however, only the departure or transfer of one of the two combatants will resolve the long-term situation. Agreeing to disagree does not work in Chinese culture.

Of course the situation rarely reaches such an impasse. Most superiors, especially those in a tight labour market, will have followed the paternalistic style of Chinese management by fostering a supportive relationship with subordinates. The boss will have secured their loyalty by attending weddings, taking his section to lunch, visiting sick family members in hospital, securing a mortgage, hiring a junior's relative, and so forth. The boss can then 'pull' on his personal relationship with subordinates to induce compliance, patch up differences among them, even give in to their privately voiced suggestions without losing face.

## Interpersonal and Inter-unit Harmony

Given the Confucian tradition of hierarchy, relationships within a work unit will tend to be familial, supportive, and relaxed. Such conflict as does arise is tinged with the kind of jealousy one often finds among siblings — the belief that one of the unit's members is specially favoured by the boss. Given that employees avoid trying to influence their equals, any such special relationship is a critical feature in a unit. Its existence prevents employees from utilizing the hierarchical strategy of appealing to the common boss about the disliked subordinate's behaviour. Many units have one or two long-standing employees who are tacitly exempted from fulfilling normal work expectations precisely because they enjoy such favoured status with the big boss. Often they are feared and suspected of acting as his or her spy. This resentment simmers below the surface, but it encourages others to seek the same favoured relationship with the boss. Such jockeying for position is universal, of course. It is, however, more pronounced in the hierarchical Chinese system, especially in a labour market where it is difficult to change jobs.

Another consequence of hierarchical allegiance is the formation of cliques. As Gordon Redding and Gilbert Wong put it:

Strength of identity with a group, however, introduces the risk of apathy about or even hostility towards other groups, and the question of the organization's internal effectiveness may well rest on whether the group to which a person belongs has aims which are in line with those of the organization.

Loyalties, being narrow, are rather more difficult to meld into an organization-wide affiliation. Usually their ambit is only as wide as the immediate boss's range of direct relationships. This consequence of paternalism often results in inter-departmental indifference, stone-walling, and competitiveness in Chinese organizations.

## Odds and Ends

A variety of topics generate considerable interest for outside observers and seem most appropriately slotted into this chapter on Chinese organizational behaviour. In turn we shall consider decision making, corruption, negotiating, and management training.

## Decision Making

Chinese in leadership positions enjoy a wider range of authority for which they are unaccountable than do those from more democratic legalistic systems. The result is that more decisions are made in private by fewer people in Chinese culture. There are a number of consequences. Firstly, the rules or principles by which these decisions are made rarely surface, since leaders are not required to justify their decisions openly. The Western apparatus of power sharing — explanation, debate, documentation, voting — is public through and through. Not so the Chinese. The result is that Western observers often label Chinese decision making 'intuitive' when they really mean: 'I have no basis for knowing what information, values, and considerations are used by Chinese leaders when they make their decisions'. For all we know, Chinese and Western leaders may use precisely the same data, emphases, and weightings in deciding how to proceed with a given situation. In fact, recent research by Leon Mann using Taiwanese respondents demonstrates that:

the basic steps . . . (i.e., 'consider alternatives . . . find out disadvantages of alternatives . . . consider how to carry out the decision . . . collect information . . . be clear about objectives . . . take care before choosing') are an integral part of decision making in Western and non-Western cultures.

A second consequence of the Confucian hierarchy is that few Chinese have any practice in making decisions and submitting them to public scrutiny. The result is that Chinese people generally lack confidence in their ability to make such decisions. Furthermore, Mann's research indicates that his Taiwanese respondents tried to avoid making individual choices. They were more likely to panic under the pressure of time, pass off responsibility, procrastinate, and rationalize away problems than were their Western counterparts. This pattern of response is understandable in a person who has been trained since his or her early years to defer to superiors or to a group when he confronts new circumstances alone.

## Corruption

The Chinese have always conferred considerable discretionary authority on those in responsible positions, preferring to trust human judgement rather than mechanistic laws. Within a hierarchy these

authorities are less subject to supervisory checks and balances than
are those in a more democratic political tradition. The stage is thus
set for petitioners to attempt to influence the decisions of such
officials through what Westerners call 'bribery'. So, an application
may be pushed to the front of a queue, a contract may be awarded
to one whose tender is not the lowest, a ticket may be found for a
sold-out concert, a coveted job may be awarded to a friend's son,
all in exchange for various resources — cash, a gift of expensive
liquor, or simply the acknowledgement of an outstanding favour,
redeemable at some unspecified future time.

Whatever their disadvantages, such procedures ensure a stable
hierarchy. Those who already have resources are better able to
command further resources and those in positions of power are able
to use those positions to benefit themselves, their families, and
their friends. The granting of 'favours' is an important component
of paternalism, as it builds a network of people tied to someone in
authority out of indebtedness and obligation. Such a network is an
invaluable resource in an arbitrary world unprotected by the rule of
law. Of course, the building of such a network requires that recipients
honour their debts and stay in contact with their beneficiary or the
pay-off will never be realized. Without that guarantee the bribery
will comprise a more immediate exchange of resources. Whether
the exchange is immediate or long term, however, such *quid pro
quo* exchanges will be more common in hierarchical societies
unleavened by the rule of law.

Where such laws are in force, as one finds in Hong Kong with
its Independent Commission Against Corruption, significant inroads
can be made. China itself launches frequent 'anti-corruption campaigns'. The acute dilemma in such crackdowns is that they are
sponsored by the Party. Given the Chinese emphasis on the morality
of leaders, the Party, especially its top echelons, must be seen to
retain moral authority after any investigation. So, none of these
key persons can be exposed, for fear of damaging the Party's
authority to lead. The mass of people are aware of this dilemma
and in consequence are cynical about the sincerity of such campaigns
when no senior officials are implicated. And so the *belief* in the
possibility of corruption at the top persists. The austerity of Lee
Kwan Yew's personal life-style and his efforts to establish judicial
independence from the government indicate what must be done to
wage an effective war against official impropriety in a Chinese
culture.

## Negotiation

Westerners tend to think of negotiation as the process by which strangers, thrown together because of some joint business opportunity, reach a verbal agreement about how they will co-operate with one another for mutual advantage. Strictly speaking, however, negotiation includes a much broader range of processes by which any two or more people reach a *modus operandi* on any matter of joint concern, be it a business deal, raising children, what film to see, and so forth. Depending on the context, anyone may be involved — intimates, acquaintances, and strangers. Furthermore, any arrangement made now is understood to have implications for future arrangements, as long as the parties have continued contact with one another.

Negotiations may be contextual as well as verbal, may involve any sphere of activity, and may span any range of time. Their success depends on consideration of the likely advantages to the participants, and on their compatibility. The Chinese take this broader view of negotiations, Westerners typically the narrower view described earlier. Out of these differences a host of literature has arisen advising Westerners about how to modify their normal practices when doing business deals with the Chinese. The general thrust of the advice is for Westerners to move closer to Chinese interpersonal practices, thereby ensuring smoother relationships during the negotiations. Westerners are advised to:

— consider sending subordinates to assess the situation before bringing in one's key decision makers;
— show restraint in both verbal and emotional expression;
— adopt a longer time frame, both for this particular negotiation and for one's relationship with the other negotiation team;
— emphasize areas of agreement rather than differences, especially at the beginning;
— expect the Chinese to discuss concessions behind closed doors, so as to preserve the impression of harmony and the niceties of face within their group; plan for frequent breaks, to allow these 'back-stage' discussions to occur;
— realize that true authority for decision making may lie outside the negotiation chamber, so that deals struck now may be subject to change later;
— pitch appeals to collective interests, not to individual advantages for the members of the opposite negotiation team;

— consider the use of third parties within the other team's social
  network to exert leverage during difficult stages in the negotiations;
— remember that Chinese prefer to deal with 'known quantities',
  so cultivate social relationships outside the negotiation chamber
  and examine carefully whether concessions should be made
  now to ensure an insider's position for future negotiations. One
  may even begin exploring now without a clear agenda, so as to
  develop a working relationship for future possibilities.

All the foregoing is sound advice at the interpersonal level. Far
more important for the viability of the project, however, is a careful
consideration of the economic, legal, and political environments
within which the Chinese function. Such considerations as the
availability of resources, the lack of effective commercial law, and
rivalries between local and central authorities are only a few of the
concerns that must always be addressed, especially when dealing
with China. These concerns define what is realistically possible, are
dramatically different from what obtains in one's home country,
and must be appreciated if one is to have any chance of success
when negotiating with the Chinese.

## Management Training

On a recent trip to China Tom Peters, management guru and co-
author of the American best-seller *In Search of Excellence*, was
bedevilled by the persistent request for formulas. 'What is the optimal
ratio of managers to workers?' is an example of the kind of question
that might have been asked during the 1920s in North America
when the 'science' of management was in its infancy. Chinese, in
their zeal to modernize, are seeking the structure that scientific
knowledge will provide to help them increase productivity. Many
universities in the West teach management programmes in China,
in part honouring Chang Chih-tung's exhortation, 'Western learning
for technology, Chinese learning for the essentials'. This pursuit of
management knowledge is also found in Hong Kong, Taiwan, and
Singapore, where business is a popular subject of study and Western
management texts enjoy vigorous sales. There are two serious
problems with this undertaking. Firstly, not all management expertise
is subject to formula. Of course many areas, like quality control,
accounting systems, commercial law, and taxation, are sufficiently
mechanical and standardized to be taught in a didactic, routine

fashion. In the 'softer' areas, like planning, leadership, communication, conflict resolution, delegation, and performance evaluation, the formulas are fewer, more contingent on a variety of factors, and often dependent on sophisticated judgements about personal interaction and needs. In these areas the knowledge base of Western management science is much shakier.

The second problem is that management knowledge in the organizational and interpersonal areas is derived from studies conducted and theories constructed *in the West*. Geert Hofstede has long counselled caution about the uncritical import of Western, especially American, management practices elsewhere. He writes:

For about 60 years, the United States has been the world's largest producer and exporter of management theories covering such key areas as motivation, leadership, and organization . . . and American theories reflect the culture of the United States of its day. Since most present-day theorists are middle-class intellectuals, their theories reflect a national, intellectual, middle-class cultural background.

The non-American consumer of management ideas should therefore proceed with considerable caution.

Hofstede offers the practice of management by objectives (MBO) as a case in point. Peter Drucker first advocated this technique for leadership, which requires the boss and his reporting subordinate to negotiate a performance contract and assessment at certain times of · the year. Hofstede writes:

it has been perhaps the single most popular management technique 'made in U.S.A.'. Therefore, it can be accepted as fitting U.S. culture. MBO presupposes:
— That subordinates are sufficiently independent to negotiate meaningfully with the boss.
— That both are willing to take risks.
— That performance is seen as important by both.

If a receiving culture does not share these core assumptions, MBO is likely to fail. Although he was writing about France, Hofstede's conclusions could be applied to Chinese cultures:

The reason for the anxiety in the French cultural context is that MBO presupposes a depersonalized authority in the form of internalized objectives; but French people, from their early childhood onward, are accustomed to large power distances, to an authority that is highly personalized. And in spite of all attempts to introduce Anglo-Saxon management methods, French superiors do not easily decentralize and do not stop short-circuiting intermediate hierarchical levels, nor do French subordinates expect them to.

More specific practices in such areas as supervision, holding meetings, decision making, and so forth cannot responsibly be presented to Chinese persons as sound management techniques until their cultural compatibility has been assessed.

By the same token Western personnel will need to alter their way of thinking and modify their behaviour if they are to function effectively with Chinese superiors, associates, and subordinates. They will have to pay greater attention to such issues as group harmony, honouring status, and general restraint than would be required in their mother country. Which party eventually accommodates to which is typically determined by political concerns and technical competence, but in reaching such agreements the Westerner must make many changes. Otherwise he will be isolated, often in subtle ways.

## Summary

This chapter has been concerned with how the many features of Chinese socialization and personal interaction appear in daily work routines. We began with a consideration of the organizational structure typical of Chinese companies and bureaucracies and then examined the behaviour of leaders and followers with particular reference to the effects of a paternalistic hierarchy. The chapter ended with a consideration of decision making, corruption, negotiation, and management training. These are practical matters of great moment which are often discussed without adequate attention to their cultural roots. Various features of the Chinese view of the world help to put these 'odds and ends' into context.

# 7

# Psychopathology, Chinese Style

> Problems within the family
> should not be discussed
> outside the family.
> Chinese adage

THE AVERAGE person in Hong Kong bet more at the racecourse in 1989 than the average person in China earned during the same year. Who knows how much more was wagered legally at the casinos in neighbouring Macau, on public lotteries, and in private and illegal games of chance? Behind these awesome figures hang the ruptured lives of many individuals and families, beggared by this addiction. Despite this incalculable pain, there is little public discussion of gambling, scant writing on the topic in Chinese psychology, and almost no treatment resources are devoted to tackling this insidious compulsion. The reasons for this silence reveal volumes about examining deviant behaviour in Chinese cultures and in comparing the results cross culturally.

No other area of psychology is more closely integrated with a people's social and historical legacy. The questions of which behaviour patterns are considered deviant and how this deviance is treated intersect with philosophical assumptions, medical practice, political ideology, societal priorities, and legal procedures as well as purely psychological considerations. For this reason I will begin this chapter by putting the study of Chinese psychological abnormality into its world-wide context. Then I will proceed to bring together what is known about 'abnormal' behaviour in Chinese society and its treatment.

## The Context

### Traditional Medical Practice

The Chinese do not make the sharp distinctions between the realms of mind and body, between internal and external that Westerners do. Instead, when Chinese are asked to assess the various causes of psychological problems, they group causes in terms of their impact on the nervous system, with a hostile working environment being equally as important as genetic weakness, and disturbances by supernatural beings accorded the same role as malignant bacteria. Similarly, they consider that internal psychological factors like intelligence or education have the same type of impact as external social influences, like interaction with other sufferers or cultural support. In short, Chinese group the causes of psychopathology differently from other cultural groups.

The Chinese consider only severe disturbances such as psychosis to be diseases while they view other disturbances as departures from the body's optimum normal balance. They believe that emotions are affected by the functioning of specific bodily organs, as follows:

happiness — heart
anger — liver
worry — lungs
fear — kidneys
desire — spleen

They therefore believe that disorders associated with these five primary emotions can best be redressed by restoring normal functioning in the corresponding organ, through physiological interventions such as medicine, diet, exercise, acupuncture, and activity changes. Elaborate theories and contending schools have arisen to support these bodily approaches to the causes of disease.

Traditional medicine thus provides a historical approach to diagnosing and treating what Westerners would often label as psychological disturbance. It rarely probes the possible social or familial roots of these complaints, nor does it require the patient to reveal his or her own assessment of the interpersonal context in which he or she is coping. It thus spares patients the need to assert themselves against their surroundings or the embarrassment of possible conflict with other people.

Western psychiatric practice is intensely interested in the client's understanding of the world he or she inhabits. The way the client assesses and relates to this interpersonal world forms the basis of many of the diagnostic categories that psychiatrists use. These categories are often linked to pathological social or familial contexts which any treatment programme must take into consideration. There is thus a potential for confrontation and social change based on individual perceptions which runs counter to many conservative, hierarchical strands in Chinese culture. Traditional medical practice poses no such disruptive threat and stands as an effective bulwark against the overzealous incorporation of Western psychiatric practice in Chinese communities.

Traditional medical writings rarely discussed more severe forms of incapacity, like psychosis and mental retardation. These forms of abnormality went beyond 'the psychopathology of everyday life', and were a matter of some mystery as, indeed, they are everywhere. These abnormalities were a source of shame, as they were often construed as a form of supernatural punishment. Families confined their afflicted relatives to the home and made no attempts to obtain treatment for them. Even today, considerable fear, suspicion, and hostility is directed towards such persons in Chinese communities. Attempts to integrate them into residential areas through 'half-way' housing schemes meet spirited resistance. Such attitudes will probably moderate as the less modernized segments of Chinese society gain an appreciation of the genetic bases of these conditions.

### Clinical Practice in the People's Republic of China

As Arthur Kleinman points out, 'Psychiatry was disrupted more than any other medical specialty during the Cultural Revolution, because the radical ideology of the period held that mental illness was wrong political thinking, not a disease process.' The obvious treatment for pathological behaviour was to inculcate correct political thinking. It was regarded as self-indulgent and wasteful of precious resources to focus upon the individual and his or her problems. It did not help that Mao Zedong declared that the study of psychology was '90 per cent useless' with the remaining 10 per cent 'distorted and bourgeois phoney science'.

Furthermore, psychiatry originated in the West and many of its core assumptions contradict the Chinese view of the world. The writings of Freud, especially those presenting his theory of infantile sexuality, were especially suspect in this regard. Only in the mid-1980s was a ban on Freud's writings, initiated in the Anti-Rightist Campaign of the late 1950s, lifted. The result of this repressive *Zeitgeist* was that many psychiatrists were sent to the countryside for re-education and the discipline stagnated for twenty-five years. There was little indigenous writing, only scanty contact with foreign colleagues, and almost no research was undertaken.

The situation is now changing. The sheer magnitude of the problem confronting China requires such a change. Kleinman estimates that there are approximately 4,000,000 schizophrenics in China, and that 'the number of patients with neuroses . . . is at the very least 5 per cent of the Chinese population, or approximately 55,000,000, and may be two or three times that number'. Defining such problems as medical, of course, helps protect the profession of psychiatry from political vicissitudes and, as Kleinman states, 'legitimizes the study of a darker side of Chinese society which has not been directly accessible to China scholars'.

Considerable progress is now evident. Assessment tests are being developed; professional identification with members of the profession is loosening and breaking the stranglehold of the work units on medical personnel, thereby promoting co-operation across the country; critical applied problems, like crime, alcoholism, ageing, and the one-child family, are being addressed; standards are being introduced to regulate the profession of psychiatry; new systems of disease classification are being proposed; country-wide surveys of mental health have been undertaken. All of these changes herald a greater future output for those interested in understanding Chinese psychopathology.

## Clinical Practice outside China

There are, of course, rich potential sources of such knowledge in Taiwan and Singapore as well as the Chinese communities in Canada, the United States, Australia, England, and elsewhere. To date, unfortunately, this potential has not been realized. Few clinical practitioners have conducted research in these locales and only smatterings of written work have emerged. The output to date has typically been based on Western theories, practices, diagnostic systems, and scales. A distinctive Chinese voice is missing.

In part this understandable state of affairs has arisen because of the Chinese tendency to seek help from traditional medical practitioners — who tend not to write or conduct research. When their treatments fail, the patients do not seek more psychologically probing services, perhaps because they are unavailable, or the clients do not know of such services or perceive them as too threatening.

However, the opportunities for Chinese outside China to train in social work, clinical psychology, and psychiatry are increasing, as are the pleas for more Chinese to work in clinical practice. Modernization will inevitably draw Chinese into these clinical professions and liberate public attitudes towards using their services, thereby increasing our knowledge of Chinese psychopathology.

Recent work in Hong Kong, for example, reveals important discoveries in the way Chinese persons classify psychological problems and behaviour disorders. It is clear that this more modern group of Chinese see *both* medical *and* social-psychological factors as causing and curing a variety of mental disorders, ranging from schizophrenia to neurasthenia. Clearly they have moved beyond the traditional bodily focus, and increasingly appreciate the usefulness of social support and psychological practitioners in maintaining sound mental health. Such studies will encourage future efforts at dealing with psychopathology in all Chinese communities.

## Chinese Psychopathology

Despite the many qualifications discussed above, our knowledge of Chinese abnormal behaviour is increasing. Before considering what is known, it is important to examine the underlying assumption on which most of it is based.

### The Disease Model of Psychopathology

A medical doctor makes a diagnosis of, say, hepatitis by collecting information about symptoms, which he or she obtains by interviewing and testing the patient. When the doctor finds a core of such symptoms, he or she is able to identify the underlying disease process and begin treatment. Each disease is presumed to present a universal syndrome or package of symptoms, so that the examining doctor's task is to collect all the pertinent information, compare them against known disease syndromes, and make an accurate diagnosis.

#### Thorough Diagnoses?

A similar approach is applied to diagnosing psychopathology. A number of important questions must be raised about this process, however. Firstly, did the examiner collect *all* the relevant information in formulating a diagnosis? If not, some diseases will be over-represented, some under-represented. Let us take, for example, the case of neurasthenia, an older name for a pathological syndrome of symptoms including lethargy, weakness, insomnia, and various physical pains, such as headache. This syndrome is diagnosed very frequently in Chinese cultures, and in China particularly. When patients classified as neurasthenic are pressed for further information about their experience, however, a very high proportion of them turn out to be neurotically depressed. Given the Chinese cultural focus on bodily complaints, it is understandable why neurasthenia is over-diagnosed and depression under-diagnosed. Obviously one must conduct a thorough assessment of symptoms to be sure that the correct diagnosis has been made.

### Similar Diseases?

This consideration raises the scientific-medical issue of what constitutes a particular disease. Even with a known viral infection like hepatitis, symptoms vary, depending on genetic adaptations, personal resistance, and so forth. In cases of psychopathology it is harder to establish a 'core' set of symptoms around which other symptoms may vary without affecting the basic diagnosis. So, for example, a report on depression commissioned by the World Health Organization concluded that the bodily aspects of the disorder varied less between people of different cultures than its social or cognitive aspects. To quote Juris Draguns, 'In particular the experience of guilt does not appear to be a universal component of depression . . . the pivotal role of guilt in the West has been linked with the development of a permanent and autonomous sense of selfhood.'

There is considerable debate about whether guilt plays a role among the Chinese, either in socialization or in psychopathology. It certainly is a less important factor than more direct social controls in many areas of Chinese behaviour. For our present purposes, however, it raises the question of whether 'depression with guilt' is a separate disease from the bodily syndrome termed 'neurasthenia'. The decision on this point may appear to be arbitrary, but it alerts us to the need for careful definitions of the core symptoms of a problem. Only when all symptoms are matched can we be sure that we are comparing similar entities.

### Functional Psychopathology?

Finally, we are concerned with patterns of behaviour, feelings, thoughts, and physical symptoms called psychological disturbances. Unlike hepatitis, which has a universally debilitating effect, a given psychological pattern may not be as disturbing or may not cause such abnormal functioning in one social system as in another. Take, for example, the findings that arise when Chinese people in various parts of the world are tested with the Minnesota Multiphasic Personality Inventory (MMPI). The MMPI is a widely used and highly respected test in Western clinical practice. It assesses the strength of a respondent's dispositions in a number of clinically relevant areas, such as hypochondriasis — the tendency to be over-concerned with physical problems, and psychopathy — the tendency to manipulate others and to engage in antisocial activities. A respondent's deviation from established norms can thus be assessed.

When compared to these norms, the typical Chinese appears to be clinically withdrawn and depressed. Similar diagnoses are common when American clinicians interview Chinese outpatients at counselling centres. Can these findings, however, be taken at face value? It seems that these response patterns may be unremarkable and within the context of Chinese social reality. They may, in fact, be entirely suitable in a culture which emphasizes harmony with one's family and self-restraint within one's social or work hierarchy.

So, we must apply the disease model to comparative studies of psychopathology with care and judgement and especially when dealing with less serious problems, like hypochondriasis and anxiety. We must find out how abnormal these conditions are and how a Chinese person copes with them within the resources offered in a given Chinese society.

## Comparative Incidence of Psychopathologies

Let us begin with Lin Tsung-yi, the doyen of Chinese psychiatrists, who has been studying Chinese psychopathology throughout his long career. He draws two broad conclusions about his subject:

First, the entire range of psychopathology observed in Western or other cultures in terms of symptoms or syndromes have [sic] also been observed in the Chinese. Second, all types of mental disorders, including the subtypes . . . have been identified among the Chinese when standard Western diagnostic criteria have been applied.

These conclusions are important because they assert that comparisons are valid and possible. Given the uneven quality of the available research, however, we can report only a very mixed collection of results.

### Schizophrenia

A study by the World Health Organization of the occurrence of schizophrenia found very low rates in Taiwan. Furthermore, the course of the disease appeared to be less harmful there than in modernized, Western countries. But the symptoms show what Juris

Draguns has described as 'a tendency of Chinese schizophrenics toward a contentious, hostile, interpersonal symptomatology tinged with paranoid ideation'.

## Affective Psychoses

Rates of occurrence, especially for depressive psychosis, are low.

## Senile Psychoses

Rates of hospital admission for this age-related deterioration are comparatively low, probably because of a greater willingness among Chinese to tolerate bizarre behaviour in their elderly.

## Alcoholism

Alcohol is widely used in Chinese culture for culinary, ceremonial, and medicinal purposes. But alcoholism has been rare throughout Chinese history, partly because of the genetic sensitivity of the Chinese to ethylalcohol. This sensitivity inhibits frequent or high consumption, thereby preventing the development of a dangerous habit. The Chinese emphasis on self-restraint, civility, and moderation further reinforces a general sobriety. Current research is, however, uncovering an increasing amount of 'hidden' alcoholism which only comes to light when financial or family problems surface. Closer monitoring may reveal that alcohol consumption is increasing in Chinese communities.

## Depression and Neurasthenia

We know from the previous discussion that *diagnoses* of depression are typically low in Chinese culture; of neurasthenia, high indeed. The latter incidence is due to the Chinese tendency to present their problems in terms of bodily symptoms, at least initially. If doctors fail to probe deeper, they will diagnose neurasthenia. If, however, they undertake more thorough examinations, they are more likely to diagnose neurotic or anxiety depression.

It appears as if Oriental people react to events which give rise to depression, such as marital impasses, work conflicts, and unemployment by exhibiting physical symptoms. Recent evidence suggests that such reactions are far more frequent in the West than was previously appreciated, especially among certain social groups. Indeed, the somatic versus psychological distinction is now being viewed with suspicion in many quarters. Far more important for future comparative purposes is to do a thorough intake interview, so that patterns of disease become apparent and valid comparisons can be made.

### Test Anxiety

There is a strong emphasis on academic achievement in Chinese cultures. We have already discussed how this influences the way pupils spend their time and the way classrooms are managed. Another consequence is that Chinese are more anxious about tests than their Anglo-Saxon counterparts. The symptoms recorded and measured include insomnia, inability to concentrate, worry about grades, and physical complaints. General health surveys of Hong Kong secondary school students show a remarkably high proportion to be 'at risk'. Given the academic emphasis in most Chinese cultures, however, many would accept these consequences as necessary.

### Suicide

A total of 52 political entities reported their rates of suicide (per 100,000 persons) in the 1986 *World Demographic Yearbook*. Hong Kong and Singapore were fifteenth and sixteenth, with rates of 13.1 and 12.8 respectively. These rates are comparable to those of many Western countries like Canada, the Netherlands, Scotland, the United States, Australia, and New Zealand, but higher than those of England and Ireland. These Chinese suicide rates are lower than those in Germany, Austria, France, and Belgium. Beyond pointing out that suicide rates generally increase with increasing wealth, it is difficult to make cultural generalizations.

What is perhaps noteworthy is that suicide among the elderly is on the increase. Thirty per cent of all Hong Kong suicides in 1989 were of people aged between 60 and 79. This figure suggests that traditional patterns of care for the elderly are disintegrating, thereby making this group more vulnerable than before. These results are disturbing in societies, like Singapore, which are striving to preserve what is best in their Chinese culture. Concerns for honouring the legacy of filial piety may well necessitate changes in policy, such as increasing the size of public housing units to accommodate three-generation families.

### Culture-bound Syndromes

No comparative discussion would be complete without mention of three syndromes that appear unique to Chinese culture. Koro refers to a panic attack focused on the fear that one's penis is shrinking. Frigophobia refers to excessive fear of the cold, in terms of temperature and food, as defined by the yin–yang distinction among foods. *Shen kui* literally means 'kidney weakness' and refers generally to fatigue, insomnia, and sexual indifference.

These are lay diagnostic categories, used especially by traditional medical practitioners. There are few statistics of their occurrence, particularly in China. Psychiatrists regard those with a sexual component as basic sexual neuroses which have culturally specific manifestations that result in their appearing distinctive.

### A General Observation

In his recent review of psychopathology around the world, Juris Draguns noted 'the more social orientation of Chinese psychiatric patients'. Patients suffering from a variety of disorders, even those characterized by social apathy and withdrawal, exhibit higher levels of interaction, conversation, and co-operation than is normal in the West. Even in distress Chinese are collectively oriented:

'Calls for help' in the Western manner capitalizing upon the person's misery and the need to find a sympathetic ear, are rarely made and would probably meet with an infrequent response in China. Psychological distress remains a primarily internal . . . subject with few if any outlets for [its] social communication. The relief of anxiety positively through food and negatively through medicine, on the other hand, represents a culturally sanctioned avenue for responding to anxiety, tension, depression, and the more general needs for understanding, comfort, and acceptance.

Patients tend to present more indirect, harmonious symptoms, as one might expect of people whose normal social behaviour is characterized by collectivism.

### Future Comparisons

Much more is needed. Methods of diagnosis must be standardized and reliably administered. A broader range of problems with important social consequences, like gambling, juvenile delinquency, minimal brain dysfunction, and intellectual subnormality, must be measured. Such investigations must include a variety of Chinese societies, so that the influences of modernization and political organization can be assessed. They must also include local, traditional systems of classifying these conditions, so that their similarities and differences with Western systems can be determined.

## Causes

It is very difficult to isolate cause-and-effect relationships in mental health. The best social scientists can do is to study a representative group of infants over a period of time. If thorough and accurate measures are taken, it is then possible to identify the biological, psychological, interpersonal, and social factors which put individuals at risk. Even then, we often find that a high proportion of those most at risk have no symptoms, the so-called 'invulnerables' or 'hardy personalities'.

Such long-term studies require resources, manpower, and social stability. Not surprisingly, they are rare in social science involving Chinese. Instead, there are cross-sectional studies which measure pathological symptoms and other factors at a particular time, and look for correlations between them. So, for example, it has frequently been discovered that patients who report having psychiatric symptoms report a lack of social support from friends and family. The seductive conclusion many would draw is that a close social network buffers people against psychological disturbance. Although this conclusion may be correct, it is equally likely that people ostracize or ignore those with psychological disturbances because of their disturbances. We must therefore be cautious in our interpretation of such results and await additional confirmation from longitudinal research.

## Social Factors

Studies of various cultural groups show that migrants, females, the elderly, and the socio-economically lower classes are most prone to psychological disorders. This general conclusion varies when we examine specific disorders. Males, for example, consistently show more antisocial or psychopathic symptoms, like delinquency. Contrary to widespread concerns, only children show no evidence of spoiled, unruly, or deviant behaviour. To the contrary, and like their Western counterparts, they demonstrate superior academic achievement.

## Interpersonal Factors

As mentioned before, Chinese who have a broad network of social support, especially from family members, and particularly from the father, are less likely to report psychological problems. Not sur-

prisingly, Chinese find disruptions to this family bond, such as
divorce, especially stressful. Indeed, this interpersonal network is
the first line of defence for Chinese in responding to problems they
label as 'psychological'. Chinese are more likely than Westerners
to select family members, especially parents, as confidants. Assuming
that this support group is effective, at least with minor problems,
the connection between a high level of support and a low incidence
of psychological problems is understandable.

Family behaviour also plays a role in *preventing* problems. Cross-
cultural studies of delinquency reveal that children whose parents
monitor them closely are less likely to commit delinquent acts. This
is true of both Chinese and Westerners. And the more the child has
been led to value the family as a unit living together, the less the
delinquency.

Undoubtedly, the close relationship between hostile parental behaviour and a broad spectrum of childhood psychopathology will
be found with the Chinese, as it has with other cultural groups.
Only recently has such shameful activity as child abuse become
subject to scrutiny and concern in Chinese culture. Studies on this
dark side of parental behaviour will undoubtedly increase, given its
key importance.

Perhaps the most widespread cause of stress for Chinese is the
push for achievement. The lack of places in good schools and universities results in the 'Narrow Gate Syndrome', as Lin Tsung-yi
calls it, with parents exerting pressure on children to achieve high
grades. Recent studies of juvenile delinquency clearly link antisocial behaviour to the value the child places on outward success.
If parents reduced their demands for such achievement the incidence of school phobia, psychosomatic disorders, test anxiety, and
failure-related suicide among Chinese school children would almost
certainly fall also.

## Psychological Factors
### Source of Control

How a person understands a psychological problem is related to his
or her vulnerability to the problem. It has been found that Chinese
people who believe that events are caused by forces beyond their
control report more psychopathological symptoms like anxiety,
headaches, and insomnia. Where these uncontrollable forces are
perceived as stable, internal, and global, vulnerability is especially
high. These results are similar to those found in the West.

The Chinese concept of *yuan* is culturally distinctive. *Yuan* is a Buddhist term referring to fate or predestination, especially in interpersonal matters. Chinese use it to explain social events. As it is an external factor, it serves a protective function in 'explaining away' negative exchanges with others, since the individual does not blame himself or herself for the outcome. Those who use the *yuan* concept in this way have fewer depressive symptoms, as one would expect.

*Ways of Coping*

Hwang Kwang-kuo in Taiwan has developed a sophisticated classification of the ways Chinese people respond to interpersonal and psychological problems. Broadly speaking, he identified two basic approaches to life's problems, the active and the persevering. Active approaches include problem analysis, self-assertion, and seeking help from others. Persevering approaches derive from the Confucian traditions of self-control, and include strategies like stopping thought, self-instruction in patience, and non-resistance. Younger persons and those from higher social classes are more likely to use active approaches. Such people tend to have psychosomatic problems. Older, lower-class persons are more likely to use persevering approaches and to experience social withdrawal and cognitive disturbance. So the type of psychopathology Chinese people experience is related to the way they approach life's problems generally. This finding provides further support for the link between cognitive factors and psychiatric symptoms.

## Treatment

### Traditional Forms

I have already discussed the medical and cultural supports for treating 'emotional' problems physically. Indeed, visits to herbalists, masseurs, acupuncturists, and so forth constitute the first form of treatment for many groups of Chinese today. There are, however, precedents in traditional practice for 'psychological' cures. Methods of diagnosis, for example, included 'interrogation'. Although Chinese rarely expressed emotions explicitly, they had many indirect and non-verbal channels for communicating such key information. Also, as David Wu has recorded, practitioners would sometimes attempt to 'rebalance' emotions by causing counter-emotions through intervening in some way in a patient's daily routines and social activities. These approaches have much in common with aspects of behaviour therapy as currently practised in the West. But they were rarely documented. Nor were they embedded within a scientific legacy involving the principles of psychological conditioning.

## Current Beliefs about Cure

Research by Luk Chung-leung in Hong Kong indicates that the typical Chinese citizen has definite ideas about treating psychological problems. The largest group of cures involves changes in personal life-style. Such characteristics as a positive attitude towards overcoming the disease, staying away from others afflicted with the disease, and seeking support from friends are grouped together and are believed to be important in overcoming *all* types of psychopathology. A second group of cures involves treatments, including professional help and environmental changes. People believe these approaches are the most effective for treating antisocial disorders like gambling, corruption, and lack of civic responsibility. To be effective, the form of treatment must be carefully matched to the type of problem, in Chinese culture as elsewhere.

## Contemporary Therapies

### Community Intervention

China faces colossal challenges in meeting the needs of its citizens for treatment. Knowledge and trained personnel are in short supply. Judiciously, Chinese authorities have responded by developing local forms of community-based therapy in a few big cities. Intervention involves mobilizing family members, neighbours, and work groups, along with medical personnel, to counsel, encourage, medicate, and monitor patients' progress. Although the collective approach of the Chinese makes such public and intrusive intervention possible, they must overcome the very same approach to permit the involvement of outsiders in their personal problems. The scientific community awaits reports of these ambitious undertakings with considerable interest. The Chinese experience in developing community psychology could well establish models to be followed in other parts of the world.

## Drug Therapy

Traditional Chinese medicine has a rich store of drugs. It is only recently that controlled clinical studies have been made of some Chinese drugs with possible psychoactive properties, like ginseng. Chemicals discovered in the West, like the phenothiazives used for treating psychosis, are being introduced into Chinese psychiatric practice. Given the different genetic characteristics of the Chinese, some useful surprises may be in store. For example, many Western doctors have observed that Chinese patients respond well to lower dosage levels of most psychoactive drugs than do comparable Western patients. Again, careful scientific studies must replace anecdotal observations.

## Talk Therapies

What most Westerners understand by the term 'psychotherapy' is the extended discussion by a client and a trained professional of that patient's experience and life situation with the shared aim of relieving the client's discomfort. Typically, psychotherapists aim to assist their patients in acquiring insight about their inner psychological processes or their social exchanges, thereby freeing the patient to make informed choices and live a more fulfilling life. The psychotherapist is a stranger, legally bound to confidentiality, paid by the state or the client, and oriented towards acting in the client's best interests.

If the above sounds like a very Western undertaking, the reader will be able to anticipate my next remarks. The psychotherapeutic process as practised in the West is extremely verbal, focused on the self and on the disclosure of personal information, change oriented, and non-directive. In short, it enshrines many of the tenets basic to liberal individualism. As such, it is simply not compatible with Chinese culture. The following constraints apply in Chinese societies:

— disclosure of personal problems may cast shame on the family;
— psychotherapy may result in changes for the client's relationships with other people of importance, and hence disturb 'harmony';
— Chinese are not brought up to be explicit in their utterances, especially about personal problems, and particularly with strangers;

— confidentiality cannot be guaranteed in a society with powerful relationship networks and an underdeveloped legal system;
— self-fulfilment is a less acceptable personal goal in a collectivist culture.

It is not surprising, therefore, to find that Chinese make little use of psychotherapy, even in countries like the United States where it is readily available from Chinese counsellors. Discussions with close friends, self-discipline, physical cures, and so forth are simply more attractive than talk therapy with stranger-professionals.

Of course some Chinese do seek professional counselling, especially those with higher education. Even this select group have different expectations about the process from those held by clients of other cultures. Research by Rhoda Yuen and Howard Tinsley concludes that the Chinese:

have less of an expectancy to commit themselves actively to counselling and [are] less prepared for the confrontation, immediacy, and concreteness that may occur as part of the counselling process. Behaviorally, it seems likely that Chinese will be more concerned than students of other nationalities with the counsellor's being courteous, respecting their privacy, and keeping their relationship distant and smooth.

It is possible to tailor psychotherapy within the confines of these expectations if the therapist assumes a more discrete, task-oriented, and directive stand towards a client. Exchanges with substitute psychotherapists, like palm-readers, temple healers, and herbalists, have always followed this more culturally appropriate form. When a distinctively Chinese mode of psychotherapy is developed, it will probably assume many of these qualities.

## Summary and Conclusions

We are on shakier ground in the area of psychopathology than in any other area of Chinese psychology. Not only is the quantity of data sparse, but it is often suspect. Statistics on particular conditions are plagued by problems of loose and inconsistent categories, incomplete diagnoses, and cross-cultural misinterpretation.

Furthermore, much of the literature has a defensive, political quality. This is understandable, given the links between clinical problems and social structure, but a combative stance tends to retard progress. The field of psychopathology needs to look more carefully and dispassionately at the often volatile points of contact of urbanization, social class, education, modernization, Westernization, political policy, and abnormality.

The tension between traditional medical practices and Western psychiatry needs to be handled with openmindedness. As the psychiatrist Lin Tsung-yi maintains, 'Chinese traditional medicine seems . . . to have exerted an inhibiting effect on the development of psychiatry as an independent system of psychological medicine'. Traditional Western practice was helpful to the development of modern Western practice, and surely greater collaboration is possible between the Chinese and Western heritages. Such a *rapprochement* requires political support and economic resources. Perhaps, then, a tactical first step is to begin to document the retarding effects of psychological abnormality on achieving the four modernizations.

Broadly, this chapter has addressed the occurrence, perception, causes, and treatment of Chinese psychopathology. I have emphasized the important legacy of traditional Chinese medicine throughout. Although useful work has started in a number of areas, future progress will depend on whether scientifically trained Chinese arise, collect data based on the social reality of China, and submit their writings on the subject to critical professional review.

# 8

# Modernization and the Loss of Chineseness

Chinese learning for the essentials;
Western learning for practical applications.

Chang Chih-tung

CHINESE intellectuals and politicians are worried that their countrymen's Chineseness is in danger of being lost to the eroding forces of modernization. From revivals of Confucianism in Singapore to campaigns against spiritual pollution in China, the concern is unmistakable — something precious is at risk when Chinese culture is exposed to foreign encounters. This agonizing began in the era of gunboat diplomacy by European powers in the nineteenth century and continues today in all Chinese societies, regardless of their actual level of modernization.

Chinese are sensitive to the charge that they are becoming 'too modern'. They have responded by developing ways of protecting their sense of Chineseness. Chinese scholars have responded by examining whether increasing modernization brings in its wake an actual loss of Chineseness and, if so, in which respects. We will examine both sides of this coin — the beliefs about modernization and Chinese identity, and the scientific evidence about the effects of modernization on Chinese attitudes and behaviour.

## Chinese Beliefs about Modernization

### The Historical Experience

Traditionally the Chinese aptly described their mother country as the 'middle kingdom' or more broadly 'the centre of the earth'. Indeed, before the age of imperialism China had no contestants for that position within its geographical area and could rightly regard itself as the seat of learning, invention, culture, and political sovereignty in East Asia — the world it chose to know. This complacency was shattered by Western gunboats and a long succession of military humiliations which the tottering Qing dynasty suffered in the nineteenth and twentieth centuries.

There then began an intense process of cultural self-examination focused on the issue of how to cope with the fruit and the poison of outside cultures. Chinese respected the technical power of the invaders, and desperately strove to obtain such material and scientific transformations for their country. Many of the outsiders' practices, however, seemed barbaric, disorderly, and shameful. How could the valued elements in Chinese culture be protected while the achievements of the West were incorporated?

I say 'the West' here because it was the Caucasians from Europe and North America who first breached the cultural self-satisfaction of the Chinese. The Japanese invaded in the 1930s, but by then the identification of technological mastery with the West was firmly entrenched. Even today, Chinese generally regard the West as the source of modernization. Note the wholesale adoption of American management texts and curricula by contemporary business schools in China and other Chinese societies as just one example of this widespread assumption. There is some evidence that this identification of mastery with the West is breaking down, however, and this changing belief is important for the use which Chinese may make of recent Japanese experience of modernizing its economy.

## Distinguishing Modernization from Westernization

A persistent theme in the Chinese world of ideas is the belief that the only way to modernize is to throw off the cumbersome legacy of Chinese culture. From the May Fourth Movement of 1919 until today, it is widely thought that this legacy and the consequences of modernization are incompatible. Representative of this stance is Su Xiao-kang, one of the creative forces behind the caustic *Yellow River Elegy* of 1987. He avers that '[The Chinese] have always tried to use their ancient glory . . . to cover up the poverty, weakness, and backwardness of modern times.' It is argued that only by renouncing this love affair with its past will China be able to proceed with the job of modernizing. Such thinking can generate considerable mobilization for change, as we saw in the student movement of May 1989. But Chinese in more developed countries than China do not see the problem in this way.

In Hong Kong, for example, people accept and endorse the idea of 'a modern Chinese' as a person who retains the essential Chinese virtues of sexual propriety, devotion to one's family, political disinterest, and social introversion. Hong Kong people contrast these qualities with their opposites, which characterize modern Westerners. They regard the modern Chinese, like modern Westerners, however, as oriented towards technical mastery and pragmatic, an achiever, intelligent, and proud of Chinese culture. Chinese believe that this creative amalgam of traditional and modern characteristics is manageable, despite pressures arising from political liberty, universal education, widespread wealth, and a free press. One can modernize without Westernizing. The virus can be contained.

This concept of a modern Chinese contrasts not only with that of a modern Westerner, but also with that of a traditional Chinese. The latter has both valued qualities, like filial piety and thrift, and also reactionary traits, like non-competitiveness, superstition, and authoritarianism. One can of course detect a certain ambivalence towards the traditional Chinese because, although he is seen as possessing fewer of the valued Western traits, he has more of the valued Chinese traits than the modern Chinese in Hong Kong.

Nevertheless, this concept of the modern Chinese identity strikes a psychological balance by retaining some of the cherished legacy along with certain prized elements from the Western tradition, without incorporating the dangerous features from the Western example.

Many observers might well ask if such a contemporary resolution to this long-standing dilemma about Chinese identity is simply wishful thinking. They look at Chinese in Taiwan, Singapore, Australia, and elsewhere and ask whether or not they have actually retained their distinctiveness as Chinese despite living outside 'the middle kingdom'. We will turn to this issue after considering the role of language in the Chinese sense of identity.

## The Language Issue

Chinese is a distinctive language, and the mastery of its written form requires considerable training. It is also difficult for many non-Chinese to speak because of its tonal nature. These characteristics make language a key factor in Chinese political discussions about preserving Chineseness, because it so effectively separates the Chinese from others behind a wall of symbolic inscrutability. It is also the language of the home and heart, so 'the mother tongue' generates considerable emotional significance for the Chinese, as it does for all peoples. In consequence the Chinese are very attached to their language traditions, and express great concern about falling standards. This is especially true in multilingual environments where parents will coach their children in their spare time or engage language tutors to keep up their children's Chinese.

Interestingly, Chinese people do not appear concerned that they will lose their Chineseness by learning English, the language of the West. In many other multicultural settings, there is a fear that, by mastering the other group's language one may lose one's identity by exposure to the language, customs, literature, and peoples of that other group. Not so for the Chinese. They regard English as the language of international communication, a useful piece of technology to master for the economic realities of the twentieth and twenty-first centuries. Responses to questionnaires which measure the ethnic identification of Chinese people with their cultural traditions consistently show no relationship between such identification and their exposure to, or mastery of, the English language. One can learn another group's language without compromising the traditions of one's own group.

One may argue that these questionnaires tap only beliefs about one's cultural identity, not one's true Chineseness. But that confirms the very point being made so far in this chapter — the Chinese perceive no conflict between being Chinese and being Western, as long as that 'Westernization' involves characteristics that are useful for modern living and do not replace the core Chinese qualities of familism, achievement, and moderation.

## The Impact of Modernization on Chinese People

One obvious effect of contact with the contemporary world is what we have just been discussing — the development of strategies for blending Chineseness with modernity. This meeting may eliminate observable differences between Chinese people and others. Those who endorse the theory of economic determinism would argue that increasing industrialization does just this.

### The Convergence Hypothesis

Modernization is a complex process. Many assume that it is primarily economic in nature, involving specialization of labour, intense capitalization, interdependent, impersonal markets, technological applications of scientific knowledge, increases in personal wealth, and so forth. Modernization also has political and socio-cultural dimensions, however. Politically, it involves the supplanting of traditional, local authorities by a single, national power, the introduction of an achievement-based administrative hierarchy, and increased popular involvement in politics through grass-level organizations. Socio-culturally, modernization involves the expansion of educational opportunities, urbanization, mass communication, and greater secularization. Modernization is thus a multifaceted phenomenon with pervasive influences on psychological development.

It is worth noting in passing that modernization began in Western countries earlier than it did elsewhere. It entailed just as dramatic changes in these Western countries as it did (and will) in other countries. To confuse modernization with Westernization is to confuse process with origin. Western countries are also changing under the impact of modernization. The question is whether all countries are converging (or developing towards the same end-point).

The psychological reflection of this societal convergence hypothesis is the assumption that we are all developing the same characteristic traits that apply in modern societies. Yang Kuo-shu has recently listed these attributes. They include:
— a sense of personal efficacy (anti-fatalism);
— low social integration with relatives;
— egalitarian attitudes towards others;
— an openness to innovation and change;
— the belief in sexual equality;
— high achievement motivation;
— independence or self-reliance;
— active participation in social organizations;
— tolerance of, and respect for, others;
— cognitive and behavioural flexibility;
— a future orientation;
— empathetic capacity;
— a high need for information;
— the propensity to take risks in life;
— secularization in religious belief;
— a preference for urban life;
— high educational and occupational aspirations.
Some of these attributes, like anti-fatalism, include traits on which, as we have seen, the Chinese are lower than Westerners. On others, like the drive to achieve, Chinese are probably higher overall. No

matter though, for the convergence hypothesis maintains that with sufficient time for modernizing forces to operate, all such differences will be eliminated.

## A Testable Hypothesis?

Modernization takes time, and different societies have been exposed to its effects for different amounts of time and, indeed, at different speeds. Should differences be found in the degree of modernity of societies and persons, one can always argue that given sufficient time these differences will disappear. The issue can never be resolved if such an intellectual trump card is played. Obviously, we must find some way to compare cultures at specific positions on the road to modernization, and to compare the psychological dispositions of their citizens. When this is done, some surprises appear.

## Evidence against Convergence

One rough measure of modernization is personal wealth, a measure derived by dividing a country's gross national product by the number of its citizens. If countries of similar wealth have citizens with different characteristics, then one could argue against the convergence theory. One needs a large number of psychological measures in a large number of countries to do this job adequately, but preliminary results are suggestive. As one might expect, wealth (or modernization) is related to some elements of the modernity profile, like equality between the sexes and observance of political freedoms. Nevertheless, countries of similar wealth still show variations in these modern characteristics. These variations can be related to psychological characteristics of the populations which vary *despite* similar levels of wealth. So, modernization may produce some convergence, but there is still plenty of room for considerable variation.

A second argument against the idea of convergence comes from evidence that the process of convergence is not the same from culture to culture. So, for example, a cluster of 'post-materialist' values has been identified which characterize the transition to modernity in North American and European cultures. These post-materialist needs include a shift towards the greater expression of what Abraham Maslow called social and self-actualization needs. No such change has been found in Japan, however, one of the most highly industrialized countries in the world.

Indeed, within Japan one can detect a combination of attitudes which appears inconsistent with any Westerner's view of modernity. As Yang Kuo-shu has written:

Strong traditional values such as group solidarity, interpersonal harmony, paternalism, and familism are coexisting with quite modern values such as achievement and competition, and . . . along with democratic values exist beliefs in hierarchical social structures and in authority, obedience, and inequality of men and women.

This pattern may be reassuring to the Chinese, as it suggests that a society can modernize without losing valued elements of the Oriental tradition.

Such reassurance is available closer to home. Yang Kuo-shu's studies on the modernity of Taiwanese people show that traditional and modern attitudes do not exist in opposition to one another. Those who are modern are not necessarily non-traditional. For example, self-reliance and assertiveness, two psychological components of modernity, are completely unrelated to conservativeness, fatalism, male dominance, filial piety, and submission to authority, the five components of a traditional orientation. Again, an Oriental culture appears to be producing a marked variation in the profile of a modern person from that one would find in a Western culture.

### Studies of Chinese Immigration

Much of the research reported in this book samples Chinese immigrants or their descendants in Western countries, especially the United States. The Chinese responses are then compared to Caucasian American responses and differences are noted. The fact that strong, pervasive differences can still be found suggests, of course, that Chinese ethnicity is proof even against immersion in a foreign linguistic, political, and social environment.

Of course a difference could still exist even if there were considerable convergence by the Chinese towards the behavioural patterns of the host population. A more satisfactory examination would compare Chinese people living in Chinese societies with several generations of Chinese immigrants in a host country over a period of time, using the host population as a baseline. In this way one could examine *which* types of Chinese behaviour are affected by immigration, how much they are changed, and at what rate. Such studies require considerable resources and are understandably rare.

One exception is a recent project led by Shirley Feldman. Her team focused on a central characteristic of Chinese socialization — parental restrictiveness. They compared the expectations of Chinese teenagers in Hong Kong, first- and second-generation Chinese teenagers in Australia and the United States, and Caucasian teenagers in both of these countries with regard to restrictions on their behaviour. Their first conclusion was that cultural adaptation appears to be very slow, with even second-generation Chinese responding more like their Hong Kong counterparts than their host Caucasians. Secondly, they found that this trend was more marked in certain areas than in others. So, for example, Chinese adapted more to local norms about social activities, like spending time with friends, than to norms for heterosexual activities, like early dating or overnight trips with groups of friends of both sexes. The authors conclude:

Although Chinese family patterns undergo modest changes when Chinese families live in the West, they nonetheless remain different from their Western counterparts, in terms of the amount of structure they provide and the extent to which they use childrearing practices which promote autonomy.

This conclusion will please many who value Chinese traditions of parental authority and are concerned about the spectre of Westernization. It should be pointed out, however, that great changes should not be expected in such central characteristics. Changes can occur quite abruptly in other areas, such as language use, clothing preferences, and friendship patterns, without causing a loss of one's distinctive Chinese traditions. Future research will need to assess this potential for biculturality.

## Conclusion

All people derive some measure of satisfaction from being members of an ethnic group and will resist any erosion in what they regard as the core elements of their cultural tradition. However, the Chinese, like many other cultural groups, are desperate to improve the living standards of their people. This struggle brings them into contact with alien, especially Western, cultures, many of the practices of which they regard as antithetical to 'the Chinese way'. This contact sparks the dilemma of modernization: how to develop without sacrificing one's cultural identity.

The Chinese are vigilant but optimistic about this process. They show great concern about the potential loss of their valued Chinese-

116 Beyond the Chinese Face

ness, but believe that they can modernize without Westernizing. They consider it possible to industrialize, to embrace democratic institutions, and to fraternize with those outside their own culture without compromising their strong family traditions, their self-restraint, and their cultural pride. In this development they are content to slough off reactionary aspects of the Chinese tradition, like submissiveness to authority and suspicion of science. They view themselves as 'modern Chinese', as distinct from modern Westerners or traditional Chinese.

This cognitive *legerdemain* is largely supported by the observable facts. Chinese who modernize and Chinese who migrate to foreign countries are still distinctively Chinese. They have adapted in ways that help them to meet the demands of a modern world and alien cultures, of course. They have and will become less fatalistic and less authoritarian, but more achievement oriented and more socially involved. In spite of these adaptations to contemporary life, their pattern of attitudes and modes of childrearing and family life will continue to be identifiably Chinese.

It seems to me that past critiques of Chinese culture [have] been too indiscriminate and were thus blind to the possibility of a mutually selective interaction between Chinese cultural values and new institutional arrangements that can generate effective configurations for modernization.

Wong Siu-lun

# 9

# Afterword

> In some respects, all men are the same;
> in some respects, some men are the same;
> in some respects, each man is unique.
> Based upon words of Clyde Kluckhohn

IT IS NOW October 1990, and I have taken a full two years to complete this integration of psychological knowledge about the Chinese people. If we are now able to see farther than before, it is, to borrow from Nietzsche, because we stand on the shoulders of those who have gone before us. The theoretical work of Yang Kuo-shu, Francis Hsu, Harry Triandis, and Geert Hofstede has been especially helpful in focusing my thought. The empirical work of all those named in the text plus a host of others constitutes the bricks from which this building has been shaped. Additionally, my dear and generous colleagues H. C. Chen, David Ho, Leong Che-kan, Liu In-mao, Leung Kwok, Chan Wai-o, and Fanny Cheung commented constructively on one or more early versions of chapters in their area of expertise. Publishers' protocol dictates that I may not name my editor at Oxford University Press, but we both know how much I value her contribution to improving the readability of this book.

The finished product is, however, my responsibility. They proposed, I disposed. It is not my disposition, however, to discard ideas or data simply because they may disagree with my viewpoint and I hope that I have not been guilty of such a failure of nerve here. My stance towards difference is embodied in verse 42 of the *Tao Te Ching*, where it is written:

> By blending the breath
> Of the sun and the shade,
> True harmony comes into the world.

In forging such a harmony, I have taken some pain to integrate the work by Chinese social scientists. They have been helpful in broadening my sensitivity to new concepts and in challenging my unconscious ethnocentrism. I need further development in these respects, but take some solace in the Chinese adage that, whereas it takes ten years to grow a tree, it takes one hundred to make a scholar! At 46, I have time enough to discover richer harmonics.

## The Golden Thread(s)

Have these two years brought me any closer to identifying what Arthur Kleinman called the 'golden thread' tying together the many strands of difference that define the Chinese as distinct from others? The answer is an Oriental 'yes and no'.

The yes's are four, perhaps five in number. Each 'yes' represents a basic theme that can be used to make sense of a variety of observations about Chinese behaviour. As I now understand things, these themes are as follows:

1. The Chinese belief in the naturalness, necessity, and inevitability of hierarchy. It is self-evident to Chinese that all men are born unequal. An efficient society requires a broadly accepted ordering of people. The alternative to hierarchy is chaos (*luan*) and anarchy which are together worse than a harsh authority.
2. The bases of this inequality are achievement, usually academic; wealth; and moral example. The last is especially important for commanding political authority.
3. Laws negotiated by men are rigid, artificial, and insensitive to the changing circumstances of life. The judgement of wise and compassionate men is a better way to regulate personal, social, and political relationships.
4. Man exists in and through relationships with others. The goal of socialization is to train children for lifelong interdependence with others by developing skills and values which promote harmony. The family is a fundamental cradle of sure support across time and requires especial commitment from its members.

The fifth theme is optional because many Chinese grow up not reading or writing Chinese characters. Where the mastery of ideographs is a necessary feature of literacy, however, it becomes an important consideration:

5. The need to master ideographs reinforces an academic emphasis on memory, attention to detail, and lengthy homework. It also strengthens a predisposition towards perceiving stimuli as whole rather than as collections of parts, and high spatial intelligence.

I have mentioned, sometimes elaborated on, each of these five themes throughout the text where they relate to the observations at hand.

What, then, is the 'no' interwoven with these five themes? Simply put, it is that the Chinese are not unique. That is, they share these basic cultural themes with other groups. Japanese also learn ideographs; Italians, too, have a powerful focus on the family; the role of law is similarly undeveloped in Burma; achievement is likewise the basis of hierarchy for Canadians; and the inherent value of hierarchy is shared by Indians, among others. These statements can only be made with some scientific certainty because, slowly, our science is becoming more cross-cultural. We are including ever more cultures in our studies of behaviour, so that patterns of similarity and difference are becoming apparent. We are discovering that in some respects the Chinese are not unique.

## Uniqueness and Shared Humanity

But of course the Chinese *are* unique! Their particular combination of positions with respect to these five themes alone would distinguish them from almost any other cultural group. If we add to these five considerations their agricultural heritage, population density, historical longevity, and numerical strength as an identifiable group, then the Chinese are distinctive, special, and different. As is each cultural group. If enough dimensions of comparison are used, any group may be seen to have a unique position.

Nevertheless, all cultural groups are united by their shared humanity. At the psychological level all children require affection and education. Each society must strike a balance between individual separateness and interdependence, between authority and freedom, between achievement and compassion, between rigidity and uncertainty. People will encounter the solutions to these choices through the process of socialization. These are the human universals, the challenges that all social groups and all individuals in those groups must meet. The Chinese way is one among many.

At least, such is my current thinking. Just as I have moved beyond my earlier understanding of the Chinese, I expect to move beyond this present offering. It is a journey closely tied to my deepening understanding of myself. I believe now with T.S. Eliot that:

> the end of all exploring
> Will be to arrive where we started
> And know the place for the first time.

How curious in light of this quotation that on my last trip on the
Toronto underground there appeared to be more Chinese people in
the subway car than from any other identifiable ethnic group!

Ye are the fruits of one tree
And the leaves of one branch
Baha 'u' llah

# Select Reading List

THIS personal list takes the reader in two directions — deeper in or further afield. 'Deeper' here refers to more detailed and more specific information about psychologists' discussions of the topics raised in this book. 'Further' here refers to the writings of professionals who work in related disciplines or to psychologists writing for a broader, general audience. The list includes both English-language and Chinese-language sources.

## Deeper In

Abbott, K. A. (1970). *Harmony and Individualism*. Taipei: Orient Culture Service.

Bond, M. H. (Ed.) (1986). *The Psychology of the Chinese People*. Hong Kong: Oxford University Press.

Brislin, R. W., Lonner, W. J., and Thorndike, R. M. (1973). *Cross-cultural Research Methods*. New York: Wiley.

Chen, H. C., and Tseng, O. J. L. (Eds.) (Forthcoming). *Language Processing in Chinese*. Amsterdam: North-Holland.

Gilen, U. P., Lei, T., and Miao, E. S. C. Y. (Eds.) (In press). *Chinese Morality: Values, Reasonings, and Education* (2 volumes).

Gudykunst, W. B., and Ting-Toomey, S. (1988). *Culture and Interpersonal Communication*. Newbury Park, CA: Sage.

Ho, D. Y. F., Spinks, J. A., and Yeung, C. S. H. (Eds.) (1989). *Chinese Patterns of Behavior: A Sourcebook of Psychological and Psychiatric Studies*. New York: Praeger.

Hofstede, G. (1980). *Culture's Consequences: International Differences in Work-related Values*. Beverly Hills: Sage Publications.

Hoosain, R. (Forthcoming). *Psycholinguistic Implications for Linguistic Relativity: A Case Study of Chinese*. Hillsdale, NJ: Erlbaum.

Hsu, F. L. K. (1953). *Americans and Chinese: Two Ways of Life*. New York: Abelard Schuman.

——(1963). *Clan, Caste, and Club: A Comparative Study of Chinese, Hindu, and American Ways of Life*. Princeton, NJ: Van Nostrand.

Hwang, K. K. (1988). *Power Games of the Chinese People*. Taipei: Jiu Liu Tu Shu Co. (In Chinese)

Kao, H. S. R., and Hoosain, R. (Eds.) (1986). *Linguistics, Psychology, and the Chinese Language*. Hong Kong: Centre of Asian Studies, University of Hong Kong.

Kessen, W. (Ed.) (1975). *Childhood in China*. New Haven, Conn.: Yale University Press.

Kleinman, A. (1986). *Social Origins of Distress and Disease: Depression, Neurasthenia, and Pain in Modern China*. New Haven, Conn.: Yale University Press.

Kleinman, A., and Lin, T. Y. (Eds.) (1981). *Normal and Abnormal Behavior in Chinese Culture*. Dordrecht, Holland: D. Reidel.

Liljestrom, R., and others (Eds.) (1982). *Young Children in China*. Clevedon: Multilingual Matters.
Liu, I. M., Chen, H. C., and Chen, M. J. (Eds.) (1988). *Cognitive Aspects of the Chinese Language* (Vol. 1). Hong Kong: Asian Research Service.
Pye, L. W. (1982). *Chinese Commercial Negotiating Style*. Cambridge, Mass.: Oelgeschlager, Gunn and Hain.
Redding, S. G. R. (1990). *The Spirit of Chinese Capitalism*. Berlin: de Gruyter.
Sun Long-ji (1983). *The Deep Structure of Chinese Culture*. Hong Kong: Yishan. (In Chinese)
Tseng, W. S., and Wu, D. (Eds.) (1985). *Chinese Culture and Mental Health*. New York: Academic Press.
Vernon, P. E. (1982). *The Abilities and Achievements of Orientals in North America*. New York: Academic Press.
Wilson, R. W. (1970). *Learning to be Chinese*. Cambridge, Mass.: M.I.T. Press.
Yang Kuo-shu (Ed.) (1988). *Chinese People's Psychology*. Taipei: Gwei Gwan Tu Shu. (In Chinese)
Yang Kuo-shu, and Tseng, S. C. (Eds.) (1988). *Chinese People's View of Management*. Taipei: Gwei Gwan Tu Shu. (In Chinese)

**Further Afield**

Allinson, R. E. (Ed.) (1989). *Understanding the Chinese Mind: The Philo-sophical Roots*. Hong Kong: Oxford University Press.
Butterfield, F. (1982). *China: Alive in the Bitter Sea*. London: Hodder and Stoughton.
Fairbank, J. K. (1987). *China Watch*. Cambridge, Mass.: Harvard University Press.
Fung, Y. L. (1948). *A Short History of Chinese Philosophy*. New York: Macmillan.
Hwang, K. K. (1988). *Confucianism and East Asia Modernization*. Taipei: Chu Liu Book Co. (In Chinese)
King, A. Y. C. (1977). *From Tradition to Modernity*. Taipei: China Times Publishing Co. (In Chinese)
Laaksonen, O. (1988). *Management in China during and after Mao*. Berlin: de Gruyter.
Leung, K. (1991). *Consumer Psychology: Analysis of Sales and Promotion Strategies*. Hong Kong: Publications (Holdings) Limited. (In Chinese)
Li, Y. Y., and Yang Kuo-shu (1972). *Symposium on the Character of the Chinese: An Interdisciplinary Approach*. Taipei: Academia Sinica. (In Chinese)
Lin Yu-tang (1935). *My Country and my People*. New York: John Day.
Marsella, A., DeVos, G., and Hsu, F. L. K. (Eds.) (1985). *Culture and the Self: Asian and Western Perspectives*. New York: Tavistock.
Mosher, S. W. (1983). *Broken Earth: The Rural Chinese*. New York: Free Press.
Nakamura, H. (1964). *Ways of Thinking of Eastern Peoples: India—China—Tibet—Japan*. Honolulu: University Press of Hawaii.
Pan, L. (1987). *The New Chinese Revolution*. London: Hamish Hamilton.
Po, Y. (1985). *The Ugly Chinese*. Taipei: Lan Pa. (In Chinese)
Pye, L. (1963). *The Spirit of Chinese Politics*. Cambridge, Mass.: M.I.T. Press.

Su, X. K., and Wang, L. X. (1988). *Yellow River Elegy*. Hong Kong: Joint Publishing Co. (In Chinese)

Westwood, R. E. (Ed.) (In press). *Organizational Behaviour: A South East Asian Perspective*. Hong Kong: Longman.

Wilson, R. W. (1974). *The Moral State: A Study of the Political Socialization of Chinese and American Children*. New York: The Free Press.

Young, G. (Ed.) (1985). *China: Dilemmas of Modernization*. Beckenham: Croom Helm.

# Index